MW00987852

THE GLASS OF FASHION

ALSO BY CECIL BEATON

The Author, from a drawing by Augustus John

CECIL BEATON

THE GLASS OF
FASHION

ILLUSTRATED BY THE AUTHOR

CASSELL

TO THE AFFECTIONATE MEMORY OF

CONDÉ NAST

IN GRATITUDE FOR HIS ENCOURAGEMENT

THROUGHOUT THE YEARS

Artillery House, Artillery Row
London SW1P 1RT

All rights reserved. No part of this book may
be reproduced or transmitted in any form or by
any means, electronic or mechanical, including
photocopying, recording or any information storage
and retrieval system, without permission in writing
from the publishers.

This book is sold subject to the conditions that
it shall not, by way of trade or otherwise, be lent,
re-sold, hired out or otherwise circulated without
the publisher's prior consent, in any form of binding
or cover other than that in which it is published
and without a similar condition including
this condition being imposed on the subsequent purchaser.

First published 1954
This facsimile edition 1989
Copyright © the literary executors of Cecil Beaton

British Library Cataloguing in Publication Data

Beaton, Cecil, *1904-1980*
    The glass of fashion.
    1. Women's costume, 1900-1953
    I. Title
    391'.2'0904

    ISBN 0-304-31629-6

Distributed in Australia by
Capricorn Link (Australia) Pty Ltd
PO Box 665, Lane Cove, NSW 2066
**Printed and bound in Great Britain by
Biddles Ltd, Guildford and King's Lynn**

ACKNOWLEDGMENTS

Some of the sketches in this book are derived from well-known portraits, others are from photographs and press reproductions, whose authorship I have been unable to trace. But I should like to thank Mr Boris Kochno for lending me his snapshot of M. Diaghilev, Lady Juliet Duff for a De Meyer photograph of her mother, Lady de Grey, and Mrs Carmel Snow for permission to utilize some fashion photographs by Mr Richard Avedon. I should like to thank M. Drian for giving me permission to reinterpret some of his early work.

My gratitude also goes to the following people, all of whom were gracious and kind enough to provide me with specific material and anecdotes which appear in some of these chapters: Mme. Edouard Bourdet, Louise de Vilmorin, Baroness Phillippe de Rothschild, Mrs Reed Vreeland, Mrs Carmel Snow, George Davis, Ellen McCoole, Mercedes de Acosta, Malvina Hoffman, Mme. Lopez-Wilshaw, Lady Juliet Duff, M. Michel Bongard, M. Balenciaga, and Lincoln Kirstein; also Mrs Edna Woolman Chase, Margaret Case, and Baron Nicolas de Gunzberg of *Vogue*.

My thanks are also due to the editors of *Vogue*, *Harper's Bazaar*, and *The New Yorker* for allowing me access to their past issues. To Mr Waldemar Hansen I am indebted for his patience and help in research work, and generally in editing and contributing so much to this book.

Some of the photographs in this book have appeared in *Vogue* magazine in America, England and France, and are reproduced by kind permission of their owners. I would like to thank the Directors of Condé Nast Publications, Inc., for allowing me to use the photographs of Paula Gellibrand (1930) and Balenciaga (1953); Condé Nast Publications Ltd. for those of Oriental Teagown (1927), Mrs Vernon Castle (1928), Lady Diana Cooper (1930), and the Wyndham-Quin Sisters (1951); and Les Editions Condé Nast for that of Madame Errazuriz (1929).

I should also like to thank Mr Augustus John for his kind permission to reproduce the frontispiece.

CONTENTS

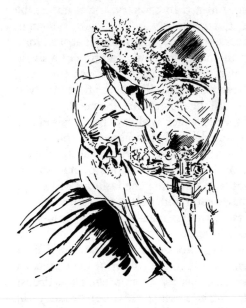

IF an Anglo-Saxon decides to write a personal record of fashion and the minor arts, he may find himself accused of being a propagandist of frivolity. He will certainly discover that, both in England and America, fashion is viewed with a jaundiced eye, feminine enthusiasm notwithstanding.

To those serious critics who would denigrate fashion, one can only reply in terms of paradox. It was Oscar Wilde who observed that we cannot afford to do without luxuries, thus making a variation on the celebrated Taoist dictum that only those knowing the value of the useless can talk about the useful. But among the Western nations France alone seems to have taken this wisdom to heart and has always laboured to elevate both fashion and *les arts mineurs* to a degree of perfection comparable with the purity of its literature and painting.

When we talk about fashion or the minor arts, we really mean the whole art of living. Its practitioners, like roof thatchers, are a disappearing race in our modern world. Perhaps it is because of an innate dislike of leisure that we Anglo-Saxons are so niggardly in praising this art. In cookery, for example, the English or Americans, unconsciously imbued with Benjamin Franklin's notion that time is money, might find it absurd for a Frenchman to spend many hours in the preparation of a single sauce. But the Frenchman, who has been criticized for being mercenary, has never been willing to stint on the time involved in a creation simply because the results are ephemeral.

As for history, that spectre which is always being raised as a criterion, it might be pointed out that fashion, the ephemeral, shares the last laugh with art, the eternal. Quite realistically, art is the only thing that outlasts all other forms of human endeavour. But art cannot help reflecting the fashions of its age, and though empires have risen and fallen, we can re-create, with astonishing accuracy, the fashions of an age simply by studying its ornaments and art.

When Marcel Proust was at work on *Remembrance of Things Past*, he sent for information as to the colour of the feathers a certain lady had worn on her hat ten years previously. Proust knew how much the fleeting expression of fashion or fancy can reflect something beyond its limited time, something haunting that whispers of the nostalgia of human impermanence and mirrors man's tragic destiny.

Any number of contemporary critics have devoted volumes to Picasso or Stravinsky, Le Corbusier or James Joyce, but little has been said about those people who have influenced the art of living in the half century of my own lifetime. This book is a subjective account of them and their achievements, as well as of the current of fashion against which they more often than not swam. If they were, or are still, fashionable, in many cases it is because they could not help being so. Some of these personalities are famous, some infamous, some outrageous; but all, in their own way, represent the styles of the past fifty years. Since the point of view is personal and I have concentrated mainly upon those of my talented acquaintances who are linked with the theme, the reader is likely to find lacunae and omissions. But I have scarcely intended a compendium of latter-day taste: we may, indeed, be too close to the subject matter for such a work.

One could perhaps divide the hierarchy of fashion into three ranks: those who play fashion's game and are the sheep; those who play the game and are the leaders; and, lastly, the real shepherds, who, though they avoid or eschew active participation, cannot help being fashionable because of the authority with which they express their tastes. All of these people appear in this book. If the shepherds dominate, that is only natural: they are far and away the most interesting and rewarding subjects.

As for those who play the game of fashion—and especially the creators whose vocations are involved—they are often tragic, for they do not have a sound basis, and find, in the end, that they have built their lives on shifting sands. The wiser give up the game as they grow older, for what older person is ever fashionable? Sooner or later, all fashion artists, whatever their medium, learn that the odds are against their survival. At most, they can successfully express their era for ten or twenty years; even the most famous dressmakers do not hold the throne longer. There is a curious paradox emerging from this: *Fashions are ephemeral but fashion is enduring*.

Mr Aldous Huxley and other Westerners influenced by Eastern philosophy have written much about 'getting out of the time stream'. This, of course, is impossible for a person involved with the moods of fashion, and it is the primary reason why fashion is often an enemy of art, just as fleeting infatuation is often the antithesis of enduring love. Only the true artist is unconcerned with time, or temporal reputations, or whether he is *a la mode* or not. He has fixed his gun sights on values outside time.

Curiously, many of the same creative forces are brought into play both in fashion and art. Standards of proportion, of measure, and of simplicity are as important to a dressmaker as to a painter. But those who work within fashion's sphere have been charmed by time and change, by the desire, above all, to be chic. They are playing a game with themselves, often a tragic game. The immediate effect is more important to them than anything else; creating something that will reflect the moment is more essential than creating something outside the time stream. The more the fashionmonger enjoys this game of artifice, the more

3

decadent he becomes. This does not mean that an artist cannot create in this medium to a brilliant effect: he can; he can become a Boldini or a Dior. But none can play fashion's game and be entirely true artists at the same time: they cannot have their cake and eat it too.

Perhaps only those who are claimed by fashion, rather than those who follow it, are the true exponents of the art of living. They have followed Emerson's advice when he said: 'Insist on yourself; never imitate. Your own gift you can present every moment with the cumulative force of a whole life's cultivation; but of the adopted talent of another, you have only an extemporaneous half-possession.'

If this book concentrates on those who have expressed themselves, however momentarily, with 'the cumulative force of a whole life's cultivation', it is because I believe that, even while writing their names on water, they have made a triumph of the evanescent. These are the people who know that abstract good taste counts for nothing, that the real task is always to express their own personalities. They are the heroes and heroines of fashion, who make the styles of living but are not made by them. Their personal, and even freakish, tastes are more important than common chic, and they have always gone against the current in order to arrive at something intensely individual.

The reader is likely to find some paradoxes and contradictions in these pages; fashion is much like ourselves—alternately contradictory and consistent, tragic and comic, compounded of the transitory and the enduring. But in spite of this, 'Drest in a little brief authority', we all have enough of the peacock in us not to be able to dismiss it entirely.

4

Sargents Madame X

CHAPTER ONE

TAKE ONE
HUNDRED LARKS

DURING the early years of this century, about the time of my birth, France was producing an ornate fashion magazine called *La Mode*. In its pages, whose paper was of such good quality that it felt like kidskin to the touch, one might have run across an Helleu engraving, a Boldini drawing, an oil portrait by De la Gandara, or a snapshot taken at Auteuil or Chantilly of some lady whose identity would barely be suggested by her initials—Madame le Comtesse A. de N., or La Princesse B. Apart from the lady's intimates, who were certain to recognize her, this anonymity added a romantic quality and an air of ambiguity to the game of fashion; for personal values and fashion still retained a mystery and discretion.

That swift tenor of change inaugurated by the First World War has carried us a long way from the Edwardian age of my birth. The distance seems, in memory, to be curiously greater than my proper lifetime. My advent into this world had coincided with first horseless carriages and electric lights. Queen

Madame la Princesse E. de B.

Victoria had died only three years previously, and Oscar Wilde was but recently buried in the cemetery at Père Lachaise. Their deaths signalled the end of Victorianism, though I think Wilde would have been quite happy in an England where affairs were being genially conducted to the aroma of good King Edward's cigars. After the monotony which had blanketed London in the latter years of Victoria's reign, there was to be a brief decade of dazzling seasons, which in their splendour were to recall if not recapture the days of Louis Philippe and of the Second Empire. Balls and entertainments became ever more lavish. At the court drawing rooms, ladies with tall Prince of Wales feathers in their hair wore trains that swept for many yards on the floor.

The Edwardian age was a period of gaiety, when life was so inexpensive that a dandy with four hundred pounds a year could go out dancing most nights of the week, wearing lavender gloves and a wired button-hole in the lapel of his tail coat. Theatre stalls cost half a guinea, operetta was in its heyday, and chorus girls, following the example of pretty Connie Gilchrist of 'skipping-rope-gaiety' fame, began to marry into the peerage.

La Comtesse T. de S. E.

The women who leaned over my crib had not yet forgone the lines of the hourglass and were laced into corsets that gave them pouter-pigeon bosoms and protruding posteriors. Perched on their heads, and elevated by a little roll just inside the crown, were hats which had grown as frivolous as the milliner's trade could make them—enormous galleons of grey velvet with vast grey plumes of ostrich feathers sweeping upwards and outwards, or they would be trimmed with artificial flowers and fruit. One of the most flamboyant and generous exponents of the prevailing styles and modes was my godmother, Aunt Jessie, who was the first woman of fashion that I ever knew.

These ladies of the upper middle classes rolled along in hansom carriages as they paid afternoon calls. Their white kid gloves were of an immaculate quality. Over one wrist they carried a small, square gold mesh bag containing a gold pencil, a handkerchief, and a flat gold wallet which held their calling cards. If the lady of the house was 'not at home', the visitor handed the servant two of her cards with the corner turned down to indicate that she had 'left cards' in person. The shining wheels of her carriage revolved on the freshly gravelled surface of the road to the next place of call, their sound muted if they

were passing a door where the sick or dying lay, for it was customary to spread a thick carpet of straw in the streets before houses of invalids.

Since the Edwardian period was a link between Victorian bourgeois security and the febrile modernity that was to follow it, the age of my birth was not unlike some rich, heavy cake with, fortunately, the magic leavening to make it digestible. The manners and morals of the time, though still strict, were beginning to yield, and a taste for spice could be detected: the opulence had a note of the frivolous; the sense of luxury was, in general, more sparkling than suffocating.

These changes showed themselves in the freer fashions of the day, though many in the upper middle classes still lived strictly by Victorian rules when it came to the exclusiveness of individual modes of dress. Exchanges of fashion confidence were unthinkable, for between the woman and her confidante, the dressmaker, there existed a relationship as private as a love affair. At times this reticence would be carried to such lengths that a lady of fashion might send her motor car away from the establishment where she bought clothes, simply in order to maintain the mystery of their origin. Exclusiveness of style

reached the point where it caused incalculable embarrassment to both parties if an identical dress was worn on the same occasion by two different women. With all the fervour of a mid-Victorian melodrama, a scene, or possibly even a scandal, might be precipitated if it was discovered that one lady had crept into the bedroom of another at a country house party to find out from which establishment the dresses had been bought, a matter easily ascertained from the silk labels sewn into the lining.

Set in such an atmosphere, it was only natural that the spangled chiffon, filigree-embroidered tulle, veils, billowing ostrich-feather boas, and, trimmed with clover, honeysuckle, or paradise feathers, the ubiquitous cartwheel hats, which had superseded the stiff satins, brocades with rigid iris or bulrush patterns, starched linen skirts, and prim boater straw hats of a decade earlier, took on an enigma comparable to that which shrouded the alchemist in his search for the philosopher's stone.

Perhaps modern chemistry, for all its amazing laboratories, has nevertheless lost something valuable that the medieval wizard, with an almost primitive belief in the symbols of his trade, possessed. Without mystery, magic disappears. Even our

9

unprofessional ladies of fashion have, today, through over-publicizing, been reduced to journalistic commonplaces. If some discreet individual becomes 'news', then willingly or unwillingly she must go into the public domain and be exploited as a 'celebrity'. If distance lends enchantment, then there is little distance in our contemporary world.

The conformist way of life, whatever its virtues, infringes on one of the fundamentals of taste and fashion—exclusiveness. Formerly it was only in an overwhelming desire for difference and distinction that fashion found its incentive. Today that incentive seems to be reversed: there is a desire to seek safety in standardization.

I was too young, perhaps, to know that the *pêche Melba* had just been created in honour of a great singer; or that Escoffier, the master chef himself, was still preparing chicken in champagne at the Carlton Hotel in London and stuffing capons with one hundred larks as a dish to set before the King. . . . But I do remember that pet Pomeranians were called Ponto, while terriers were named Egbert. Anyone who dropped the ball was 'a

silly duffer'. Grown-up games included the Diabolo, which was played with an hourglass spool balancing on a string between two sticks. My aunt Jessie's gramophone had a horn of crimson enamel, like some huge, exotic tropical flower, on which she played arias sung by Tetrazzini, Albani, or Caruso.

At Madame Sherwood's dancing school we children wore our patent-leather shoes with their silver buckles and learnt the polka and the hornpipe. The young girls were wrapped in Shetland shawls at children's parties and carried their dancing shoes in a bag, bronze leather pumps with an elastic round them and a little bead on top. Inevitably they were accompanied by their nannies, who would roll the sausage curls of their wards around their fat fingers. These curls were like rolled-up slices of bread and butter, or the ginger brittle rolls known as 'elephants' tongues' that were served together with tea and ices. Fire stations had scarlet doors and white horses that were trained to rush out at the sound of a big brass bell, rearing and flaring their nostrils like the stallions in the chariot races of the *Decline and Fall*, at which the nursemaids screamed or

fainted, for women were more hysterical then than they are today.

My inward child's eye, even as my adult vision, always sought out the detail rather than the conception as a whole. A particular trimming on a dress seen in childhood could make a profound impression on me, and certain details have remained in my memory to this day, with acute combinations of colour that have influenced my own creative work.

Thus it was always a thrill when my mother, who was a fair reflector of the feminine fashions of the day, would come to say good night to me, perhaps going out to a dinner party, dressed in miraculously soft materials. On one occasion she wore a large special bunch of imitation lilies of the valley on her bosom, pinned to a pale green chiffon scarf. This sunburst of artificial flowers was a revelation, because I had not thought lilies of the valley could be simulated.

I soon discovered that my mother had an entire drawerful of artificial flowers. She would fasten a clump of slightly crumpled 'old-rose' coloured roses to her waist if she was going off to an 'at home', where the baritone (one singer, I remember, was named Hubert Eisdale) might sing 'Down in the Forest Something Stirred'. Sometimes, when she decided to spend the afternoon 'calling', my mother would perhaps choose a huge rosette of Parma violets. When she went to Ascot, she wore real flowers—three Malmaison carnations, fully five inches in diameter. To keep each of these flowers in place a pale pink cardboard disc had been fitted behind them, with a centre hole for the carnation stem to pass through.

Like any other hostess of the period, my mother gave luncheons or dinner parties. The day of these events she would be too busy to give any but the most cursory attention to her personal appearance, though the flowers were always tastefully arranged on all the occasional tables. The masterpiece of decoration, most usually sweet peas, was saved for the centre of the dining table, which would be dotted with olives, salted almonds, sugared green peppermints, and chocolates in cut-glass bowls or silver dishes. These were the signs of a gala, as they were never on the table in the ordinary course of events. At Christmas time preserved fruit made its appearance—splintery wooden boxes of glacé pears and greengages, which I seem to remember came from elsewhere than France, possibly Sweden or Denmark. There were also tins of caviare sent from Riga, and huge blue-and-white vases of preserved ginger from India, via Whiteley's or Harrod's.

The period of elaborate coiffures had not yet passed. Since she had no personal maid, my mother was usually obliged to dress her own hair. It was worn wide at the sides, stuffed out with pads and garnished with amber, tortoiseshell, or imitation diamond combs. On black Mondays, after a long solitary session with her arms upraised, putting the waves and curls into place, the effect might still not please her.

Then she would take out the rats, glancing with alarm into the looking glass as the whole business started over again. Her face became flushed, her arms would be aching, and by the time she had finished she was more than late for dinner.

On special occasions a man with a moustache and sepia wavy hair parted in the centre would come to the house with a brown leather bag. He was shown to my mother's bedroom, where, armed with the spirit lamp or stove, he heated his tongs over a blue flame. I can still, in memory, conjure up the exciting scent of methylated spirit and singed hair, an accompaniment of the transmutation in this wonderful adult world which I watched with such spellbound admiration. There were almost regular intervals of alarms and a last-minute rush for a dinner party or a visit to the theatre. My mother's room, by the time she vacated it, looked as if a tornado had passed; powder was spilled on to the dressing table and floor, while the bed and chairs overflowed with discarded garments, trimmings, and feathers.

Another great thrill for me was provided whenever my mother indulged her interior decorating fancies. Sometimes this coincided with spring cleaning, for spring cleaning caused a great upheaval in those days: the whole house was taken to pieces and put back together again. Invisible gnome-like creatures appeared early in the mornings to clean out the chimneys and were gone before you had rubbed the sand out of your eyes; carpets, pictures, looking glasses, and furniture were covered with dust sheets, while for days on end most of the house was 'out of bounds'. It was not unlike fumigating a ward where patients with contagious diseases had been segregated.

At this time of year my mother might well decide to alter the colours of her rooms, choosing curtain materials or chair covers for the drawing-room or the 'library' (a room in which, strangely enough, never a book was to be seen). One springtime the school room was redecorated in grey and mauve, somewhat half-heartedly after the fashion of the *art nouveau* movement. There were pale mauve curtains of muslin with frills on them and what must have been daring touches of simplicity in grey papered walls edged with a geometrical mauve border. The pale grained furniture included a set of tall backed chairs of grey wood, having stylized roses carved out of their centre panels. Later, when it became my privilege to accompany my mother on shopping expeditions to Hanover Square, new vistas and wonders were opened as I watched her choose flowered cretonnes, shot taffetas, and purple brocatelles.

With the passing of time I was not only conscious of colour and detail, but became aware of line and pattern and crystal-

Sunday luncheon aftermath: my mother in hammock

lized more developed aesthetic experiences. It was then that Bessie Ascough's fashion plates, which appeared each day in the *Evening Standard*, began to excite my curiosity. Soon I was in virtual paroxysms of impatience while awaiting my father to bring home the paper in which this lady's latest pen drawing would be ready to be smeared with my water-colours or oddly smelling silver and gold paints. Sometimes, on red-letter days, Bessie Ascough sketched a picture of a lady in court dress, replete with feathers, bouquet, and train; or she might draw a *robe de bal*, giving a wonderful facsimile of all the embroidery on the dress. Her particular skill was manifest in the roses that she drew, roses like balloons or billiard balls, with great round centres. Often a whole cluster of them would be held by a worldly bride. At first my father may have attributed my excitement to his return from the city, though he could not have been long in remarking that the *Evening Standard* was the focal point of my attention. One evening he said he had forgotten to bring his newspaper home with him, and I was deeply hurt by his callousness in the face of such an important event. The next day I was told that Miss Ascough was on holiday and that her fashion plates would not be appearing for a while. Later I discovered this was not the case at all. The truth was that my family deemed it unwise to allow these apoplectic expectancies for Bessie Ascough's artistry to continue: the child was becoming peculiar.

Philosophers tell us that as we grow older we come closer to childhood. I was still a child when King Edward's death closed the covers of the book of opulence, if not forever, at any rate for my lifetime. I am glad that my early roots were Edwardian, for that period gave me a sense of solidity and discipline and helped to crystallize a number of homely virtues and tastes by which, consciously or unconsciously, I have been influenced in my life.

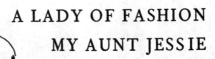

CHAPTER TWO

A LADY OF FASHION
MY AUNT JESSIE

AUNT JESSIE was my mother's eldest sister. She was too short to be considered beautiful, inclining towards the petite and the plump; but her nose was one of the most beautiful noses I have ever seen—straight and small, of perfect classical proportions—and her personality, at any rate, was built on heroic proportions. There was something Falstaffian in Aunt Jessie's laugh and her infectious sense of the comic; she was grand and gaudy and gay. Though in later years she was to become a tragic little figure, it was tragedy imposed from the outside, the common tragedy of the passage of time, and not one which was innate in her. During her lifetime, and especially the first half of it, she was an ardent devotee of fashion, scurrying to keep up with the latest hats from Paris, much as the Red Queen raced across the squares of Lewis Carroll's chessboard.

Aunt Jessie had startled her family by marrying a Bolivian, had gone off to South America, where she was reputed to be the first white woman who had ever sailed up the green-walled

17

c

My aunt Jessie, with Madame Avelino de Aramayo & Princess Glorietta.
from a photograph 1899.

My aunt Jessie in 1913

Amazon in a canoe and had succeeded in keeping her poise on a mule's back while moving through remote Andean mountain passes that were quite likely too narrow for her hat or her hair-do. When she reappeared in London, it was in the official position of the wife of the Bolivian minister, and with a marked foreign accent that haunted her native English tongue whenever she spoke it for the rest of her life. True to her flexible nature, Aunt Jessie became hostess to a whole tribe of South Americans who sat around with their tongues clacking like castanets in their native Spanish, or roaring with laughter at whatever makes South Americans laugh. She was rich and flamboyant, with a heart of gold; and so full of the joy of living that a child at once became over-excited in her presence.

It was Aunt Jessie who provided the greatest treats and pleasures for me when I was a child. She was my *tante gâteau,* and was probably regarded askance as not being the best influence on me. For, had I been left to my own devices, I would surely have spent all my time at Aunt Jessie's, where I was certain to be stuffed and petted, returning home with too much enthusiasm and an understandable colic. If she had borne children, she would doubtless have spoiled them, even as she spoiled her pet animals. She was empress in a domain that could only be a Cloud-Cuckoo-Land for a child, where the rare and the special were always to be found.

Even to wash one's hands in her house was a treat. Instead of the yellow soap we had in the nursery, a cake of that wonderful, wine-coloured Pears soap, with a texture of petrified jelly and an elusive but magical scent, was placed on the side of the wash basin, whose blue and white irises were forever embedded in its china surface, the whole lifting up to revolve on a pivot and empty into the unknown below. Likewise, how pleasant it was to go to her lavatory, with water lilies decorating the porcelain pan, surrounded by a solid encasement of mahogany and equipped with a gold handle which one pulled up in order to bring about a discreetly gurgling flush of water.

Downstairs there were enormous gilded baskets with silk bows, filled with pineapples and mangoes, custard apples and Brazil nuts, while the air was redolent with white lilacs out of season. Aunt Jessie provided wonderful grown-up things, things to eat, like Dutch chocolates and *marrons glacés*, a cuisine of highly spiced or peppered Spanish dishes, and exotic-tasting sweets (on the tongue of a child her food was always excessively hot or excessively cold).

My aunt had an assortment of pets, many of which she had imported from South America, including a marmoset that would chatter and shiver and shriek from a vantage point on her shoulder or keep itself half hidden in her muff. This minute creature was named Chinchilla after Aunt Jessie's favourite fur, which she wore on every possible occasion as a stole, a muff, or in the form of trimming on dresses or hats. Her selection of dogs included Ronnie, a fluffy black ball of a Pomeranian, a small yapper called Tiny, and a quivering, black silk skeleton of a Chihuahua with protruding eyes. Later there was a bright red squirrel with the appropriate name of Tango, who used to run up the green silk brocade walls of her drawing-room and

around the elaborate cornice of the ceiling, believing itself to be still in the jungle beyond La Paz or Cochabamba.

On special occasions I would be allowed to come into her dining-room at the tail end of a luncheon party, just in time to savour the aroma of melon and cigar smoke. Such brief glimpses would be enough for my imagination to build upon, and I created a mental picture of the aura of fashion and luxury in which she lived, an aura that surrounded her like the spirals of cigar smoke created by the men of the party, all so foreign and enigmatic, yet amused, in their black morning coats, striped trousers, and pearl tiepins.

To Aunt Jessie I owe my first real glimpse of the world of fashion, of that whole grown-up world from which a child is so often excluded while he waits for the key of the years to open it for him, like an Alice too small to reach the table top where the key itself lies waiting. I had no idea then that Aunt Jessie was not entirely representative of the most restrained in taste,

though when I finally made the discovery it did not matter very much. She was one of those women who enjoyed fashion, and managed to give you a sense of *her* sense of fun; so, good taste, bad taste, Aunt Jessie's taste for life was, at any rate, always impeccable. In the end she not only resisted judgment, but was outside its laws, making it invidious to laugh at her instead of with her, in those great gales of laughter that swept up from nowhere and carried you along in their wake.

Several times a year my aunt would make buying trips to Paris, and her return was always something of an event. I have no idea how her servants managed to haul the enormous black trunks with gilt hinges and locks up the stairs, past the stained glass window on the landing, for it was surely a feat comparable with bringing the *Queen Elizabeth* into harbour.

Most of these gargantuan coffins were filled with dresses, others with shoes and corsets, ribbons and ruffs, and aigrettes done up in black tissue paper, or materials with which to make

Aunt Jessie's hatboxes

more dresses; beaded embroidery by the yard, and lengths of velvet, brocade, lamé, and chiffons gaily iridescent with sequins. One particularly large box was entirely filled with face lotions, pots of cream, boxes of powder and beautifiers of every description. Then there were the hat boxes—great square containers that held six hats apiece. In those days, mesh moulds were pinned on the sides, top and bottom of a box so that the crown of a hat could be placed over the mould and fixed into place by a long hatpin piercing the mesh. In such manner, six hats could travel in a box without being crushed. And such headgear! Vast discs covered with funereal plumes of black ostrich feathers or white ospreys; hats for the evening and hats for the afternoon; hats for her garden parties.

Aunt Jessie's garden parties were special events for me, since I was *persona grata* and allowed to circulate among the guests, while all the South American children (none of them Aunt Jessie's, for she was childless) peered with envy from the windows above a marquee which was set up on these occasions as a place for rest and refreshment. I remember once seeing an enormous American woman with grey hair, named Madame Triana, seated in the marquee eating an ice and wearing a dress of pale grey and apricot. I had never before seen a combination of those two colours, and their effect on me was extraordinary. Frederick Ashton was to observe to me years later that certain childhood experiences are of such a nature as to pay dividends for the rest of one's life. Thus I was to remember this apparently extraneous moment and to make use of it again and again.

Aunt Jessie was a martyr to fashion in the grand style of Sainte Geneviève. On holidays, in order to reduce, she would put on a rubber corset, take her racquet in hand, and go out and play strenuous sets of tennis until the sweat poured in cascades from her head. For long hours she would cover her face with cold cream or a special mask of white ointment. Sometimes chicken fat would be in vogue as a beautifier, and she smeared her features with that. Throughout the years you could always find the rind of a lemon left by her washstand, a tell-tale clue to some astringent process or other.

Aunt Jessie loved to dress up to the hilt for any special occasion, and she relished the fact that her appearances involved hours of preparation. For reasons more of splash than of economy she did not frequent the best Paris dressmakers, often preferring to buy six 'models' rather than one good dress. Then it was her habit to convert her sitting-room or an extra bedroom into a makeshift workshop, where odd little women, who looked as though they could be hatched only from the world of needle and thread, bobbin or paper pattern, would come to copy in ever more flamboyant colours her existing dresses and elaborate evening gowns.

It was a great treat to watch behind the scenes, but the greatest excitement of all was when I was allowed as a child to go down in the morning to see her being dressed for court, since at that time the court drawing-rooms were held at noon. On these occasions it took her four or five hours to make herself ready.

By the time we had arrived, she would be standing in front

*Lily Elsie, Gertrude Glyn, my aunt Jessie and my uncle Pedro
from a snapshot taken at Biarritz*

of a cheval glass, her hair already arranged and the plumes fixed
in place, her face a mask of powder and rouge, desperately set
and serious, for court days were scarcely a laughing matter and
the customary gales of laughter were banished from the scene.
My father disapproved of women painting their faces, a moral
judgment that could only be calculated to intrigue me, and it
was delightfully shocking to see how Aunt Jessie would cover
her face, neck, arms, and back with a thick paint which by some
was called enamel but which my family referred to as whitewash. Her eyelids were painted mauve, her cheeks a bright
carnation pink, while the lips were cerise. Her jewellery would
already be round her neck or hanging from her ears. Aunt
Jessie had a rather odd collection of stones embedded, after the
fashion of that period, in rather small diamond settings that
showed an *art nouveau* influence in their arabesques. She was
fond of black pearls and would have a pendant, necklace, and
earrings with enormous black pearls as the centre of the
ornament.

Now the dressmaker would be sewing the court train on to
her shoulders, a train sometimes made of rather surprisingly

flimsy material. One train, I remember, was of embroidered chrysanthemum design in black and silver sequins that were shaped like tadpoles, the whole being edged with swansdown. At a somewhat later period she wore an entirely magenta court dress and train, while her hair (which was always going through some new phase of russety tinge) had been dyed a shade of dark brick red to complement the dress and was set tight on her skull with Spanish kiss curls around the forehead and in front of each rouged ear.

I have Aunt Jessie to thank, not merely for spoiling me by giving me a glimpse of the grown-up world, but for introducing me to my great childhood heroine, Lily Elsie, who at that time was the queen of London's musical comedy, the English creator of *The Merry Widow*, and perhaps the first actress of her genre to captivate the popular imagination by means of her ladylike restraint and dignified grace. At a children's party given in the Carlton Hotel I found myself, one Christmas, comparatively soon after I could walk, undergoing the extraordinary sensation of having favours bestowed upon me by a beautiful actress. I rose to the occasion by peremptorily ordering my Bolivian uncle to buy her an enormous bunch of Parma violets.

With the passing of the years Aunt Jessie was to suffer a serious reversal of fortune. My uncle's Bolivian investments failed; without his money and accompanied by his wife, he returned to South America, where he died. After his death Aunt Jessie came back alone, bringing her black and gold trunks with her, calling early one morning from the garden before anyone in the household was awake, a strangely pathetic creature in her tussore coat and skirt, her cream-coloured calf skin shoes with their high patent-leather heels and blunt, round knobs of toes. They were old and out of fashion by then, those shoes—a relic of the past—like the trunks that she had brought back with her, out of which she was to live for the rest of her life. She had panama hats that lasted her lifetime, and there were things of such quality that, indeed, they saw her through to the end.

It was as a comparatively penniless widow, however, that Aunt Jessie had come to stay with us. Though the former dazzle and glitter of her life were no longer available to her, she man-

Lily Elsie as the Merry Widow, 1909

My aunt Jessie: Greek style 1914

aged to enjoy herself. Even when she was well over eighty years old she continued to savour, with the greatest relish, all of the simplest things that life offered. She would apotheosize a garden, or a leaf, literally anything, with that extraordinary knack of making the best of things. Everything can be used in a lifetime, Aunt Jessie seemed to imply; and so she utilized all the relics of her former grandeur, though the black pearls were eventually sold, while the chinchilla stole turned yellow with age as she steadfastly refused to give it up. Somewhere amid these things the black ostrich feathers could still be found in a box, together with the embroidery left from the magenta dress.

Perhaps the most tragi-comic touch of all was that the mesh shapes—those souvenirs of great hat boxes carried up the stairs past the stained-glass window on the landing—came into their utilitarian own at last: they were used for straining the soups and sauces when she concocted Spanish and Argentine dishes in the kitchen. For in her widowed days Aunt Jessie loved to cook.

I remember bringing a friend from Harrow School home to luncheon. My adolescence had its moments of mistaken snobbery, one of them being that I was a stickler for formalities. I had hoped for a gracious meal with all the odds and ends attended to by the servants, while my mother and aunt would converse sedately with the young but sophisticated guest. It seemed scarcely proper for Aunt Jessie to be bustling about the kitchen, straining things through her hat meshes and tossing up *empanadas* and Spanish puddings, though I was later to realize that the gesture was far more in good taste, more natural and unaffected, than my own stilted and genteel proprieties. One of the sad things about life is that we are always appreciating things too late, belatedly seizing the quality of an experience or a person, as though they had to grow in us with the years before any fruit of meaning could appear. The more I think about Aunt Jessie, the more retrospect reveals her great gifts to me. In her own unintellectual way she had a rare wisdom and philosophy; she knew a lot about life and people and possessed qualities of gaiety, pluck, and courage.

Aunt Jessie lived on until well after the Second World War. She was constitutionally as strong, not as the proverbial ox, but (I think she would approve of the simile) as a Rolls-Royce engine, a fact one doctor was to observe; and, were it not for cancer, she might have lived to be a hundred. Although her last days were passed in frightful pain, she never complained, sipping a spoonful of tea as though it were nectar, while any little attention was an anodyne to her suffering. One dark, drab morning in mid-winter she was obliged to be taken from her bed of agony to the hospital for X-ray treatments. Instead of lying back resignedly in the ambulance, she sat up, peering interestedly through the windows for a glimpse of the bare branches of the winter trees, or some sight of that outside world which she must have suspected was already diverging forever from her own.

Visiting her as she lay dying was an experience that was to be most haunting for me. She lay in bed, ravaged. Above her head a photograph depicted her at the height of her youth, with diamond stars in her hair. Having dispensed, by her good nature, with any sense of style, she had accumulated around her, through the years, all the flotsam and jetsam of things that she had liked. Her room might have been some strange beach where extraordinary objects had been washed up with the tide of the years: madonnas collected in South America were to be found juxtaposed with pictures of herself or her family; relics and rustic souvenirs mingled without the slightest self-consciousness. She was ardently Catholic, and I like to think of her as having had a 'catholic' taste.

When Aunt Jessie died, a part of my childhood died with her. She represented something that even my own parents could not supply, for parents are often, of necessity, the arbiters of reality and must keep a certain discipline for the sake of the grown-ups their children are to be. By contrast, Aunt Jessie was the outsider, the magic relation who provided those special treats and fantasies that are so dear to childhood. She made one feel that one went back to reality after leaving her.

When Pandora's box was opened and let forth all the evils into the world, Hope was left behind in the bottom of the casket. It might equally well have been Aunt Jessie's chinchilla stole. Grey and apricot, marmoset and mesh moulds, and Aunt Jessie dressing for court—I suppose I am guilty of being more utilitarian than sentimental, for I keep all these memories as my aunt kept her shoes, or her ostrich feathers, or her magenta train. After all, everything can be used in a lifetime, and Aunt Jessie was of such quality that she will see me through till the end.

CHAPTER THREE

FOOTLIGHTS
AND POWDER

WE make a mistake if we think that the important influences on our tastes are necessarily the genuinely
aesthetic ones. Often they are of questionable artistic
value. Bad poetry and bad fiction have been known to inspire
even the greatest writers. Mozart and Bizet drew inspiration
from the popular songs of their day, while Henry James could
find the subject of some of his work in the gossip of old ladies.
Our own painter, Graham Sutherland, once surprised me by
telling me that he, like myself, admired the drawings of Gladys
Peto. The work of this 'bastardized' Beardsley of the twenties
consisted entirely of trees, chandeliers, and decorations on
dresses—all executed in a careful mosaic of futuristic balloons.
Thus I am well aware that the men responsible for decorating
the first stage productions I ever saw were possibly not artists
of any high distinction. Yet their work was to be a stimulating
incentive to my most serious efforts in the theatre many years
later.

31

Early in this century the stages of the serious theatre were bathed in an amber glow that gave a rich effect to scenery and costumes but drained them almost entirely of colour nuances. On the light opera stage, pale candy colours were, almost without exception, all that were ever seen. The ante-room at the Marsovian Embassy would be decorated with marble columns, tapestries, Aubusson carpets, and hydrangeas, all confined to sweet-pea colours. Likewise, the ladies were attired in pastel shades. In its own limited way, this was extraordinarily pretty and created a magic of its own. Among the items listed on the theatre programme, together with the usual credits of 'Cigarettes by Abdulla', 'Scenery painted by the Harkers', and 'Shoes by Raynes' there was the inevitable line, 'Colour schemes by Comelli'. I never discovered who Signor Comelli was; but as the invisible wizard behind the scenes, he correlated in wonderful harmony the opalescent mauves, blues, and pinks that dominated his strange world.

The leading lady's gowns were inevitably made by Lucile and were masterpieces of intricate workmanship. It was the fashion for women to wear high-waisted Directoire dresses, falling straight to the floor, where the wearer's feet would be encumbered by bead-fringes and possibly clinging trains. Lucile worked with soft materials, delicately springling them with bead or sequin embroidery, with cobweb lace insertions, true lovers' knots, and garlands of minute roses. Her colour sense was so subtle that the delicacy of detail could scarcely be seen at a distance, though the effect she created was of an indefinable shimmer. Sometimes, however, she introduced rainbow effects into a sash and would incorporate quite vivid mauves and greens, perhaps even a touch of shrimp-pink or orange. Occasionally, if she wanted to be deliberately outrageous, she introduced a bit of black chiffon or black velvet and, just to give the *coup de grâce*, outlined it with diamonds.

In private life Lucile was Lady Duff-Gordon and a sister of the romantic noveletist, Elinor Glyn. She had suddenly developed her own utterly personal *métier*. Nowadays her work is sometimes disparagingly referred to as 'boudoir lampshade stuff'. All fashionable dresses become costumes in time, how-

Lily Elsie dressed by Lucile for 'The Count of Luxemburg'

33

ever, and in her heyday Lucile's artistry was unique, her influence enormous. She was the first Englishwoman to create a name equally well known in London, Paris, Chicago, and New York. Until Lucile's advent the Paris dressmakers had displayed their clothes on mannequins of no particular looks. These models wore black satin 'maillots', with high necks and long sleeves, over which went the evening dresses of Doucet or Worth. It was considered shocking to see a lady's skin in daylight. Lucile discarded the black undergarment and employed beautiful young women as mannequins for her clothes. The fame she brought to the outstanding Hebe and Dolores is legendary. Drian, the painter, has described these tall women mincing about in their turbans and trailing trains as looking like impertinent lobsters.

Apart from these innovations, Lucile was responsible for the training of a number of good designers, including Edward Molyneux, who started his career by making drawings for her on a landing at the turn of the great staircase in her Hanover Square establishment.

Just as ladies' costumes were limited to sweet-pea colourings, so their make-up was of a more restricted palette: lips were touched with coral instead of carmine, complexions were peaches and cream. Hair was pale nut-brown, and I remember that the yellow or peroxide hair which we now call blond was, at that time, considered unfortunate. Perhaps, in comparison with today, the art of physical embellishment was somewhat naïve; yet there was a dancer in *The Merry Widow* and *The Dollar Princess* who knew a thousand tricks of make-up.

Gabrielle Ray was not a talented actress, not even a good dancer, but her parakeet features were not without possibilities. By sheer cleverness she was able to fascinate an audience and make it susceptible to her self-created prettiness. She metamorphosed herself into a sort of Maude Goodman nursery-picture-book unreality, with masses of soft, silky curls falling about her raised head and a straw hat hanging over her shoulder from a ribbon. The effect was as though butter would never melt in her mouth, yet there was an intriguing perversity about such excessive prettiness. Gabrielle Ray was the precursor of the

Gabrielle Ray

Marie Laurencin school of pink-and-white feminity. Lily Elsie, the star of the operettas in which Miss Ray appeared, was to tell me many years later of some of her colleague's experiments in make-up. A past mistress of *pointillisme,* Gabrielle Ray would, for her stage appearance, put mauve and green dots at the edges of her eyes, with little red and mauve dots at the corners of her nostrils. As meticulously as Seurat working over one of his canvases, she shaded her eyelids and temples in different colours of the mushroom, while her cheeks were tinted with varying pinks from coral to *bois de rose.* The chin was touched with a hare's-foot brush dipped in terracotta powder, and the lobes of the ears and the tip of the nose would be flicked with salmon colour. Thus painted, Gabrielle Ray appeared before the audience enamelled like a china doll.

Perhaps better than any other actress, this dancer knew how to pose for a photographer. Doubtless she was one of those forerunners of photographic facial surgery, for she would have a piece of silk thread held under her nose by assistants who stood at either side of her, uptilting the nose just the amount that she wished. With little talent but much imagination Gabrielle Ray, during her brief career, turned herself into a small work of art.

The reputation of actors or dancers may or may not live after them, depending upon their artistry or their importance to a given age or epoch: ballerinas like Taglioni or Carlotta Grisi still live on in legend and in nineteenth-century engravings, perpetuating the spirit of romantic ballet; actors such as Coquelin or Sarah Bernhardt have their names in theatre history. There are any number of personalities, however, who, like the *Ephemerae*, those mayflies that are born, live, and die in a single day, vanish completely and leave scarcely a trace behind them. It seems unlikely that anyone born after 1920 may ever have heard of Gaby Deslys, who was also something of an actress and something of a dancer, but whose ambitions, indeed, lay more in the achievement of luxury than the fulfilment of talent. When I was five or six years old she was already in her heyday; by the time I was sixteen she had died.

Aunt Jessie may have given me my first glimpse of the grown-up world of fashion, and Lily Elsie, the star of *The Merry Widow*, may have personified romance; but Gaby Deslys was the first creature of artificial glamour I ever knew about, one of that species of *rara erotica* calculated to bring forth all the emotions that might be dreamed of by a boy who has not yet reached the age of puberty. I was never allowed to see Gaby Deslys on the stage, but, though my mother felt that my enthusiasm for such a soubrette should scarcely be encouraged, I followed her career with the greatest interest. No doubt my family must have read or heard of the gossip that this actress wisely allowed to gild her name. She made no secret of her private life or of her belief in free love, and said to American reporters, with disarming candour: 'Money is woman's only bulwark against the world. I give nothing back.' Her bejewelled value had even been calculated in terms of her weight. It was estimated that, with all the diamonds and pearls and emeralds in

Gaby Deslys

place, Gaby Deslys was worth something over three thousand dollars a pound.

Apart from photographs which appeared in magazines and which I pounced upon with the enthusiasm of a botanist discovering a new plant, my only human contact with Gaby Deslys was through the medium of Aunt Jessie. My aunt would tell me of a matinee she had attended, describing how the star had shed an enormous cloak of feathers, or the manner in which she had removed her hat, a pyramid of precious ospreys, that was then thrown across the stage landing on a chaise longue while the audience gasped with delight. That same audience knew, just as Aunt Jessie suspected or as I guessed from photographs, that the pearls she was wearing were priceless, that her emeralds were far from being paste, and that ladies had to invent more than the Gaby Glide to acquire such things.

Gaby Deslys was something of a key transitional figure—the successor to the grand Parisian *cocottes* of the nineties on the one hand, and, since she was a theatrical figure, the precursor of a whole school of glamour that was to be exemplified twenty years later by the Marlene Dietrich of the Cinema screen. Her critics were in agreement that her voice was like a canary's and that she was not even a particularly good dancer, but what did it matter if her aura of glamour was artificial? The world loves nothing so much as artifice, and I was not alone in my worship of Gaby Deslys: her success was phenomenal.

Plump as a partridge she was, but though her features were far from classic, one did not feel that they could be improved upon in any detail. Her nose was rather fleshy, pear-like and thick-ended, yet somehow in perfect harmony with the cherry lips. Indeed, something about Gaby Deslys' whole esculent appearance called to mind a basket of fruit, real or imitation. Her breasts were round, with unpointed nipples. Even the colour and texture of her complexion cried aloud to extend the metaphor, for it was like fruit and cream. Her silky hair was dyed a greenish marzipan gold, possibly like Dorian Gray's, but more like that of a child in a perambulator. Set in the cherubic face, two eyes as warm and sad as those of a Saint Bernard dog painted by Landseer looked at you with liquid compassion

38

GaBY DESLYS · 1912·

39

from beneath their heavy lids and luxuriously sad brows. The cherry lips were parted in a smile that showed seed-pearl teeth, a smile that revealed the sensuality, the gaiety, and the good nature behind it, as well as reflecting a distant strain of something tragic, an awareness that the days of the waltz could not last forever.

Upon this physical foundation Gaby Deslys walked the tightrope of a near-barbarous taste with a rare audacity, scarcely regarding the sheer drop to utter vulgarity below her. The spirit behind her self-adornment was not unlike that of some African chieftain strutting his panoply and plumage before the tribe. Her taste ran amok in a jungle of feathers, diamonds and chiffon and furs, creating the pattern for the *Folies Bergère* costumes to be worn by Mistinguette and other *vedettes* who came after her. Most of those who copied her, however, did so without taste, an observation which is intended to be neither ironic nor paradoxical, since Gaby's personality alone was fully capable of sustaining those outfits for which the word 'bizarre' must take on new overtones.

Yet, though fantastic, her clothes had their own grace. They were an adaptation of the fashions of the time. With a high Directoire waistline, she might wear a harem skirt and a huge bonnet towering with bows. She wore, indeed, virtually anything: jewels, lace, furs, beaded fringes of the lampshade school, and, always, feathers galore: swansdown, paradise, osprey, egret, even cock and chicken feathers. When she entertained the soldiers during the First World War, she dressed as they would have liked her to dress—swathed in black satin lined with cerise velvet and trimmed with chinchilla, cascades of pear-shaped pearls hanging from her neck, and, on one side of her head, a tea cosy rampant with bill hooks of paradise tails.

Contrary to the fashions of her time, which favoured high *décolletages*, Gaby Deslys showed as much of her bosom as propriety permitted. She made a point of revealing her legs, too, well-rounded legs encased in lace stockings. Her small feet were shod with stub-toed shoes whose buckles glittered, whose incredibly high heels were studded with flashing rhinestones.

The climax of any costume display, however, was her hat, resembling aeroplane propellers or a Brancusi bird. These huge constructions of gauze were rampant with the ubiquitous feathers of tropical birds, parrots, or flamingos. She was, in short, a human aviary. On occasion she might employ a slightly pyrotechnical theme by wearing a jewelled cap which, like the last of some fireworks display, sent up the inevitable great sprays of egret plumes.

In the theatre Gaby Deslys must have lived up to the off-stage legend she had created, and no doubt went through a performance that was sure to delight an audience. Her success was made to be enjoyed by others. Like a Midas, everything she touched turned to gold. The signature was luxury, scrawled on her motor cars, clothes, jewels, and feathers; and the more luxurious and scandalous her life, the more people loved her. She created a morality of her own immorality, with a vitality that obviated any unpleasant undertones of 'kept woman' or worse.

Then, too, at that time nobody felt guilty for adoring luxury. Even the stagehands were impressed and pleased to see some enormous limousine waiting at the stage door for her, with a chauffeur and a footman in attendance, their livery splendid in its colour and chic. The Renault, Daimler, or Rolls-Royce might have a canework body, or it might be painted white or elephant's breath, a sort of off-mustard yellow that was popular at that period. As she drove off, people would see her sitting framed in the window, creating an effect comparable to the passing of the Queen of Sheba. I myself first caught a glimpse of her in this fashion near the Ritz Hotel in London. The effect was like seeing someone from another world: through the window of the motor car her complexion had an extraordinary luminosity; and, as the Rolls-Royce purred past, it left a scented trail of unbelievable luxury and allure, spiced with a breath of naughtiness that escaped, at least by a narrow margin, being trashy.

Her news value, for obvious reasons, was inevitable. On holiday in Monte Carlo, or 'roaming the Riviera', each picture of her added a new note to the evergreen reputation. It was not just a case of Gaby Deslys being photographed walking along an esplanade; rather, each costume she appeared in was the apotheosis of something new, something exaggerated, perhaps, but nevertheless an inspiration. If Gaby wore an ecru-coloured tussore suit with a coal scuttle of full-blown roses on her head, or a dress of velvet and *diamenté* trellis, I might well feel I had discovered a new continent. Her fantasy spread to embrace even the little Chihuahuas she kept as pets, Mexican creatures so spindly and fragile that one felt certain they could not survive a winter in subtropical Nice unless they were wrapped in dark Russian sables. And they were.

The day came when I was to see Gaby Deslys at close quarters. It was at an open-air entertainment, one of those theatrical garden parties where I had been taken as a schoolboy. The event was for charity, and actresses appeared as saleswomen, selling ice cream or their own photographs, shouting through megaphones and shouting without megaphones. Gaby Deslys appeared in a magenta dress of very fine lace. On her head she wore an enormous cock-eyed propeller of magenta osprey. Magenta orchids trembled at her breast; magenta were her lace stockings, and her shoes were of magenta satin with magenta ribbons crisscrossed up her legs. Pale magenta cheeks and lips had been painted on a face the colour of marshmallow. Vulgar? Perhaps, but by whose standards? The gesture seemed to transcend vulgarity and create its own allure.

42

Gaby Deslys had appeared in London as early as 1903, as a dancer and soubrette in musical comedy, but it was not until she established herself as a vaudeville turn, singing slightly naughty French songs, doing somewhat acrobatic dances, and wearing fantastic clothes, that she came into her own. Gradually the flames of her reputation spread. There was never a greater fire in the forest. Gaby soon gained international attention as the mistress of the young King Manuel of Portugal, who had, indeed, spent a king's ransom on her and had given her a rope of pearls as long as herself. Newspaper stories of the day would have it that the Portuguese people revolted against the extravagances of their young monarch, whose bills for Gaby Deslys must have appalled his Treasurer. More than likely it was only the straw that broke the Portuguese camel's back. Be that as it may, the actress severed her liaison with King Manuel after the loss of his crown and, taking her pearls, went triumphantly off to make her American debut. Contracts were signed with both Ziegfeld and the Shuberts, and her salary, from the very beginning, reached $18,000 a month, an astronomical figure in those days.

Reporters enumerated the $320,000 worth of jewels that 'Gabrielle of the Lilies' had brought with her to America, or told how she forbade her press agents to use King Manuel's name in connection with her own, as she wished to shine on personal merits. Since she had come to epitomize the most fantastic in European glamour, New York was quick to recognize her genius. A number of shocked suffragettes only just failed to prevent her from appearing on the stage of the Winter Garden. Yale and Harvard students adored her and made her their Zuleika Dobson.

Though she appeared in New York in the winter and bought her clothes in Paris, Gaby Deslys lived in London, in Knightsbridge, where she had a house with leaded windows and rows of scarlet geraniums in window boxes. The interior was decorated in sumptuously bad taste. Typical of a good-natured *vedette*, she allowed the newspapers to take photographs of the bed in which she slept, an elaborately carved and gilded ecclesiastical four-poster in an alcove reached by three steps. Sometimes

44

other photographs showed her having lunch with her sister, seated against the oak wainscoting beneath a deep beamed ceiling. In front of her was an ostentatiously decorated table with, as centrepiece, a huge silver tureen filled with orchids. I can even remember the heavy cut glass on the long refectory table.

When Gaby Deslys went to call on Sir James Barrie, who at that time lived in a top flat in Adelphi Terrace, she completely beguiled the author, then as she left, ran down the staircase, ringing the doorbells of all the other apartments. Sir James fell in love with her and wrote a starring vehicle with the rather literary title of *Rosy Rapture*. At the first day of rehearsal Gaby walked to the footlights and leaned towards her admirer sitting

45

in the stalls. 'I can't dance,' she said, 'I can't act, I can't sing, but I can do it.'

Even today, when thumbing through some old bound copy of *The Sketch*, a tremor of excitement runs down my spine if I come across a photograph of Gaby Deslys. Perhaps it is a picture of Gaby in ruched tutu and windmill headgear performing the Gaby Glide; or 'at home' in a negligée of spidery lace, her elbow poised on a knee, chin resting on her extended fingers as she smiles tragically into the camera. Whatever else she may have been, she was always individual. To me, she remains mysterious.

Some may well say that Gaby Deslys was a freak, that she did not really represent style or fashion, but the nature of glamour is ill understood, and women of doubtful reputation have often possessed this most elusive of all qualities. The individual representatives of any given period are always apt to be somewhat *outré*, in any case. What would not be considered vulgar on the African chieftain might have been judged adversely when worn by Gaby Deslys. Why? The answer is obvious. A condemnation of her taste is based on the limited conventions of ourselves and of our society. If we find that the African and his costume are really in the best of taste, it is because we are suspending our arbitrary notions of fashion to see him in his own light. Taste, after all, is variable; conventions are variable. Conventions in taste are much less interesting than the taste of the individual.

It was Francis Bacon who said that 'there is no beauty which hath not some strangeness in its proportions'; and Gaby Deslys certainly had more than her share of exoticism. In the last analysis, style is not created by the imitators, nor even by the couturiers, whoever they may be. You can lead a woman to a Dior dress, but how she will look in it is another matter. Only personality creates style. Indeed, personality not only can impose its bizarre aspects on a period, but even, to some extent, creates the period itself.

Like many good things, it was thought that Gaby Deslys was an import from Paris, though, as it later transpired, the French could not claim her for their own, and her exact nationality and origin remain to this day a matter of mystery. As had Webster's Duchess of Malfi before her, 'she died young', leaving all of her money to the poor of Marseilles. Even the manner of her death was surrounded with a certain romanticism. It was said that she had an incurable throat ailment and that, when doctors advised surgery as the last possible means of saving her life, she chose death rather than scar her throat. Several lawsuits contesting her estate were carried on for some ten years afterwards, together with secret-service investigations, their purpose being to establish the identity of a woman who, enchanting as she was, showed more of an inclination to ambiguity than to mystery in her own lifetime. Some said she was Hungarian; some claimed to be illegitimate daughters, showing birthmarks to prove that this was so; and thieves, a decade after her death, made a hole in the wall of her mausoleum at Marseilles.

For me, Gaby Deslys is the individual embodiment of the pre-1914 war epoch, a symbol whose depth goes far beyond herself. No one may know or remember the names of the ten best-dressed women in the world at the end of good King Edward's reign, if indeed such a list ever existed; but there are still a few, like myself, who remember Gaby Deslys with all the nostalgia of a popular song or a summer's day picnic. Like fashion itself, she represents the triumph of the ephemeral.

47

CHAPTER FOUR

THE
DEMI-MONDE

BOTH in life and in literature the *demi-monde* has always been identified with romance, tragedy, brief gaiety, and enlarged hearts. A candlelit world of its own, far from the decorum of respectable society, it exists now, alas, only in the brilliant evocations of Marcel Proust and Colette. The *déclassée* women, exotic blooms, who were nurtured in the hothouse of all that money can buy, thrived in an easy atmosphere that created a tacitly agreed place for them in the social scene. Houris of the rich, they enjoyed a half century and more of poignant splendour before the changes following the First World War forced the leisured classes into a less ostentatious pattern of social behaviour, and spelled the end, at least in its outward and dazzling social forms, of this perhaps somewhat touching way of life.

During the age of romantic ballet, the *cocotte* had already began to wage her victorious campaigns from the vantage point of a theatre loge. Here, through opera glasses, she was

the cynosure of the young bachelors and married men whose cheque books were often as large as their hearts. Perhaps one of the highest peaks in the history of the *demi-mondaine* coincided, paradoxically enough, with the outwardly respectable eighties. But these often brilliant and cultivated creatures continued to sit at private tables at Maxim's and privately screened theatre boxes until the First World War, inspiring their dressmakers and the creators of luxury to the most dazzling flights of fancy. One of their dressmakers described these elegant women strolling up and down the lawns at Longchamps or Deauville as looking like 'fillies paraded before their backers prior to the trial gallop, adorned with furs and hypertrophic plumes; the strut of a bird, the gestures of a queen, a magnificent carriage of the head. When one draped them in a chinchilla cape, it showed its ten thousand louis' worth. One knew what one had for one's money. They were women born for luxury. Competition made them achieve the impossible, since all the Parisian dressmakers outdid each other in invention and daring to assure the triumph of their latest creations. Sometimes on the very morning of the opening of a race meeting, dressmakers' assistants would be still sticking pins into a gown that was to be displayed that same day.'

But 1914 was to bring their world, among so many others, to an end. After the war, Harry Melville complained that the *cocottes* had become so 'golf-linksy'; and today, the *poule de luxe* is almost non-existent, an anachronism or, in her newly vulgarized guise, a forever altered entity who can scarcely lay claim to the genius of her feathered predecessors.

The goddesses of that vanished half-world were tarts of the highest calibre. Without being restrained in their styles, they were also obliged never to offend by their vulgarity the men of taste who financed them. Thus they deserved their riches, their servants, their stocks and bonds. The greatest of these ladies of immodest means lived in large houses or apartments of their own. They knew how to command servants, how to order good food and wines and entertain their men friends in a faultless style, but with a levity, an atmosphere of improvidence that the gentlemen could scarcely find in their own homes. No

duchess could have excelled in dignity the bearing with which some tart with éclat alighted from her carriage to air her Afghan hounds in the Bois. Nor were these women any less gracious as they entered their dress shop, to be received, perhaps, by the ambassadorial-looking Monsieur Doucet himself, with his Vandyke beard and carnation buttonhole. In fact, the duchess and the *grande cocotte* never came face to face, for not for

Airing Afghan hounds in the Bois

another twenty years were their worlds to coincide, and when they did the *cocotte* had become something quite different.

In their great days the tarts showed no desire to become respectable or move into the legitimate world by marrying the men who kept them. Sometimes, as in *Chéri*, they fell in love with young men of their own class, but their profession was sacrosanct. If a gentleman was seen at a restaurant by a lady of his world in the company of a *grande cocotte*, there was never any question of 'cutting' him or of acknowledging his companion's presence: while dining with this enigmatic woman, resplendent in her pearls, lace, and picture hat, the gentleman was as invisible to his respectable friends as if he wore a magic cloak. He did not exist.

Some of these spectacular and well-publicized ladies had vague connections with the stage, and in magazine photographs, attired in frothy negligées or reclining in their ornate

drawing-rooms, they would be called 'the well-known actress'. Most of them blossomed in the luxury of Paris, though a few thrived in London.

Perhaps the last of these great 'actresses' was Forzane, an incandescent blonde of Swedish extraction, who appeared a short time before the First World War and had disappeared by the end of it. With her exquisite grace and original line of body, her luminous pallor, her small chubby nose and fully fashioned, divided rosebud lips, she was a clarion call to sex. Her Negroid eyes, set in a long pale face, had the same hot, somewhat queasy look that her rival, the actress Lantelme, possessed. But Forzane was more subtle, more restrained and ambiguous than her sultry blonde rival. Forzane's appeal was never vulgar. She seemed to breathe in the rarefied atmosphere of parma violets and gave the illusion of the unattainable.

Her long fair hair was worn straight and swathed close to her head, in a modification of the Greek classical style: she foreshadowed the neat boyish head of the twenties. At a time when it was fashionable to lean somewhat forward, in the manner of a swan triumphantly carving through the surface of a lake,

Forzane

55

Forzane adopted a contradictory stance, leaning backward with her pelvis brought forward, one foot trailing behind the other. A tightly rolled umbrella would be tucked under one arm, while the other arm was almost pulled from its socket by not one, but two borzoi dogs on a leash.

Her clothes, in comparison to others of the day, were sparsely trimmed, relying for their effect on a fluid line of drapery. Forzane's special allure could be seen to its best advantage when she wore white and grey chiffons falling in fluted columns from high Directoire waists. Another striking appearance was achieved by severe *tailleurs* of broadcloth, complemented by spats and tight-fitting toque trimmed with uncurled heron feathers. An impressionable friend of mind described the delighted shock of seeing her descend from her electric brougham to go into a shop, a vision in pigeon-throated grey, with a draped hobble skirt slit to the knee, chinchilla at neck and wrists, and a turban sprouting a vast aigrette.

Both Forzane and the *demi-mondaines* knew how to sustain interest, not only in their men but in their public. Perhaps

Forzanne
1911.

it was easier to create a sensation in those days than it is today. When Forzane entered the restaurant of the Savoy Hotel in London, people stood on their chairs to get a better view. Her very original form of allure must have been even more startling in its day than it would appear now. Like other women of real chic, Forzane triumphed over the ephemeral fashions of her day. In the legacy of photographs that have been left to us, the quality that elevates her above others is vividly apparent.

It is difficult for our age to estimate the novelty of many of these women's appearance. So many copies have since been foisted upon us that we have become inured to the shock of the original. Before the actress Eve Lavallière appeared, for instance, no fashionable woman would have dreamed of accentuating a slightly Mongolian face by tying her neat dark hair in a bow, just as the wearing of 'little boys' natty suits was an innovation with her.

An undoubted sensation was caused by the spectacle of Lantelme entering a box at the theatre accompanied by the South American millionaire, Edwardes. Cocteau has given a graphic picture of them: Edwardes wearing a soft shirt instead of the usual boiled front and tail coat; while his lady friend, with the huge mouth of a carp, her hair a mass of frizz, possibly with a tight dog collar of diamonds around her neck, declined to sit upright in the customary manner, but slouched so low over the rim of the box that her pearls fell in cascades to the light brackets below.

Many of these women were inventive and strange in their public appearances. They had an artist's eye for effect. Some were accompanied by curious pets or exotic servants. One lady brought back a middle-aged, weather-beaten-looking midget from Australia to be her perpetual bodyguard. Polaire, the actress with the tiniest waist and the boast that she was the ugliest woman in the world, capitalized on the appearance of her huge mouth, evil slanting eyes, and wild hair cut in a fringe by returning from a visit to America with a Negro servant boy around whose neck she had hung a plaque that read, 'I belong to Polaire. Please send me back to her'. In *The Tatler* dated December 13, 1911, 'Priscilla in Paris' wrote:

Lantelme

59

Lantelme, 1910

'The Dress Rehearsal of the Folies Revue is one of the important functions of the winter season, and Polaire created quite a sensation by arriving in her box with a youth who looked about sixteen. Such a baby boy! Uncle dear! A little pink and white face, violet blue eyes, and smooth flaxen poll. I'm sure he was wearing his first dress suit, and he looked so conscious of his "prettiness". He seems to be the celebrated actress's latest toy. She takes him everywhere with her. The other night she was invited to sup at the Café de Paris by a delightful Englishwoman who is a great admirer of the little Algerian actress's talent. Well, Polaire accepted the invitation, but she brought the baby. I think she carts him round because she has an artistic eye for contrasts, and certainly you cannot imagine anything more piquant than the extreme blondness of the youth next to Popo's very swarthy little self.'

Gina Palerme, a delightful actress who became an adornment to the musical comedies at the Palace Theatre, brought the

POLAIRE. *La femme la plus laide du Monde*. 1912

glamour of the French *cocotte* to London. Her off-stage appearances were as sensational as her stage escapades. She would appear in a chinchilla cape that touched the ground, embellishing the effect with a saluki dog. Sometimes she wore a velvet tam-o'-shanter and men's riding breeches while relaxing in the richly ornate gilt of her Maida Vale drawing-room.

One day, perhaps, an historian will write a book about these unique women whose breed has vanished from contemporary society. In respectable social terms they served little or no purpose. But then, the world in which they lived was not a world that had any need of justification. It was neither threatened from within nor from without. Our concept of 'usefulness' has, alas, been narrowed to a rather prosaic definition in modern times. Baudelaire, in the middle of the nineteenth century, could write that nothing was more horrible to him than a 'useful person'. He was making, beneath the shock of the statement, a profound judgment on the hypocrisy of moral values. We do not ask of nature that it be useful: flowers are the most useless of all things; yet we pursue, cultivate, nurture, and foster them, spending hundreds on our greenhouses and gardens. If people do not come under the same category as flowers, then perhaps Baudelaire would have said that they should. Many of these *demi-mondaines* graced their epoch with a true expression of luxurious personalities flowering in a free environment. Admittedly they were social orchids, and the conditions of their cultivation are no longer possible. They have died out. But their extinction has scarcely been our gain, nor has the passing of their world been superseded by any substitute which possesses those qualities of the bizarre and the picturesque.

Gina Palerme

CHAPTER FIVE

CHANGING
WORLDS

WHEREAS Queen Victoria's reign lasted for more than sixty stolid years, the Edwardian age of opulence proved to be a short-lived wedding party, confined to one brief decade. Someone has said that each age is an age that is dying, or one that is coming to birth; but the nostalgic eye always seems to choose to regard change as a form of dying. Meanwhile, though it would have been difficult to foresee the war that was to come four years later, King Edward's prestige was such that his death in 1910 brought a first suggestion of the profound organic break-up which many of the component parts of Western European society and culture were to undergo in the next three or four decades.

The most significant aspect of England's mourning period for King Edward was the social event that came to be known as 'Black Ascot'. At the first Ascot racing season after the popular monarch's death, society appeared dressed from head to foot in black. The men wore black silk top hats with morning or frock

coats, black trousers, black waiscoats, black ties, while in their black-gloved hands they carried tightly rolled black umbrellas. Their funereal ladies must have seemed like strange giant crows or morbid birds of paradise strutting at some Gothic entertainment. As far as the eye could see there were black dresses trimmed with long black fringes, black lace parasols and huge black hats, wider than they had ever been before. Fashions tend to extremes before being dropped, and the elaborate headgear had now become like the last spurt of a Catherine wheel. These vast picture hats, perhaps set on one side of the head and piled high with black ostrich feathers mixed with osprey or black paradise feathers combined with black tulle, were worn not only in mourning for a king but for a glory that had gone forever.

The glory had not entirely gone, if one is to be accurate. Certain personalities in society and on the stage or in opera came into their own during these transitional years between

King Edward's cigars and cigarette smoking. Not the least of them was the unforgettable Lina Cavalieri.

Lina Cavalieri was said to be the most beautiful woman in the whole world. Though time made her a contemporary of Gaby Deslys, the two could not have been less alike: Cavalieri was not a music-hall entertainer, but an opera singer; and if there were *demi-mondaine* aspects to her career, she was unquestionably a woman of innate distinction. Music critics were in agreement that her voice was not of the calibre of a Tetrazzini or a Geraldine Farrar. Physically, she was hardly a woman of heroic proportions, being of medium height and slender build. But Cavalieri was undeniably a great beauty in the classic mould. Her features were of a blunt, Roman cast, a magnolia complexion that complemented the black wavy hair, which was parted in the middle like that of a Spanish dancer and gathered in a bun at the nape of the long neck.

Even as a young woman Cavalieri had the gestures, the bear-

Lina Cavalieri

ing, and the grace of a woman in her prime. Until the 1914 war women did not seek to appear as youthful as they do now: on the contrary, maturity was the keynote of feminine beauty, and Cavalieri had the air of sorrow and experience that comes only with years of living. Her Italianate aura of sad perfection was dominated by large eyes, compassionate and sombre, set beneath eyebrows raised not in question but in inner sorrow. Her equally sombre but sensuous mouth completed features that seemed to have derived from a painting by Murillo.

In the *demi-monde* in which she occasionally appeared, though often only through being publicized in newspapers side by side with stars of a more unsubtle and dubious social position, she created the appearance of Athene mingling with a group of doxies. Cavalieri's ladylike bearing gave her the appearance of a czarina or an empress. She possessed the cool impassivity of a statue. The line of her back merged with the nape of her neck to create a noble column. Whatever the origin of

66

her instinctive physical perfection, it lent authority and even grandeur to all bodily movements. She used her Italian opulence with a wonderful and probably unconscious distinction, a Mediterranean Valkyrie on a small and graceful scale. Her arms were employed for flamboyant yet beautiful gestures, which have been immortalized in the photographic poses where the right hand is idly fingering a long string of pearls, or where, with arms locked behind her head, she outlaws the vulgarity that such an odalisque gesture would normally imply. Often there might be a picture of her with one arm curved upwards, the palm of the hand with its pointed fingers resting on the crown of her head, while its counterpart was placed on hip.

About the same time as Gaby Deslys, Cavalieri made her New York debut as an opera singer and entered into a brief marriage with a wealthy American. During the First World War, Cavalieri returned to her native Italy, where, as a young girl, she had worked as a factory hand. After hostilities had ended she returned to America with Lucien Muratore, a French tenor and her second husband. Together they toured in opera, and Cavalieri began to make a series of silent motion pictures.

As late as the early thirties, the Italian diva (who may have inspired Edward Sheldon's perfumed theatre piece, *Romance*) could be seen in Washington Square circles, where I caught sight of her one evening at a party. Years had passed since her prime, yet the magnolia complexion and black satin hair still created their dazzling effect. She had the same carriage with straight back and the high proud poise of the head. Her dress was of black velvet, severely cut, like that of Sargent's Madame X, and was unadorned by jewellery. After that evening it was a long time before I heard of Lina Cavalieri again. The real tragedy of people is always lived out in time: what irreconcilable deserts of years lie between the opulent New York of 1913 that feted this beautiful diva and the impossible rubble of the Second World War under which Lina Cavalieri was killed in a bombing raid on Florence in 1944.

To speak of Cavalieri is to speak indirectly of Lady Diana Manners and 'The Souls'. Towards the end of the Edwardian

Mrs Aubrey Herbert as a bride. Bay leaves fastened by paste brooches were invariably worn by 'The Souls'

age in London there had appeared a coterie of somewhat intellectually inclined aristocrats, bohemians, and statesmen, who called themselves (it is to be hoped with a tinge of irony) 'The Souls'. They were earmarked by a revived interest in poetry and literature and cultivated aesthetic tastes and were not without a capacity for creative activity. Their members included Lady Wemyss, Lady Desborough, Lady Ribblesdale, Lady Islington, Lady Lytton, Lord Balfour, Harry Cust, and Evan Charteris. Yes, there were male 'Souls', and one particularly 'uneasy spirit' in the guise of the Countess of Oxford and Asquith, a 'charter' member who was to observe many years later: 'I was born with sufficient enterprise, affection, and observation to discern, even among the young, those who were likely to become permanent; and there was not a member of "The Souls"—the name given to me and my friends—who did not earn world-wide reputation. . . . There is no social circle of the same kind today, because prominent political opponents, who had seldom spoken to one another, met in our house. This was an innovation which was almost as good as a scandal and was what first brought "The Souls" into fame.'

Apart from their peripheral political activities, 'The Souls' had a considerable influence on the aesthetic trends of their day. Their taste might generally be described as being expurgated pre-Raphaelite or day-nursery Yellow Book. The vivid colours of Rossetti were banned in preference for the almond greens and pale greys of Kate Greenaway. Their houses were decorated with discreet Morris chintzes, while leaves replaced flowers in the category of beauty: a sprig of jasmine might be found in a single 'specimen' glass on a mantelpiece, and other vases around the pale-coloured rooms would be filled with sprays of rosemary or thyme or magnolia leaves. Bay leaves fastened by paste brooches were invariably worn by the ladies, who went in for long draperies and pleated dresses.

One of the immortal 'Souls' was Violet, Duchess of Rutland, a great beauty who wore her hair in the Greek manner, with a fringe and a big chignon, and was partial to trailing tea gowns of coffee colour, combined with a lace cap that was tied under her chin. She had three daughters who were dressed in unusual clothes and reared along the remarkable and original lines of their mother's high aesthetic aims.

Lady Diana Manners, the youngest and most beautiful child, was very fair. Instead of being enveloped in the ordinary white muslin dresses of the times, she was scrupulously clothed by her mother in black velvet. When the young girl Diana was of an age to make her debut, she did not appear in the pink-and-white dress which was standard for other debutantes, but was garbed by her mother in stone colours, greys or other off shades that made their wearer's opalescent complexion seem even more glowing. When she went to Ascot, Lady Diana Manners, unlike the other girls of her age, who wore straw hats trimmed with a rose or a ribbon, was outstanding in a black picture hat with sheaves of gold and silver wheat on it, and in another hat draped in grey lace. At the popular historical pageants of the day, in which important personages appeared for charity as well as for their own amusement, Lady Diana always arrived in some surprising guise. Once, instead of appearing as a queen of England or a French king's mistress, Lady Diana, together with a group of other young ladies, decided to be a swan. Her mother, without informing the others, arranged for her daughter to be the black swan of the brood.

All the Duchess of Rutland's children received a similarly unique guidance. One piece of advice issued to them was: 'If you wish to comport yourselves in the most graceful and dignified manner possible, if you wish to assume beauty, if you wish to have the grace of a great lady, then you cannot do better than to study every detail and gesture of Lina Cavalieri.'

Perhaps Lady Diana's sister Marjorie, with her dark hair, took this advice most to heart and became Cavalieri's most adept pupil. Today her children, the granddaughters of the old Duchess, are very beautiful women, married and with children of their own. Whether they realize it or not, their mannerisms —from the surprised eyebrows and the arched back to the bold gestures of the arm, the sensitive twisting and untwisting of the pearl necklace—all of these idiosyncrasies are derived from Lina Cavalieri. Thus Cavalieri lives today: a school has been established, based on this woman whose personal magnificence

Lady Diana
Manners –

was a living proof of how great natural gifts of distinction can be found in those not born in the highest spheres. That a wise old English duchess, conscious of the best when she sees it, should select as a paragon of behaviour for her children a woman who worked in a tobacco factory and rubbed shoulders with the *demi-monde*—all of this has the ring of a short story by Isak Dinesen.

Among the stage personalities in the years before the 1914 war, none was (or is, since she is still alive) more vivid than Cécile Sorel, who represented that rare thing, an actress with the ability to display a great deal of taste in her off-stage life. Since her earliest days, when she was photographed by her sister, the well-known Reutlinger, flamboyantly posed in the most exaggerated fashions of the day, with heroic hats, draped silks and furs, Cécile Sorel brought the glory of Racine into the drawing-room. Likewise, there has always been a panache about the way in which she lived. With the advantages of a great deal of

CÉCILE SOREL
AFTER DRIAN

money to spend and the advice of the Count Boni de Castellane and the architect Whitney Warren, this actress turned her nobly proportioned apartment on the Quai Voltaire into a thing of extravagant beauty. Everywhere she displayed her penchant for leopard skin. Though the taste was derived from Largillière and Nattier, Cécile Sorel's predilection was to wield considerable influence for the next half century. She possessed some rare pieces of furniture, including a particularly beautiful chaise longue shaped somewhat like a gondola, upholstered in a wonderful old green-blue velvet, and a set of magnificent chairs signed by Cressant. The fine *boiseries* were of eggshell blue and gold. Against a magnificent Coromandel screen she placed a couple of Jacob fauteuils covered in lobster-scarlet velvet.

In the bedroom, in an alcove and on a raised dais, stood her magnificent Louis Seize bed. The bookcases held many beautifully tooled bindings, and the pair of Oriental dragons with beautiful mounts of ormolu, the phoenix in Turkish green,

Cécile Sorel.

every object was chosen with an extraordinary instinct. Sorel's 'smaller drawing-room' could easily be in the home of an enlightened Rothschild today. But it was the dining-room that perhaps displayed her sense of grandeur to the best advantage. The floor, of white and pigeons'-blood marble squares, was spread with leopard skins, while the marble walls, of an eggshell brown, were hung with medallions of carved stone. The dining table of marble was copied from one at Versailles and was covered with a cloth of gold tissue. For her dinner parties fat garlands of scarlet poppies or red carnations, raised at given points to attach themselves to a huge still life of purple grapes, were hung in festoons the length of this table.

Early in the century Sorel's apartment was photographed in colour. From the reproduction that appeared in a magazine, it is astonishing to realize how little the evanescent or trumpery found its way into her rooms. There were no fussy cushions, no palms or ferns, no overcrowding.

A corner of Sorel's bedroom

This is an example of classical taste allied to an individual point of view, though the personal touches have been so widely copied that it is difficult for us today to realize the full force of their original impact.

Outside fashion, and yet immeasurably more elegant than most of the heroic beauties of her Edwardian heyday, was the American heiress Consuelo Vanderbilt, who became Duchess of Marlborough and later Madame Balsan. Though she was immensely tall and exceedingly slender, with a long stalk-like neck and wasp waist, there was nothing willowy about her, even in early youth. Something like an idol or a Cretan goddess, she was poker-backed and poker-faced. With her etiolated but compact contours her movements were ceremonial, and she seemed to spend her life simplifying her own silhouette.

From the time that Consuelo Vanderbilt wore the famous

74

Sorel's drawing-room

stomacher of diamonds and transcended the essential ugliness
of the peeress's robes at the coronation of King Edward,
through the period of boaters, picture hats, sunbonnets, cloche
hats, and until she became the white-haired woman in an early
Victorian trilby of parma violets, she has retained her easily
recognizable primness. The minute face as symmetrical as a

Consuelo, Duchess of Marlborough

primrose, the pursed smile and the tiptilted nose with triangular nostrils were captured by Helleu, Sargent (who made an heroic family portrait to hang at Blenheim Palace), and many other painters of her day, but no one succeeded better than the painter of fashion, Boldini.

Surely no other artist ever slashed his canvases more vigorously to produce an effect of brio and verve. With a few aggressive strokes Boldini could produce the incandescent effect that women felt they were able to create when seen at their best.

The bulk of the canvases of this extraordinary little Italian reveal duchesses and *cocottes* caught in some terrible contortion on parquet floors so shining and slippery that you wonder how they are able to maintain their balance, especially when they are wearing such high-heeled, pointed-toed shoes. Perhaps, for safety's sake, a mushroom-coloured fauteuil is painted nearby, where the subject can collapse if one of her posturing poses should prove too arduous. Boldini inevitably pictured his

In the manner of Boldini

sitters as caught in the extreme affectation of their times. Like birds about to take flight, the ladies seem barely at home on satiny chaises longues that seem to be spinning round in mid-air. The tulle scarves, pointed fingers, elaborately coiffed hair, silver tissue trains, and aigrettes are all caught in a frenzied whirl of succulent paint.

Boldini had an awareness of fashion far more acute than that of Sargent, and instead of painting his subjects in the somewhat nebulous draperies that the American painter erroneously supposed would not 'date', the Italian immortalized his sitters in the dress of one particular season. Mrs Lydig walks in the Bois in a *tailleur* from Callot, or someone else wears an evening gown recognizably from Cheruit. Boldini was able to create on his lightning-struck canvases an apotheosis of all that the Rue de la Paix and the Place Vendôme could offer. As the years advanced, his canvases became bigger and his art debased, until he finally attained a vulgarity that gave birth to the schools of Van Dongen and Jean Gabriel Doumerge.

The early and smaller sketches of Boldini—ladies in *broderie anglaise* drinking tea in the garden, interiors of dress shows, or sitting-rooms shuttered against the afternoon sun—are tender and sensitive and are as yet underrated for their consummate skill and artistry. But however superficial or meretricious his work became, he was always able to pass on to the spectator his enjoyment of the nonsense he was portraying. Even the most outrageous of his portraits imply the greatest fun.

Of the poor, pathetic phantoms of the past, a faint memory of the day before yesterday, the Baron de Meyer is forgotten today by all but a few who still appreciate the contributions he made to this time in *Vogue's* pages, where his best work appeared.

Baron de Meyer was a German who settled in London with his ultra-fashionable and spectacular-looking wife. He was the continuation of a tradition based on the Scottish Octavius Hill, a mediocre painter who became a remarkable photographer. But the Baron's intentions were very different from those of the Scot. De Meyer wished to avoid reality except when it con-

From a drawing of the Duchesse Graẓioli by Boldini

formed to his particular idiom of grace and distinction. He succeeded in overcoming the mechanical limitations of the camera with the surest and lightest touch, and created impressionistic pictures of the ladies of his day that brought to the surface their innate elegance with an uncanny and varied mastery and spirit. His was the triumph of mind over the matter of mechanism. By using a soft focus lens of particular subtlety he brought out the delicacy of attractive detail and ignored the blemishes that were unacceptable. Utilizing ladies in tiaras and silver lamé as his subject matter, he produced Whistlerian impressions of sunlight on water, of dappled light through trees. As in the instance of many true artists, De Meyer managed to convey his enjoyment of a subject, and he never conveyed too much: he was not afraid of producing an almost empty photograph.

With his dashingly dressed wife, his house, and his entertainments, Baron de Meyer was a man of flamboyant taste, the first photographer to possess a wordly sense that came through his work. He was a great snob, and if he photographed a certain woman, the implication was that she had attained a high position in the social scene. The innate discrimination of his touch could be seen in every photograph: if a bibelot appeared on a table in a corner of a picture, it was certain to be an exquisite bibelot, just as the table itself bespoke quality. He was the first of the editor-photographers and would take a hand in choosing the dresses he was to photograph for the magazines: then often he would improve upon the look of the dress he was photographing by giving some slightest readjustment to a sleeve or a bow. The Baron brought many innovations to photography, and, though even technicians are ignorant of his name, much of the photographic work being done in studios and moving pictures today can be directly traced to him.

It was a great event for me when at last I was able to meet the man whose photographs had had such an indelible influence on my own. I wanted so much to discover the sort of person responsible for making such a variety of pictures that had all been touched with the sacred fire of an artist. Alas, I never made the discovery.

De Meyer drove down the precipitous path to my small remote house in the Wiltshire downs in an enormous open racing car which was painted bright blue. At its approach, stones, little lumps of chalk, and rabbits scattered in all directions. Inside the car, driven by a chauffeur in livery to match the motor car, sat the Baron de Meyer, a tall, ageless-looking man in a bright blue suit and beret, with hair dyed to match.

My rather bucolic guests were somewhat surprised by this apparition, and I must confess to feeling embarrassed myself by his mannerisms. I fear the wretched man did not make as successful an entrance as he had expected. Perhaps it was because of this lack of sympathy that, out of nervousness, he took refuge in a dreadful affectation and artifice, talking with raised eyebrows and a plum in his mouth, in a high-pitched voice that was like a stage caricature. Each word that he spoke seemed more unfortunate than the last. He giggled nervously. Alarmed that things were so disappointingly different from

what I had expected, I felt, before all was lost, that I must
make a speech and tell this man how he had been my god for
years, instilling into his pictures a magic whose recipe it had
long been my ambition to discover. As I continued with my
set piece, I could see the man's face becoming rigid and resent-
ful. I had done something wrong. To talk about photography,
I realized, was unpardonable. It was just as much of a blunder
as if I had asked him whether he himself fixed his pictures in
hypo.

Perhaps if I had been given other opportunities to know this
strange creature I might have been able to discover a rapport
with him, to learn the secret of which the hard core of his
aesthetic integrity was composed. But the blue motor and its
blue-clad occupants soon rolled up the hill again, and with them
went the close-guarded secret that has survived the critical
scrutiny of many years.

De Meyer's early photographs, taken from 1900 onwards,

are in a class by themselves, with as touching and sensitive a quality as the impressionist paintings of Berthe Morisot. Nothing could be more simple and restrained than Madame Errazuriz in black taffetas, with feathered exclamation mark in her toque, sitting forward expectantly and almost turning her back to the camera, yet giving more than a mere indication of an impression of the personal appearance, character, and atmosphere of this great individual than any conventional literary portrait could have hoped to achieve.

Only in the Baron's photographs of Lady de Grey (later Lady Ripon), resplendent in silver cloth and tiara, do I find a corroboration of all that I have heard about this great social figure, of whom, alas, I was never able to catch a near glimpse but whose name is a byword for elegance, graciousness, and charm of an earlier period.

As for the pictures of the fabulous Nijinsky, they alone do not seem to destroy a legend. We have heard of the leap, the lightness, the dynamic agility. It is hard to reconcile the simpering, muscle-bound clod of the Bassano pictures with the verbal reports that have come down to us; but the frivolous De Meyer, with his camera, pioneer spirit, and touching zest, spent an afternoon photographing *Le Spectre de la Rose*, the Faun from *L'Apres-Midi*, the Slave in *Schéhérazade*, and the Prince of *Le Pavillon d'Armide*. The results of that afternoon lead one to appreciate that this strange-looking dancer did, in fact, possess a steel-trap agility, the gaiety of youth, the lyrical and exciting qualities which have now become a part of history.

It was only after a long career of documenting the gloss of an epoch that Baron de Meyer became the Boldini of photographers, and his work changed to the exaggeratedly affected. Even then he was able to pass on his admiration for, and his enjoyment of, the frivolities of the moment. From the curving spines of his sitters with an inevitable hand on a hip and their proud heads, and *profils perdus* caught in frieze-like poses, to the sparkle on the silver lace, the tissues, the pearls, the shells, the sunlight catching the pristine petal of a madonna lily, the sheen on parquet floors, the shimmer on mirror-panelled doors, the fireworks bursting among the arabesques of a crystal

1911

chandelier—all of these details have been frozen out of time by the unique art of fashion's first and most individual photographer.

De Meyer, Boldini and his ladies, Cécile Sorel, Lina Cavalieri, and 'The Souls' played their roles in a world of changing fashions. Indeed, the barometer of feminine styles never ran a stranger gamut than in the years preceding the First World War and throughout the war itself. Paris was never captured during the war, thus allowing its continuing catalytic influence as the world's fashion centre. Though ten million men were killed in that period from 1914 to 1918, the war was still (and not so ironically by present-day standards) a 'gentleman's' war. There was no pin-point bombing, no saturation raids on the civilian population, no prolonged deprivations. It is not too cynical to say that, with a few outward bows to wartime conventions, certain aspects of social life in Paris continued much as they had before.

On the eve of world catastrophe the mode had become so disparate and varied that to be fashionable in all ways was out of the question. With half panniers and suggestions of Directoire and Empire styles, as well as a partial return to early Victorian bustles, elegant ladies were able to be in the height of fashion while adopting the most divergent of styles. Every leading house had its personal preferences: Paquin was not like Laferrière, nor Doucet like Vincent-Lachartrouaille, nor Reboux like Camille Roger, nor Worth like Redfern. Premet had gone back to the dress of 1880; Beer favoured the periods of Watteau; while Doeuillet expressed preference for Second Empire styles. One half of Paris was wearing Victorian basques as tight as possible, while the other adopted the tunic that hung without touching from shoulder to knee. The pitch pipe of change was sounding different and discordant notes with each season.

These changes of style were not unrelated to the breaking up

Every leading house had its personal preferences

of the social scene: like the shadows cast on the wall of Plato's cave, they reflected the mutations of the times. Suffragettes insisted on woman's emancipation, while paradoxically the styles asserted themselves as being more feminine than ever; morals and modes of behaviour were being shaken up like the first cocktail. Automobiles were bigger and more powerful, trains were longer and faster, aeroplanes were feasible, and life became a whirl. A craze for dancing swept in. The *thé dansant* became a social function, a rendezvous for illegitimate flirtation. With it came the 'lounge lizards', the unescorted wives and enthusiastic businessmen who left the office an hour earlier to dance the tango, which had been 'smuggled' in from Argentina, to wriggle to the maxixe, hug in the Bunny Hug, glide in the Gaby Glide, and walk the Castle Walk, for Vernon and Irene Castle were at the peak of their popularity.

When Mrs Vernon Castle suddenly appeared, she was greeted with the shock of recognition that people always re-

Fillette delivering hats. Place Vendôme 1910

Suffragettes, 1910

serve for those who—as Wordsworth once said—create the taste by which they are to be appreciated. Her advent introduced a completely fresh note in women's appearance, but at the same time this surprise had the familiarity of understanding: when we take up the 'new' it is only because we have had a secret need of it and have unconsciously prepared for its coming. It is no accident that Stravinsky's early music and Picasso's cubist period coincided with the success of a woman who was to be one of the most remarkable fashion figures the world has known. Mrs Castle was as important an embodiment of the 'modern', in the social and fashion sense, as these artists were in the world of art. No doubt there were many ears that rejected the *Sacre du Printemps*, just as many eyes could not appreciate *Les Demoiselles d'Avignon*. With the passing of the years, those same eyes and ears came to accept the painting and music which they had at first rejected so violently. In the case of Mrs Vernon Castle, no such time lapse existed: women are much more open to changes in fashion than the public is open to revolutionary trends in art.

In the spring of 1911, when England was on the eve of George V's coronation, New Yorkers were heralding Victor Herbert's operettas, Oscar Straus's *The Chocolate Soldier*, or the *Pink Lady* with Miss Hazel Dawn. Mr Irving Berlin was about to popularize a new kind of jazz with his song, 'Alexander's Ragtime Band'.

The waltz, the Boston, and the two-step had been the dominant forms of the dance, but now the tango and the one-step were 'all the rage' and Mr and Mrs Vernon Castle were the embodiment of this new modernity.

There must have been an unconscious wisdom in the newly-married Castles' choice of temporarily turning their backs on the American scene, though in fact the entertainment in which they had been appearing in New York had closed, their immediate prospects were nebulous, and the groom had vague plans to appear in a revue in Paris.

Thus the Castles set sail for France, there to meet with a cycle of bad luck. Disappointments followed close on one another. Vernon and Irene Castle were sitting in some obscure pension on the Left Bank at the nadir of their fortunes. When all theatre prospects had failed to materialize, they were finally offered an engagement to appear as a dance team at the Café de Paris. An announcement was posted together with a display of their photographs in the lobby of the restaurant: '*Tous les soirs, au souper, Vernon and Irene Castle, dans leur danses sensationelles*'. These '*danses sensationelles*' were to be performed in costume, and possibly included some wilder versions of the new, fashionable jazz steps.

The evening preceding their engagement the Castles were invited, as a magnanimous gesture on the part of the management, to dine at the Café de Paris. As they sat somewhat timidly watching the world around them while they ate their dinner, they were recognized from their photographs by a Russian count at a nearby table, who persuaded them to dance for him then and there. The young couple found themselves taking the dance floor, not from the wings nor in costume, but from a table among the guests wearing evening dress, Mrs Castle in her wedding dress replete with train and a Dutch bonnet, which was later to be copied all over the world. Perhaps they were obliged to dance with more reserve than if they had worn their theatrical costumes. Mrs Castle's short train limiting her to non-acrobatic movements. The result was a *succes fou*.

From then on there were unlimited invitations and offers. It became the Castles' specialty to appear in ball dress, to rise for their exhibition dance from a table among the guests. When they returned to America a year or so later, the Castles were international celebrities. Soon they found themselves the king and queen of Castle House, a restaurant for *thé dansants* and dancing school in East Forty-sixth Street of New York, from which they sent forth the rules of modern dancing.

They performed at a night club which opened on top of a theatre called, appropriately enough, Castles in the Air. On the stage they became the stars of *Watch Your Step*, earning as much as six thousand dollars a week. From cheap Left Bank pensions they had travelled to a country house in Manhasset, where Vernon played polo and kept sporting dogs.

The dance craze was meanwhile at its zenith. Endless new dance steps emerged, including the fox trot of 1915, which was to prove to be the most enduring of all. Many restaurants engaged similar dance teams to rival the Castles, among the leading contenders being Maurice and Florence Walton and later Mae Murray and Clifton Webb. It was as the winner of one of the so popular dancing contests that Rudolph Valentino came to the fore. Moralists attacked the new dancing, saying that it encouraged loose behaviour, but the upheaval in manners was consolidated and the dancing continued, its vitality being

Mrs Vernon Castle

personified by the genial new ambassadors of youth, Vernon and Irene Castle. Even middle-aged people found themselves joining the quadrille. When we think that today one scarcely pays attention to an older man or woman taking the floor at a night club, we must realize how the attractive personalities of Vernon and Irene Castle were important elements in the creation of such a *laissez-faire* attitude.

Irene Castle's appearance was unlike anyone else's, yet overnight people accepted it and emulated her wherever possible. The primary effect that she created was one of an exquisite grace combined with an extraordinarily boyish youthfulness. There was something terrifically healthy and clean about her. In her whiplike and taut bearing she hinted at the wonderful play of muscles beneath the surface, as a fine-bred horse betrays its beauty by a ripple. There was something blade-like and steely about her muscles and her limbs. She used her hands with such a bold grace that one had the notion that she gesticulated rather than gestured. Previously dancers had made softer use of gesture; but Irene Castle moved her hands sharply, with a masculine boldness, the wrists arched, the fingers straight as bread sticks. She walked with very long strides, with no daintiness, swinging along with wonderful, live, big gestures. She invented a whole balance of movement, with the pelvis thrust forward and the body leaning backwards, giving her torso the admirable lines and flat look of Cretan sculpture. This stance necessitated, if she were standing still, the placing of one leg behind her as a balance. Within the compass of these basic axes she turned her body to the four winds, raising a shoulder against the direction in which she was going. The 'trademark' of the raised shoulder became a sort of fetish that many women were to copy. Such movements seemed possible only with an extraordinary sense of balance and an innate sense of design. It was as if a gyroscope were inside her, always stabilizing the body's framework no matter on which tangent it moved off.

Yet Irene Castle's boyish impression was counterbalanced by an extreme femininity, an equally strong suggestion of allure, despite the fact that she employed none of the usual feminine attributes. Her complexion was rather like a boy's, dun in colour; and her hair was a nondescript mouse-brown. The features were knobby and blunt as those of a marmoset. With the heart-shaped face, the high cheekbones, and the incredibly long eyebrows that ended like a mouse's tail at the corners, Irene Castle was not a beauty in classical terms at all; but the relationship of her features to one another was good, and her face became the prototype of a cast of looks not at all uncommon today. Very few women, up until that time, had possessed high cheekbones or slightly protruding, rather Egyptian mouths, almost simian in their pout. Even Mrs Castle's eyes, small but of an extraordinary brilliance, proved how unimportant is the notion that eyes have to be large. The upper lids tapered downwards to give a sad, compassionate, sympathetic expression, belying the lower lids, which, in contrast, screwed upwards, so that she looked as though she were always laughing. She created a strange combination of sadness and gaiety.

Like many works of art, it was not symmetry that made Mrs Vernon Castle so alluring; she, too, proved that real beauty can often be irregular, and she created a dominant and striking personality from assets which any other woman at the time might well have regarded as liabilities.

In fashions Irene Castle was an instinctive leader. When she cut her hair very short, everybody copied the Castle bob. She had a completely personal way of dressing, utilizing the fashions of her time for her own purposes, and always in an unusual manner. Though she stands out in memory as being the personification of her epoch, she was responsible for many innovations in the prevailing fashions: above all for an innovation in appearance—her marvellous balance of femininity and boyish simplicity was congruent to the latest ideal that women had created for themselves, to replace the golden curls and valentine sweetness of a Mary Pickford.

Since her professional appearance was seldom theatrical in a flamboyant sense, it was easy enough for Mrs Castle to adapt the very feminine fashions of the period for her dancing clothes. The impression she created was rather as though the most elegant woman in a restaurant or night club had been induced to give an exhibition on the dance floor.

Wherever she travelled she would find some costume of a foreign country could be adapted to her purpose. Sometimes Mrs Castle wore boys' caps or men's riding coats, even donning glen plaid or striped tail coats for evening dress. In spite of her short hair, these outfits were always extremely feminine, and if she wore a man's top hat there would always be a loose curl in the middle of her forehead.

In general, she dressed in soft, flowing materials. Though some of the dresses Lucile made for her might be elaborate, they were always simple in outline: there was little trimming about her—she was a statuette conception with nothing pinned on.

In effect, Mrs Castle put the backbone to femininity, showing its vertebrae instead of its dimples, and was thus an important reflection of the social attitude of her period, an embodiment of woman's declared emancipation. This attitude genuinely defined her personality, even down to the buckled shoes that trod on slippery floors with a sure unerring step, the step of her utterly frank, open, and bold personality.

Irene Castle had the certainty of an artist. You knew that she was never fussed, that the comb went through the hair once, and once was enough. She did not need a second chance. She was the kind of woman who could dress without looking in the glass, for she needed no assurance from a mirror—if she felt right, she could go out on to the dance floor.

Of her dancing it was said that she was like thistledown, and an observer remarked: 'Not until you have seen her dance do you really understand what a breeze is like; she makes a breeze visible.' Yet it is said that Irene Castle was not as fine a dancer as her husband. Her grace and poise were a perfect foil for Vernon Castle's 'lithe authority'.

Not only were the Castles the precursors of modern ballroom dancing, but by their grace and distinguished example they opened the hearts of millions and sped 'modernism' on its way. The dance craze that they symbolized promoted a freer, less restricted social exchange between men and women. It was only a step in the revolt that, at its peak, would bring in the shingle and knee-short skirts. When Vernon Castle was killed

Choosing hats for spring 1913.

at Fort Worth, Texas, in 1918 as the result of an aeroplane crash, his death marked the end of an era—the era of the First World War—and the beginning of a new one, the era of the twenties.

No doubt the war of 1914-18 had hastened the demise of the tightly swathed skirt as being impractical for the new role that women not only envisioned for themselves but were actually fulfilling. These narrow costumes had never been in keeping with those early struggles for feminine freedom, and suffragettes in hobble skirts and picture hats had had a hard time

when chased by policemen. Now the pendulum was to swing to the other extreme; by 1915 and 1916 fashions returned to an eighteenth-century feeling and skirts became bell-shaped. 'Flare and the world flares with you, cling and you cling alone', was the adage that fashion magazines applied to the new skirts. Some dresses were tiered, and *robes de style* or 'picture dresses' became popular. There came in the ravishing fashion of peg-top skirts, or skirts with Fragonard panniers of taffetas. A full-blown rose was tucked in at the waistband, at the culmination of a fichu which fell in ruffles or drapery from the neck. Stripes were popular; and Nattier blue became the fashionable colour. Shoes were pointed, trimmed with huge buckles, and laced with silk ribbons. Suffragettes tying themselves to the railings of Buckingham Palace now wore Dolly Varden shepherdess hats tipped up at the back, with a bunch of ribbons under the rear of the brim.

By the winter of 1916 these extremes had been somewhat modified, though femininity in the form of frills and fichus did not utterly disappear until a stubborn peasant girl from Auvergne in turn created her revolution.

These were the changing years that preceded and ushered in the even more changing twenties. To an older eye the death of Edwardianism must have boded no good, and a decade or so later there were to be those who would look back fondly on Black Ascot, the Castles, and hobble skirts, witnessing the advent of jazz age with horror. But from our present vantage point, even the twenties are beginning to charm some of us once more. Time not only heals, it reconciles.

James Laver has written well on the theory of the relativity of taste itself in his *Taste and Fashion*, and has even established a table to indicate the probable historical perspective on a given fashion as time ultimately brings it round to be reconsidered as romantic and beautiful. The implications of such a theory are less disturbing than a similar view of history, such as Toynbee's cyclical conception of the world. That empires rise and fall we agree; but to conceive of the breakup of Western civilization, as we know it, is more difficult to enjoy than the idea that all fashions, their hour come round at last, will be

magical and alluring when seen through the rose-coloured
glasses of the ages.

CHAPTER SIX

I T is difficult to speculate upon the social or psychological
reasons that prompt the periodic revivals of Orientalism in
our diametrically opposed Western culture. But maybe the
real significance of a Napoleon's expedition to Egypt, or the
opening of a King Tutankhamen's tomb, is that the West has
an absolute need to inject not only the colours of the East into
its pallid spectrum of browns and greys and blacks but also its
qualities of the bizarre and the alien.

Whatever the reason may be, Orientalism had in 1909
affected European fashion many times before it again struck at
the heart of London, Paris, and New York. This time it was to
come via Russia, with the young Diaghilev and his artist Bakst
as the spearheads of the invasion. A rising Parisian couturier,
Poiret, was to filter Bakst's imaginative *élan* down to the public
itself; or, acknowledging that Poiret may have been the innovator when he claims that his personal Orientalism preceded
that of Bakst, we may say that Paul Poiret exploited a parallel
vein to the fantastic Orientalism which the Russian Ballet was

to foster. As a matter of fact, Poiret's obsession with the East continued to impose itself on the world of fashion for a long time after the influence of Orientalism had waned. It is a tribute to his stubborn genius that he sent women off to the races wearing turbans and padded kimonos embroidered in gold peacocks, and perversely made them accept his taste when time had already by-passed the spirit that animated it.

Diaghilev's talents were rare for any period. He was one of the baker's dozen of powerful personalities who have helped to nurture the arts since Renaissance individualism. The vision, initiative, and daring of such men of taste have often stamped the style of their age with the authority of a king applying his signet to sealing wax. These impresarios (and how that word has become vulgarized today) leave imprints which are not soon forgotten, influencing aesthetic trends for many years afterwards. None has ever surpassed the achievement or influence of the remarkable Sergei Diaghilev.

So much has already been written about Sergei Diaghilev that he threatens to become a legend under our very eyes. Though he has been dead only twenty-four years, the world that he represented and the splendour that he materialized out of thin air already have an odd quality of history. His capacities for organization, combining music, painting, and the dance, created modern ballet as we know it today and fostered a public consciousness which has largely helped to breach the gaps caused by the difficulties and obscurities of modern art.

This extraordinary figure, so quiet and discreet, known intimately by a handful of initiates, moved in the rarefied world of Monte Carlo and the most carefully winnowed circles of London and Paris. Yet today, audiences throughout the seven continents of the world, whether consciously or not, are applauding his taste and the results of his wonderful talents, for no one man has ever had a greater aesthetic influence on the years that immediately followed his death. Perhaps the reason for this is that Diaghilev, in his own lifetime, had an uncanny instinct for predicting the newest tendencies. His instinct was so *avant-garde* that, years later, audiences are accepting Diaghilev's discoveries as reflecting the spirit of their own age.

Diaghilev

Those who knew the impresario could scarcely forget his arresting physical personality. He was a *grand seigneur* in every sense of the word, in dress, speech, and manner. Beneath the slow-motion gestures, the quiet air, and the utter lack of pretentiousness, Diaghilev's authority manifested itself the moment one came into his presence. That presence was as much public as private: he was not averse to appearing in public and could often be seen dining out in Paris and London, or drinking apéritifs at Florian's in Venice, usually in conversation with Lifar or one of the artists allied with the Ballet Russe, perhaps a composer, director, or scenic designer whose efforts would be under discussion.

To the observer, Diaghilev must have looked rather like an imposing seal, with his long, wide mouth, flat teeth, and sleek, plump body. His cheeks would be powdered, and the chinchilla hair was liberally streaked with white. Inevitably the spectator's eyes came to rest on the immaculate and aristocratic hands with their calm gestures. In attributes of dress he was always the dandy, immaculate beneath his fur-collared coat, and usually wearing a pearl tiepin.

The man behind this impressive physical façade was always something of an enigma, even to his intimates, and became considerably more of a mystery after his death. Not that he was shy—far from it. Diaghilev was on intimate terms with every member of his company, charmed them with his frank manner, tamed them with his authority, and could be ruthless if the occasion demanded. His intimates had the impression of a simple person with a schoolboy sense of humour and a lively curiosity about other people that often took the form of unusual interest in their intrigues: he adored bedroom gossip. As for his own private life, he made no secret of it and could often be seen having kipper or haddock suppers at the Savoy Grill with the latest favourite.

Like all truly original and powerful personalities, he disregarded criticism. His taste was impeccable, and he was as much a man of the world as an artist of the world, bringing the same refinement of choice to ordering a meal as he would to commanding a new concerto. He knew where the best intimate restaurants were, just as he knew where to find the most provocative sets and costumes, or whom to go to for a ballet scenario. His way with waiters was as knowing as his way with a temperamental star.

But whether dinners or ballets were at stake, Diaghilev had little business sense in any ordinary meaning of that expression. Indeed, his utter lack of vulgarity could hardly have allowed him one. But as though to compensate for that, he had untold energy at his command with which to raise money for each new ballet season from the patrons who, unknowingly, were contributing to one of the last great expressions of culture that the leisured classes were to produce.

Sergei Pavlovich Diaghilev was born in the Tsarist Russia of 1872. As a wealthy young Russian aristocrat of impeccable and varied taste, he had edited a remarkable art magazine which showed unmistakable signs of the master's originality and indicated his flair for discovering unknown painters. Later his interests were to turn suddenly to music, and later still he was able to fulfil his dream and combine these two early passions by creating the Russian ballet.

Before Diaghilev's advent there had indeed been wonderful Russian dancers. As a single instance, the fame of Anna Pavlova was already independent of this great impresario, and she had made a number of grand tours before the Russian ballet dazzled Paris with its opening seasons in the years immediately preceding the First World War. But the popular ballets at that time were very different from the great romantic age of ballet which, some fifty or sixty years previously, had launched Taglioni and Carlotta Grisis and had given to its repertory such unforgettable works as *Giselle* and the *Pas de Quatre*. The ballets in the first decade of the twentieth century were, indeed, little more than advantageous vehicles to display the technical efforts of the leading virtuosi. Little artistry went into their presentation of these ballets, and the décor and *mise en scène* were utterly banal.

An ordinary person entering this scene of balletic desuetude would have been discouraged and downhearted. But Sergei Diaghilev was a man of vision, and paradoxically, in his own aristocratic, impractical way, he was enough of a businessman to bring that vision into being. His many friends included rich patrons of the arts. Like a magician materializing a little world out of a hat, Diaghilev gathered together the necessary funds to launch such a spectacular luxury as the Russian ballet.

His personal tastes served him well in the enterprise, for he loved the old while manifesting the keenest interest in the new. This combination of traditionalism with a taste for the modern was to create a new ballet such as had never been seen before— a ballet where mime would be as important as the dance itself and where music, décor, and costumes, far from being relegated to the status of supernumeraries, were to become an integral part of the complex aesthetic expression.

To carry out such a programme, Diaghilev sought the aid of Stravinsky, whose new music had already aroused both enthusiasm and criticism. For the décor and costumes there were Benois, Sert, and Léon Bakst, whose work had been featured in

Diaghilev's art magazine. Bakst's vivid colours, extravagant materials, and flamboyant exoticism were destined to light up the international sky for quite a long spell, and their influence on fashions led to a whole new phase of dressmaking. Together these three giants brought the dream into its initial realization.

The early seasons of the Russian ballet in the several years preceding the First World War are still spoken of with bated breath by those who were fortunate enough to see the miracle of Nijinsky leaping fifteen feet to the stage as the Spectre of the Rose, or Karsavina as Cleopatra being fanned by Nubian slaves. Working in close collaboration with Bakst, Diaghilev had wrought a miracle. For the first time the colours of a modern painter were brought to the scenery workshop. The emerald-green curtain of *Schéhérazade* and the cobalt-blue walls in *Carnaval* were quite staggering in their impact.

Great dancers seemed to appear from nowhere, created by the master himself. The fantastic assembly of talents that he coordinated gave a note of history to each new season. Diaghilev went forward on a wave of new discoveries, never willing to rest on his laurels. Each time the curtain rose on the première of a work, he produced a surprise. But it was never surprise for its own sake; rather, each ballet asserted the changing and dynamic flow of creative values. Diaghilev never followed *Thamar* or *Petrouchka* by a ballet of its own type; on the contrary, new talents were continually being unearthed.

But any portrait of Diaghilev, however condensed in scope, would be incomplete without an awareness of the colder side of his nature. Possibly this stemmed from some Asiatic, some primitive vestige in his sophisticated heritage. Diaghilev, so sensitive, so vulnerable to youth and beauty, possessed also a banked ruthlessness that could be fanned into overt cruelty. For many years he and Léon Bakst were the closest of friends, and it was through association with this designer that Diaghilev first acquired his greatest ballet successes.

Suddenly he broke off relations with Bakst. Bakst was at a loss to understand the reasons, for there had never been any quarrel or misunderstanding. The impresario explained to mutual friends who came to find out why he had rejected Bakst: 'Léon Bakst has done his best work for me already. I do not consider he will be able to produce anything of interest to me any more.'

In defence of the heartlessness of his behaviour, Diaghilev went on to explain: 'I live only for the ballet. Everything must be sacrificed to that. I feel that Bakst is becoming old fashioned. I want to have my new ballets decorated by younger men—Picasso, Derain, Rouault, even Pruna. No, I am through with Bakst.'

The shock of this breach of friendship may well have caused the illness from which Bakst died a few years later. It could be of little solace to the artist who had created the visual splendours of *Schéhérazade* and *The Sleeping Beauty* that, after his death, Diaghilev suffered agonies of remorse. Those who know or read of this incident can draw their own moral. It would seem that art, however important, is not life itself: and to set up a code of 'art for art's sake' can at times prove equally as in-

human as any political dogma which is fostered and held above human values themselves.

The extraordinary reign of Diaghilev and the Russian ballet lasted less than two decades, ending with the impresario's death in 1929. Yet one can safely say that ballet has been feeding upon those years since Diaghilev withdrew the life force that had been the Russian ballet's mind and heart. It is sad to think that at that time the impresario had to rely solely on private patrons and subsidies, while his seasons inevitably showed a financial loss. Today, throughout the world, ballet companies have been commercialized, to the benefit of many a business tycoon. The art of the dance has latterly become as popular as Gilbert and Sullivan and is no longer a high-brow institution or in any sense special. The *Sacre du Printemps* has given place to festival ballets, and Alicia Markova is a star able to compete with the most renowned comedians on gala programmes.

Since the death of Diaghilev we have found nothing new in ballet, little that is new in the dance or in painting. One wonders whether this is because Sergei Diaghilev is not here to make the discoveries or whether he died in 1929 because there were no further discoveries for him to make. Each age is heard to murmur that 'somewhere has passed a glory from the earth'. Yet even the most open critical examination would indicate that the tremendous activity in art that opened the twentieth century has slowed almost to a standstill. It may well be that factors of environment beyond our control influence the productivity of art. One would like to think that art can blossom in any soil and at any time.

We can be grateful to Diaghilev for the influence he created and for that which has survived him. Nowadays it is not at all uncommon to see modern painters of note working on the décor for a ballet or a play. But until Diaghilev appeared on the scene no artist of even the stature of a Bakst or a Poiret had designed for the theatre. It took a Russian aristocrat, single-handed, to lift the stigma and open the field of designing to the highest talents. Alas, the lowest talents have profited as well, like the jackal at the kill. There can be no doubt but that the dance sequences in any mediocre Hollywood musical comedy are today reflecting, in a watered-down and bastardized fashion, the innovations that the master launched forty and more years ago.

Even in respectable ballet we find the restatement of the aesthetic principles that were utilized by Diaghilev. It was that impresario who discovered George Balanchine early in his career; and today Balanchine, of all living choreographers, is the one most worthy, perhaps, to wear the master's crown.

In the highest and lowest fields of artistic activity, we find that we are still living off dividends from the past. Life thrives mysteriously out of death, roses spring from dung heaps, and all modern art seems to stem from a few powerful artists or personalities whose influences have echoed down the years. Perhaps Diaghilev, in his turn, was influenced by certain others whose names are unknown to us. There is nothing new under the sun, and in art as in evolution, each new manifestation is merely the last link in a chain that stretches back to the beginnings of human consciousness, when the cavemen were scratching their first drawings on the walls of primitive caves.

The new exoticism that Diaghilev had launched was well personified by Ida Rubinstein, whose dancing was perhaps not respected by him, though he felt that her grace of line and move-

Ida Rubinstein
1913

ment more than made up for her lack of technical skill. She mimed her way through *Cléopatre* and a number of other thous-and-and-one-night ballets. An incredibly tall, thin woman, the proverbial 'bag of bones', Ida Rubinstein's slender height allowed her to wear the most outlandishly remarkable dresses, often with three-tiered skirts that would cut up almost any other figure. In private life she was as spectacular as on the stage, almost stopping the traffic in Piccadilly or the Place Ven-dôme when she appeared like an amazon, wearing long, pointed shoes, a train, and very high feathers on her head, feathers that could only augment an already giant frame.

It was her habit to put kohl round her eyes, while her hair was often dressed like a nest of black serpents, giving her an appearance which was not far removed from a mixture of Ichabod Crane and Medusa.

Schéhérazade was Bakst's great moment and to this day is the one ballet of Orientalism that is still successfully performed, though lacking the splendour of the original production. With the excitement engendered by the dance and the vivid colours, a whole debased and bastardized spirit of Orientalism was let loose. Costume parties and fêtes followed in the wake of the new sultan's dream. Society women gave *tableaux vivants* dressed as Eastern slaves, with gold bangles on their ankles and headache bands over their eyes. Baron de Meyer took photographs of ladies in Paris and New York in a flash of gilt tissues and the metallic brilliance of the Orient. London's society beauties were caught by the objective lens of less romantic cameras doing nautch-girl poses, with metal cymbals on their fingers and bells on their toes. A fashion world that had been dominated by corsets, lace, feathers, and pastel shades soon found itself in a city that overnight had become a seraglio of vivid colours, harem skirts, beads, fringes, and voluptuousness. Later there would be bright futuristic scarves of checkered or harlequinade triangles and squares, all of which could be traced traced back to Bakst.

A Frenchwoman remarked at a futurist exhibition: '*C'est d'un mauvais gout épatant!*' For futurism, with one eye cocked to the Orient, had swept into the home. Wide zebra-striped cushions were placed at the ends of an orange- or purple-covered sofa, lotus blooms floated in shallow bowls, walls were painted emerald green or were covered with gold and silver paper that ordinarily would have been put inside a tea cabinet, and sharply angular furniture was made out of lemonwood. The ash from a Pera cigarette would fall on to the thick pile of a black carpet.

From the Russian ballet brilliant colours passed to musical comedy and revue. As a schoolboy, one of my greatest thrills was to go to see Miss Ethel Levey. She was a remarkable and fascinating American jazz artiste with an aquiline nose that, in profile, made her look like a ram. She would strut the stage on her very trim little feet like an exotic bird and was able to do high kicks above her head with consummate ease. Ethel Levey invented the jazz ruse of singing with her arms stretched wide, pecking her head at every turn to make a sort of syncopated frieze.

It is certain that through her artistry Ethel Levey created a sort of refined barbarism, singing with the deep contralto of a sophisticated coal heaver. Her sense of rhythm was unsurpassed by even the Southern Negroes. She possessed enormous éclat, and there was something indefinable about her provocative personality: her particular form of chic was unique, a quality that intrigued all artists. It was not surprising that Diaghilev once asked her to appear as Zobeide in *Schéhérazade*.

Ethel Levey inaugurated many fashions. When she first wore a top hat to ride in the Bois she was ridiculed; but soon every other woman wore a top hat for riding. Virtually her 'trademark' was the omnipresent slave bangle on her ankle, and she claims that by never being without at least half a dozen golden bracelets hung with coins and charms she originated costume jewellery.

One of the costumes that Ethel Levey wore in a revue which had been designed for her by Bakst was of mustard yellow, white, black, and emerald green—such a combination of colours as I would never have thought possible. Bakst also helped her with the decoration of her London house in Gloucester Terrace, which was extremely daring for its epoch.

Jules Bertaut has remarked that the *ballets russes* were a note in the history of French aesthetics. The influence they wielded was certainly not confined to France alone. What could be more stark than a revolution that overnight guillotined prettiness and set exoticism upon the throne? Or what more startling innovation than the replacement of the pastel colour schemes of Comelli by the violent beauty of Diaghilev's world? From Comelli to Bakst is the difference between an aquarelle and an oil painting.

The reigning dressmaker in this new harem world was Paul Poiret, who with his blazing hyperthyroid eyes and short beard looked to the young Cocteau 'like some sort of a huge chestnut'. Both innovator and a reactionary, a fashion tyrant and a generous, idealistic dreamer, Poiret was a complicated personality, perhaps the most paradoxical in many ways that fashion has known in our day, when couturiers have come into

Jean Cocteau

their own as arbiters of taste. To appreciate his revolutionary influence on the prevailing mode, one must consider the kings he dethroned.

Worth was probably the emperor of the presiding geniuses of Paris fashions during the Edwardian period. That had been an age of 'ceremonial fashions', and the velvets, brocades, and broadcloths had been worn with an almost religious pride. For in spite of the latest outward signs of gaiety, the Edwardian age was still a ceremonious one, sustaining much of the spirit of Victorianism in its continuing regard for bourgeois manners and ethics. The men, too, in their frock coats, with beards and Ascot ties studded with great pearls, comported themselves as if for a ritual rather than celebration. Presiding over this world, Worth, Doucet, and Linker had little notion that they were soon to be ousted by a revolutionary who was to sweep all before him with his violent influence.

Paul Poiret's origins were humble. The son of the owner of

Paul Poiret

a small textiles business, Poiret had at a very early age demonstrated his facility for improvising costumes. As an umbrella maker's assistant, he stole small pieces of silk in order to dress up children's dolls in the Oriental taste. It was during a two years' sojourn with Doucet that the youth served his apprenticeship as a dressmaker, an apprenticeship that was terminated when Doucet, sensing that the young man's talent warranted something better than a subsidiary display, advised Poiret to launch forth on his own. Poiret, however, was to hide his light for a time at the Maison Worth, until at last his rebellious spirit gained the sense of authority it needed to start an upheaval that revolutionized fashion.

'I waged war upon the corset,' boasted this irrepressible dressmaker, 'and, like all revolutions, mine was made in the name of liberty—to give free play to the abdomen!'

'Yes, I freed the bust, but I shackled the legs! Women complained of being no longer able to walk, nor get into a carriage.

Have their complaints or grumblings even arrested the movement of fashion, or have they not rather, on the contrary,
helped it by advertising it? I made everyone wear a tight skirt.'

Modesty was one of the qualities completely lacking in the
young anarchist, and he was willing to let his theories be heard
from the housetops.

'The taste for the refinements of the eighteenth century had
led all women into a sort of deliquescence,' he complained. 'On
the pretext that it was "distinguished", all vitality had been
suppressed. Nuances of nymphs' thigh, lilacs, swooning
mauves, tender blue hortensias, niles, maizes, straws, all that
was soft, washed out, and insipid was held in honour. I threw
into this sheepcote a few rough wolves—reds, greens, violets,
royal blue—that made all the rest sing aloud. I had to wake up
the good people of Lyons, whose stomach is a bit heavy, and
put a little gaiety, a new freshness, into their colour schemes.'

Baron de Meyer wrote in *Vogue* magazine during the 1914

war, 'It is astonishing how, during these last few years, colour seems to have been used indiscriminately, almost felt as a necessity, perhaps to counterbalance in some way all the sadness and mourning that pervades Europe. Never have we heard more of a shortage of dyes, never were they more scarce and costly, and yet, never have we had such an orgy of glowing oranges, greens, or reds as during these last months.' The shop windows of Marshall and Snelgrove displayed colour schemes in emerald green and blue, and Monsieur Cartier mixed coloured jewels together for the first time, announcing, '*Je trouve ici un grand avenir pour le vert et le bleu*'.

We may find a partial explanation for the rise of Poiret in the parallel advent of the Russian ballet, which naturally turned many enthusiasts to Orientalism. Yet Poiret himself vehemently denied any eclectic influence of Bakst, and I have been assured by his nephew, Monsieur Bongard, that there was no real or substantial link between Poiret on the one hand and Bakst

and the Russian ballet on the other. This is somewhat reminiscent of the cubists' denial that they had ever seen African Negro art before launching their movement.

To enter Poiret's salons in the Faubourg St Honoré was to step into the world of the *Arabian Nights*. Here, in rooms strewn with floor cushions, the master dressed his slaves in furs and brocades and created Eastern ladies who were the counterpart of the Cyprians and chief eunuchs that moved through the pageantries of Diaghilev.

Poiret had no respect for 'good taste'. He forced his victims to wear chin straps of pearls, slung them with white foxes, stabbed them with fantastic ospreys, imprisoned them (as one hobbles the forelegs of a horse to prevent him from running away) in harem skirts. Wired tunics like lampshades were hung round the ladies' hips, heavy capes enveloped them, and they were laden with tassels and barbaric jewels. This violent Orientalism, which shackled and bound some of Paris' most respectable women, was even more extraordinary when one considers that Poiret himself had at the time never been out of France.

Thus, Poiret, the egocentric genius, ruled despotically for nearly twenty years. His activities were widespread. He designed clothes for the stage and claimed that he was the first designer to co-operate with the scenic artist. He created perfumes.

In the field of interior decoration a school and workshop were opened. There was, at this time, a penchant for indoor trelliswork, geometric edgings and borders to plain walls, stylized or Hispanian roses on cretonne or cushion—a taste for what might be termed a '*gazette du bon temps*' or a 'depraved Kate Greenaway'. Poiret was accessory *directoire* to this crime. Much of the furniture he encouraged was ugly, in the *art moderne* vein, with colours of pink and yellow and salmon. Yet he launched special fabrics for curtains and draperies that are still used today. Many excellent artists were commissioned to design materials for him, and Dufy invented for him certain mordant dye processes. Thus the best of Poiret's influence has filtered down to us in many indirect ways.

If he was rude and tyrannical, Poiret was also lavishly generous, taking groups of his friends to North Africa in his yacht, or giving fabulous parties where the guests received valuable presents. In his spare time he developed a passion for astronomy, together with an interest in serious painting, his art collection including Dufy, Dunoyer de Segonzac, and Matisse.

Eventually, however, the splendour of his reign dwindled; his daring and wit and *Arabian Nights* magnificence slowly began to lose their hold. By the end of the twenties Poiret was more or less an exile from the field of fashion. His nephew tells a touching story of the early thirties, when the designer was occupying the two top floors of the Salle Pleyel, with no money to pay the rent. The young man had taken Poiret to lunch, and his uncle spoke of some businessmen who were coming later that day from Liberty's in London to discuss a transaction whereby he would design some prints for mass copy and cheap distribution in England, receiving ten thousand francs in advance for his work. On the strength of this deal the uncle then invited the nephew to lunch the following day. When Monsieur Bongard duly arrived, he remarked that his uncle looked extremely fatigued. 'Yes,' replied Poiret, 'I am, and little wonder. I have spent the night with Venus!' He explained that he had been up all night looking at the stars through a newly acquired telescope. The ten thousand francs had been entirely spent on the telescope and upon a refrigerator which he now began to display with pride, naïvely explaining its mechanism, and opening its door to reveal innumerable chilled bottles of champagne from the remains of his wine cellar. They drank the champagne and conveniently forgot the lunch.

During the war, under German occupation, the ageing dressmaker moved to the South of France, where his poverty became so intense that he wore a suit which he had ingeniously cut himself from a beach peignoir. He had little or nothing to eat and often sat in the restaurants, hoping to charm the patron into giving him lunch or a bottle of wine. Any occasional money was flung to the four winds as rapidly as it came his way, and almost immediately he would be penniless again.

The cultivated Poiret, with his fantastic memory and his passion for astronomy (didn't the Persians have a passion for astronomy too?), still rude and truculent, and proud when he could ill afford to be so, spent his declining years inveighing against the new ways of the world.

'The last of the truly elegant ladies,' Poiret might sigh sadly, 'was Forzane, who invented a new silhouette for women, with poses rather like a kangaroo. Do you remember her mornings in the Avenue du Bois, with her immense parasol? She could have been sketched as an ellipse. Since her, there has been nobody.'

Poiret was right when he asserted that modern women are afraid of wearing fashions which have not gained public approval. He saw, and stated clearly, that wealth and luxury are not necessarily the enemies of democracy. Fear or reticence are the real fifth column and can be stultifying in their influence.

Mask of Poiret by Marie Wassiliew

CHAPTER SEVEN

MRS LYDIG

AS fantastic as any character in romantic literature, Mrs Rita de Acosta Lydig graced the opening cycles of the twentieth century with a perfectionism that would have been rare in any period since the Renaissance. A woman of unusual intensity, she lived up to the extraordinarily high standards and ideals that she had set for herself, paying dearly in that most difficult of all causes—to make of oneself a work of art. That she achieved her aims was a tribute to her original and dynamic personality. Yet Mrs Lydig was in some ways a tragic figure, playing out her life in a setting that was not hers by choice: through circumstances, she had become a legendary woman of fashion but was destined to remain a displaced person in fashion's glittering world.

Rita de Acosta was born in the security of 1880, the eldest girl of a family of eight children. Her father, a political exile from his native Spain, had settled in New York a few years previously, marrying a beautiful and distinguished member of the

Spanish family of Alba. No doubt the Spanish blood was to account, in part, for Mrs Lydig's passionate and intense devotion to the art of living, just as it was to provide her with a natural cosmopolitan outlook that would permit her the free development of her rare aesthetic tastes. All that was lacking was money, and by an inevitable contingency the wealth that allowed her unique combination of talents to mature came to her.

When scarcely more than a child Rita married an eccentric multimillionaire, William Earl Dodge Stokes, a sportsman who was apt to be too ready to bring out his gun. It was a misalliance in every way. The groom was not only old enough to be Rita's father but displayed such parsimonious habits that he wore the same overcoat until it turned green from age. Perhaps it is a proof of the attraction of opposites, or merely a justified irony, that Stokes should have married a woman who possessed such an innate gift of extravagance. Under the circumstances it was scarcely surprising that the marriage lasted only four years. In spite of his parsimony, Stokes gave his young wife the largest divorce settlement that had ever been granted at the time, thus enabling her to give full rein to her luxurious tastes. The liberality began at once and was to lead Rita to become one of the most fanatical spendthrifts of her age. Three years later she married Philip Lydig, an unimaginative man who belonged to the best clubs; it was by his name that she gained fame as 'the fabulous Mrs Lydig'.

Mrs Lydig needed but little time to perfect *l'art du salon* and soon became a remarkable hostess. She dominated her round table with the authority of a virtuosa, manipulating the conversation and demanding of her friends, both artists and raconteurs alike, the best that was in them. Floating from group to group in her magnificent drawing-room, Rita Lydig would encourage her friends to shine with a wave of her hand or an admiring, an understanding word. As she passed on, another group would feel the thrill of her master presence, reacting to some electrifying phrase with renewed spirits. Malvina Hoffman observed: 'Whenever Mrs Lydig appeared there was a quiver in the air; and wherever she appeared she made the occasion her own, or else she wasn't there.' Someone else has appended: 'It was as if, when the felts of a piano are worn down, no sound comes when the keys are struck; but Mrs Lydig, with her long brittle fingers, could always pluck the most wonderful sounds from the keys.'

During the years between the turn of the century and the twenties Rita Lydig must have spent more money than any personage of a royal household. When she travelled, it was in the company of seven servants—hairdresser, masseur, valet, personal maid, secretary, chauffeur, and footman. On arrival at the Ritz Hotel in Paris or Madrid, her rooms would at once become transformed by the *objets d'art*, bibelots, flowers, pictures, and statuary she inevitably brought with her. Her luggage comprised fifty trunks as large as coffins, containing a more fabulous wardrobe than any that has been bequeathed to us during this century.

Yet Rita Lydig was the least ostentatious of women. She could never have been accused of the slightest vulgarity, for her taste in all things was infallible. Of the value of money or material things she had little sense. Her only desire was to surround herself with beauty in all its forms. If a friend admired some object in her possession, Mrs Lydig was apt to give it away regardless of its value, for she had no knowledge of the worth of an object beyond its aesthetic appeal.

Her passion for collecting was both fastidious and eclectic, ranging from laces, furniture, bibelots, and jewellery to interesting people connected with music, science, philosophy, painting, and the theatre. It must be admitted that, when it came to artists and notabilities, Mrs Lydig was something of a snob, preferring only the greatest. Bergson and Clemenceau were friends and correspondents; Sarah Bernhardt, Réjane, Caruso, Paderewski, Mary Garden, Toscanini, and many poets, writers and painters would make their headquarters in her home whenever they were in America. Not a few of these artists treated her house as their own; and since Mrs Lydig was incapable of restraint, especially in the encouragement and propagation of talent, she would pay out huge sums whenever an unfortunate artist found himself in financial difficulties. On one occasion she put on a play for which the entire Garrick Theatre was redecorated; and when she arranged for the first New York exhibition of the paintings of her compatriot, Zuloaga, the whole of Duveen's gallery was transformed. It was Mrs Lydig who brought Jacques Copeau, Louis Jouvet and Valentine Tessier, among others, to perform in America. With the best talent of the day appearing at her parties, little wonder that invitations to the house of this brilliant and witty woman were eagerly coveted.

The personality who could rally such a social life about her must, of necessity, have possessed a remarkable charm and magnetism. So great was this gift that her mere presence converted men into her adoring slaves. When Puccini came to New York in 1910 for the première of his new work, *The Girl of the Golden West*, he abandoned several rich dowagers who had invited him to the opera, having caught a glimpse of Mrs Lydig sitting in the diamond horseshoe. For the rest of the evening the composer stood like some forlorn and hypnotized bird at the back of Mrs Lydig's private loge.

On her way to luncheon one day Mrs Lydig's eye was caught by a very beautiful rug in the window of a Fifty-seventh Street *antiquaire*. She entered the shop to scrutinize the work of art. After a moment she decided: 'I'll take that.'

The salesman expostulated, 'It's a very expensive rug, madame. The best I can do for you is sixty thousand dollars!'

'That will be all right,' said Mrs Lydig. 'Call the footman in my motor to take it out over his arm.'

In 1910 she was living in a house on Fifty-second Street built for her by Stanford White. Its furnishings included antiques of the fifteenth and sixteenth centuries. But with the beginning of the First World War, Mrs Lydig dismantled the house, and the contents were sold at auction. During those war years she came to feel the inappropriateness of any display of luxury and devoted herself with enthusiasm to charity or welfare, masking the hard work that she accomplished by making light of it all.

At the end of the war Rita Lydig divorced her husband and moved to a Georgian house in Washington Square. Here she created what was considered to be the most discriminating collection of *objets de vertu*, complete with the best English silver and crystal chandeliers. Her rooms, in which no piece of furniture was ever allowed to be placed catercorner, were somewhat sparsely furnished, for with the purification and deepening of her tastes the sifting process had dispensed with all but the most select and special art. One beautiful rug, her Flemish tapestries, her Titian and Zurbaran, were among the sole objects she chose to keep. She had always had a rare discrimination in all the arts and from the very beginning was a great patron. The curators of museums throughout Europe respected her knowledge and taste.

Mrs Lydig lived alone in the Washington Square house. Her servants (who, like everyone else she had ever employed, loved her so faithfully that they were loath ever to quit her service) slept over the garage. Yet she would never allow the front door to be locked, and the ground-floor windows were often left open. When her mother remonstrated that she might be burgled, the dauntless Rita replied, 'I have an accident of wealth. If anyone who has an accident of poverty needs these things more than I, they can have them.'

But Mrs Lydig was never robbed. A radiating spirit, she had a generosity that gave out a feeling of generosity to others. She was the sort of woman whom no one could ever resent, natural in all things and, in spite of her stateliness and proud carriage, as simple as a child. All who saw her felt her feminine magnetism. Without any conscious effort she was able to get anyone to do for her anything she wished.

Mrs Lydig was never a public figure. Yet with her pale face dusted with lavender powder, her high collars worn tight up to the ears, her eighteenth-century tricorne hat and pointed shoes, the appearance was so spectacular that people who did not know her would follow her admiringly when she went to the Louvre or walked in the street. Her sister, Mercedes de Acosta, told me that on an occasion when they were getting out of her motor car in the Place Vendôme, a complete stranger came up to Mrs Lydig and said, '*Que Dieu vous bénisse, madame!*'

Every artist whom she sat for considered it a rare privilege to work with so co-operative a subject. She inspired Rodin and Bourdelle to sculpt her; Sargent, Laszlo, Carolus Duran, Soralla, and Helleu painted her. It was Sargent who called Mrs Lydig 'Art in its living form'. Boldini was completely fascinated by her. Having painted fourteen portraits of her, he was always begging her to sit for another drawing inspired by some pose she had naturally assumed.

Mrs Lydig's arresting appearance was partly due to her complexion, which was so pale that she was known as the alabaster lady. It was indeed in alabaster that Malvina Hoffman sculpted her. Her nose was long and flamboyantly uptilted, her lips thin and pursed. She wore her ebony, silken hair (so beautifully brushed that it shone like patent leather) in a huge pompadour and, in later years, *en brosse*. She ate seldom and sparsely, with the result that her long thin legs and arms gave her the effect of some wonderful spider. Possessed of a natural grandeur of bearing, Rita Lydig always held her head high and seemed to float across a room with unusually lithe movements. Isadora Duncan observed that Mrs Lydig was one of the few people who understood one must dance as one walks. She never forgot that the whole personality had to be employed, and never permitted herself any liberties with or indifference to her own style. In public Rita Lydig seldom smiled or laughed. When she was amused she lowered her head; her face would become screwed up and her shoulders would shake a little.

Independent of time, Mrs Lydig dressed in her own fashion. Yet for all her strangeness and fragile appearance, she created many new styles. She was the first woman to wear an evening dress cut to the waist at the back. Appearing thus for the first time, sitting in her box at the opera with a great black fan in her hand and surrounded by men, Rita Lydig created a sensation. In those days such trifles seemed to mean much. The newspapers were scandalized. Then after a week all the women who had taken exception to the new fashion copied it.

Mrs Lydig financed the Callot sisters in their dressmaking business, for her clothes always came from that distinguished firm. Yet throughout the years she never went to their shop for a fitting, considering it the height of vulgarity to go to a dress shop. Even the jeweller came to her rather than she to him; likewise, the furrier brought his furs. Dress fittings at Mrs Lydig's house were frequent events.

Mercedes, her youngest sister, has described how the fitters would arrive with their vast boxes, thimbles, silk paper, and scissors. Some would be kneeling with their mouths full of pins, while others, hovering, gave their opinion and exclaimed, '*Que c'est ravissant, madame!*' After the fittings all were given port and cakes. Everyone who ever worked for Mrs Lydig inevitably received a lavish appreciation. Sometimes she put her hand in her pocket and distributed loose emeralds. Her sister admitted, 'Everyone who fitted Rita got emeralds!'

Such an individualist would naturally despise uniformity of dress. Mrs Lydig's clothes were never modern or *à la mode*, belonging to no period. They were the expression of a unique personality that loved ancient brocades and velvets, was a fanatic of rare laces, and developed a style of dress to which she remained faithful despite all fashion changes. She never ordered one thing of a kind, but duplicated each item by the dozens, with only slight variations in material, lace, or design. It was not unusual for twenty-five copies of one coat to be made. Mrs Lydig's adoration of clothes was not for purposes of display, but because they gave her the satisfaction of a work of art. In her own bedroom she would wear, as a dressing-gown for her own pleasure, a circular skirt made from one piece of seamless eleventh-century lace. The price she paid for this garment was nine thousand dollars.

Her wardrobe included black velvet dresses for day; low-cut, bare-backed evening dresses; jackets and coats made of rich and rare materials and worn with velvet skirts by day or satin culottes for evening; nightdresses and underclothes trimmed with medallions incorporating classical figures in lace as delicate as the skeleton of an autumn leaf; black lace mantillas as light as gossamer; heavy lace tunics that appear like armour; blouses of embroidered batiste, needlework, or bobbin lace with the exaggeratedly high collars; cobweb-thin stockings with rare lace insertions; rose-point petticoats, small sable hats, fezzes of unborn lamb, and an umbrella stick of platinum with the name 'Rita' set in diamonds on top.

Although she walked very short distances, Mrs Lydig possessed at least three hundred pairs of shoes, shoes that have never been seen before or since. These were made by Yanturni, the East Indian curator of the Cluny Museum, a strange individual with an extraordinary gift for making incredibly light footwear that was moulded like the most sensitive sculpture. The conditions under which he would supply a few favoured customers were somewhat unusual. Yanturni demanded a deposit of one thousand dollars, from which he would subtract the price of each shoe or boot supplied, though delivery often took two or three years. Once he had agreed to work for a customer, he made a plaster model of both feet, on which he would then work and mould his materials until they were as flexible as the finest silk. Mrs Lydig's shoes were fashioned from eleventh- and twelfth-century velvets, with variations in long pointed toes or square-ended toes and correspondingly square heels. Her evening and boudoir slippers utilized brocades or gold- and silver-metal tissue. Some were covered with lace appliqué and leather spats that fitted like a silk sock. Mrs Lydig collected violins expressly so that Mr Yanturni could use their thin, light wood for his shoe trees. With its tree inside, each shoe weighed no more than an ostrich feather. She preserved these shoes in trunks of Russian leather made in St Petersburg, with heavy locks and a rich cream velvet lining.

But it was not merely in fashions that Mrs Lydig was unpredictable and provocative. Pleasure-loving and capricious, she was a Medici; her soul was Latin. In her behaviour to her female friends she was apt to be somewhat offhanded and continually created difficulties for herself. In her fight for perfection she would send some object back to a shop as many as fifty times, until it was as she desired. So, too, her friends had to attain her ideals. Any deviation from her standard of good taste was an outrage to her. She never allowed them to use slang expressions in her company, and suffered beyond control if their rooms were ugly. Seeking beauty, she was a deeply religious creature of super-sensitivity who gave herself wholeheartedly to all adventures of the spirit. Rita Lydig never knew what it was to be bored. She had the mind of a lawyer and would dash off indignant letters, her irony and sarcasm phrased in scholarly language. It was her contention that any opponent could be defeated by humour. In politics her views were radical; she became a leader of the Equal Franchise Society, advocating woman's suffrage. Long before the subjects were mentioned in polite society, she fought for birth control and was a rabid antagonist of the drug traffic, though ironically enough she herself later became a victim of morphine. One day while riding in her carriage Mrs Lydig became injured in an accident with a runaway horse. She never recovered from the effects. Yet in the face of misfortune she showed gallantry, courage and charm.

With little notion of practical things or business. Rita Lydig slowly accumulated so many debts that, finding herself incapable of meeting the bills, she sought a sister's help to cut down

expenses. Mercedes de Acosta ran through the items in the monthly books. 'A thousand dollars for flowers! But you must do without the white cyclamen, the lilies, the gardenias, and the lilies of the valley!'

'I knew you'd say that!' Rita cried. 'But why should you take away that one beautiful thing from me? I can go without food. You must cut out the butcher for me, but I will not be without my white flowers.'

Eventually the house and all it contained were sold. Duveen paid forty-one thousand dollars for a Flemish tapestry, but still Mrs Lydig could not pay her creditors. She had run through her fortune and, appalled that she owed anybody anything, was obliged with the greatest humiliation to declare herself bankrupt. The incident was the first of a number of vicious blows that fortune was to deal her. Overnight Rita Lydig found herself dropped by the conventional and fickle world of society that was incapable of feeling any real understanding or sympathy for her, yet had pursued her at the summit of her power.

She fell in love with the Reverend Percy Stickney Grant, the rector of the Church of the Ascension on Fifth Avenue and Eleventh Street. But the Episcopalian bishops decided that no clergyman could marry a divorced woman. Bishop Manning refused to sanction the marriage and, rather than leave the Church, Grant broke off their engagement. Mrs Lydig felt she had been betrayed, suffering deep disillusionment.

When I met her in New York in 1928, less than a year before her death, her skin was still as smooth as that of a gardenia. I was surprised to see that even during the daytime she wore the bodice of her black velvet dress cut audaciously low, revealing a considerable portion of her pearly, globose bosom. The effect was particularly startling at a time when fashion dictated that women should be flat-chested. I remember that her movements were sharp and brittle, that she had the rare quality to shine, reminding me of a large china cat.

I did not realize she was suffering at that time from a mortal illness that caused her great physical pain. During an operation an electric pad on which she was lying had short-circuited, burning her so badly that the wound never healed. She was unable to lie on her back. Yet even in the bouts of unspeakable suffering she never accused or complained, saying, 'Accidents can happen to anyone. Suffering can be overcome by all, and it only makes us stronger.' The victim of careless and unscrupulous doctors. Mrs Lydig had become dependent on morphine.

The final years of suffering ended in October of 1929, when she died at the Gotham Hotel in New York City, with her sister Mercedes near her. Towards the end Rita Lydig had become reconciled with the Catholic Church, possibly as much for the sake of her Spanish forebears as for spiritual reasons. Spain, indeed, must have been much on her mind. As she lay dying, Mercedes lifted her to fan her. Lethargically Mrs Lydig asked, 'What are you doing?'

'I am only fanning you,' her sister replied.

'Is it a Spanish fan?' she asked. They were her last words.

After her death her sister gave a wonderful collection of Mrs Lydig's personal belongings to the New York Metropolitan and Brooklyn museums. There all the details of her extra-ordinarily personal wardrobe are tended with the care they deserve. Although her clothes belonged to a period now some-what piquant in our eyes, of matinee hats and cloaks, of the New York and Paris of the First World War years, they have a timeless character that is essentially Spanish, austere and uncom-promising, a character which, in fact, has much in common with that of the Spaniard Balenciaga, the greatest dressmaker of today.

Like all giant personalities, Mrs Lydig was the target of much gossip and censure. Yet there is no one who denies her the quality of distinction. The painter Sargent said that she had the grace and beauty of the Old World and the courage and spirit of the New. Frank Crowninshield was to write of her: 'With her beauty, her allure, her personal extravaganzas, and the long succession of tragedies that befell her, she was not, in her essence, a true embodiment of her time. She belonged rather to the days (and to the novels) of Balzac, to the pages of Turgenev, the stories of Maupassant. There was even, in her battle with destiny, a haunting suggestion of the tortured and heartbroken Emma Bovary.' Crowninshield also compared her to Balzac's Duchesse de Langeais; and, with her wealth, her romantic flair, and her religious fervour, the comparison is apt.

Frederick MacMonnies, the sculptor, added his own eulogy: 'Few of us ignore the majesty of seeming realities and the powers that seem to be . . . she lived her own life in her own beneficent way, heedless of criterion . . . she became a perfected personality, radiant, individual, of consummate style and judgment, a delicious comrade for any emergency, in fact, a masterpiece of civilization.'

 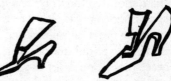

CHAPTER EIGHT

THE BEAUTIFUL
AND THE DAMNED

THERE has been no period in my lifetime more abused, more ridiculed, more hailed as damned, ugly, and wild than the twenties. Perhaps I am rare among my contemporaries in finding that that period was, on the whole, remarkable and vital. If we try to re-examine it, we find it was in some ways like the one we are now passing through—a postwar period marked by restlessness and diversion-seeking. In literature the first 'lost generation' was in command. Many people were building their lives on false, shifting, materialistic, childishly romantic, or epicurean values. Women were cutting their hair short, as they do today; and if skirts were up to the knees, whereas today they are down to the calf, it may be merely due to the fact that the Second World War created a hiatus in fashion such as did not occur in the years from 1914 to 1918.

There were beauties in the world too. I am of the opinion that styles are at no period really unbecoming. If a woman adheres to the proportions and the formula of a given epoch, she will aquire an allure, a feeling of rightness that makes her sense she is attuned to and in equilibrium with the times. By embracing a particular fashion and using it with an instinctive feeling for its organic relationship to the moment, she can make it her destiny.

To me the fashions of the twenties are infinitely alluring. Looking through a fashion magazine of 1926 or 1927, one is above all struck by the simplicity of line with which the fashion illustrators sketched those longer-than-life ladies who, with their short, tubular dresses, cigarettes in long holders, cloche hats, bobbed hair, plucked eyebrows, bands of diamond bracelets from wrist to elbow, and earrings hanging like fuchsias, symbolized the visual aspect of the period.

For all the deleterious values that are generally associated with the decade of *The Green Hat* and *Our Dancing Daughters*, bathtub gin, speed, the precipice-bound excitement of youth, gangsters, and immorality, some people seem to forget that it was also a period of immense creativeness. Since then we can point to few writers, actors, artists, or cinema stars whose personal contributions have been so great. Literature produced Huxley, Virginia Woolf, E. M. Forster, Fitzgerald, Faulkner, Hemingway, and Thornton Wilder; the films created stars— Garbo, Gloria Swanson, Charlie Chaplin—of a magnitude never since equalled. Art yielded Dadaism, the post-cubist period of Picasso, Klee, the German expressionists, and Brancusi; sport was represented by Suzanne Lenglen, playing incredible tennis and looking hideously chic in a knee-length shift, her head bound up in a sunset-coloured turban. In the theatre, Noël Coward, Gertrude Lawrence, Helen Hayes, Pirandello, and Eugene O'Neill were exercising their literary or dramatic talents.

In America, Miguel Covarrubias' cartoons in *Vanity Fair* were eulogizing Harlem, and Carl Van Vechten had just written *Nigger Heaven*. The *Blackbirds* revues and the Cotton Club were at the peak of their success. People somehow found the energy to visit Harlem from midnight to dawn, crowding night clubs where the frenzy of the jungle was added to the expert rhythms of the new dancing. Though diluted and popu-

*Glass baubles of
the twenties*

larized jazz had been the rage for a long time, the white people
were now seeking it at the source. Negroes came down to
teach the Charleston and the Black Bottom in Park Avenue
apartments. By degrees and in dribbles Harlem moved to
Broadway and then made its way to Paris, where there were
'Bricktops', Negro night clubs in Montmartre, and miscegen-
ation. It even became fashionable to look like Negroes, and
Negro fashions were copied.

In interior decoration the Chinese influence flooded Georgian rooms with bibelots of every dynasty from Ming to Tang.
Large lacquer screens were placed to hide the serving lift, coffee
tables were made of lacquer, and sometimes even the walls were

boiseried in imitation lacquer. Chinese figures held up pagoda-shaped lampshades, while gilt lotus flowers sprang out of empty accumulator jars of rough glass, or a shallow floating bowl contained dried poppy heads stippled in gold paint. Large brocade floor cushions would be trimmed with bunches of purple cotton-wool-stuffed grapes.

It has been said that a complete change in women's appearance comes about after every war. The French Revolution led to Greek draperies, the Second World War led to the New Look, and the 1914 war preceded an utter revolution in the concept of femininity, a revolution which, with its planes, straight lines, and flattening out of bosoms and silhouettes, is more than superficially related to cubism in art, and to the tubular world of Fernand Léger. For in the aftermath of 1918 fashion began to show strong signs of the influence of modern art.

Mrs Vernon Castle may have been a slight indication of the future, since coming events cast their shadows before; but there was nevertheless a complete metamorphosis, in which Chanel soon took her rightful place as the guiding hand of the period. She made every woman look entirely unlike the women of the past. This time it was a complete innovation, with no reversion to any style of history. The days of grandeur and flamboyant elegance were as dead as Queen Anne. Thirty years previously it had taken ten yards of material to make a skirt; now it took perhaps a yard. Chanel was the first designer to make her clientele feel that it was smart not to look rich. Comfort and freedom were opposed to straight-jacket luxury and were expressed in the simplicity of the new uniform.

The standard explanation of these styles is that emancipation had become the slogan of the post-war period. In 1920 women had been given the right to vote, and their new-found freedom was expressing itself in dress. Together with their recently acquired legal, economic, and political equality, they wanted to look as much like young men as possible; Chanel helped them. In the Edwardian age women had been magnificent, handsome, statuesquely beautiful, but they never felt the desire to appear youthful. Now youth and boyish beauty became the ideal and the password. Lillian Russell and the Gibson girls had turned

1929

into Rosalind in the Forest of Arden. Skirts crept upwards like the mercury column on a midsummer's day, hair became shingled or Eton-cropped, ever shorter, hats more and more bell-shaped until, by the late twenties, the accepted look had become as standardized as a prison uniform, and there was scarcely any difference between the styles for a child of eight, a flapper, or a woman of eighteen, twenty, or fifty-eight.

It was La Rochefoucauld who once said that few people know how to grow old. In the twenties they didn't have to. Women became younger and younger, as though fashion had decided to reverse time.

The personification of the new type of woman was the Duchess of Penaranda, a Spanish beauty who appeared wearing a short white tunic with a deep scooped neckline and a skirt that stretched barely to the knees. She wore sunburn stockings with white satin shoes whose Spanish spike heels were fully six inches high. Her hair, brilliantined to a satin brilliance, was drawn back as tightly as a bullfighter's. The Duchess's complexion matched her stockings, for she was burned by the sun to a deep shade of iodine. Two enormous rows of pearl teeth were bared in a white, vital grin, complementing the half a dozen rows of pearls as large as pigeons' eggs that hung about her neck. The uncompromising simplicity of this sunburned body and white dress, coupled with the straightness of her back, was quite unique. Perhaps if any counterpart could be found in England it took the form of Lady Louis Mountbatten, though her shoulders were always hunched as she teetered on her high heels to present the silver cup to the winning polo team at Hurlingham, or sat myopically in a sequin sheath at the Embassy Club.

The Duchess of Penaranda was one of a whole coterie of women who, in Paris during the twenties, invented their own styles, and the dressmakers kept an eye on them, rather than the reverse. Being women of taste, ingenuity, and a certain artistry, as well as having a private income, they were able to make a work of art of their games of invention.

The Honourable Mrs Reginald (Daisy) Fellowes was among the outstanding members of the coterie. Half French and half

137

Lady Louis Mountbatten : 1928.

American, her Gallic bent predominating, she lived for the most part in Paris, though making occasional cross-Channel trips to England. Mrs Fellowes was much publicized as the best-dressed woman in the world. Such a title would seem to imply frequent changes of wardrobe; but, on the contrary, she earned the distinction more for the brilliance of her studied simplicity. Other women would often be furious to see her wearing the same dress perpetually for day and evening wear. It was Daisy Fellowes who invented the sequin coat cut like a man's dinner jacket. She wore it with audacity and a green carnation sprouting from the buttonhole, until, indeed, she wore it out. But whatever the occasion or the clothing, Daisy Fellowes always had a scrubbed classical look, an unparalleled air of slickness, trimness and cleanness. Her hair was sleeked back whether it was cut very short or folded in a tight knot. Her general appearance bespoke no fussiness: she had the air of having just come off a yacht, which she very likely had.

With apologies to 'Faceless Freddie' and his sketches of Mrs Reginald Fellowes

The Honble M^{rs}
Reginald Fellowes.
1930.

Daisy Fellowes enjoyed making other women appear foolish, and would wear plain linen dresses when everyone else was
dressed to kill. These linen suits, though simple in tailoring and
often of identical shape, were ordered in dozens of different
colours and complemented by barbaric jewels—handcuffs of
emeralds, necklets of Indian stones, or conch shells of diamonds.
She even wore jewellery with her beach suits. At the races,
while her rivals would be wearing enormous picture hats of
chiffon or transparent straw that sprouted fireworks of feathers,
Daisy Fellowes might turn up hatless. The effect, of course,
succeeded in making the others appear overdressed and slightly
ridiculous. Mrs Fellowes enjoyed her 'appearances', though
often they were as inconsequent as a masquerade. At an hour
when most luxurious women, in appropriate dresses, were being
driven to cocktail parties in purring limousines, she would be
seen on foot, turning a corner of the Place Vendôme under a
cloudless sky, on her way to a secret date, wearing a neat coat

140

and skirt, with an umbrella under her arm. The piquancy of the picture created its charm.

On an occasion when she wished to appear at a court in Buckingham Palace, Mrs Fellowes was determined not to conform to the usual white or pastel shades that women wear when presented. To provide herself with a suitable excuse for widow's weeds was not difficult: like most Frenchwomen, Daisy Fellowes had a widespread family tree, and a little cursory botany sufficed to discover, on some outlying limb, the recent death of a fifth cousin twice removed. With the funeral established, she appeared at court in a dangerously short black jet dress adorned with a black train and set off by a spray of black Prince of Wales feathers on her neat head.

Once she went to a supper dance wearing a black tulle dress decorated with puffs of beige ostrich feathers, and was subjected to the rare and embarrassing incident that every woman dislikes: another member of the party was wearing the same outfit. Calmly, while talking to the others, Daisy Fellowes equipped herself with a pair of scissors and cut all the feathers from her dress. When she rose to move on to the dance floor, she waved the bunch of cut feathers nonchalantly, like a fan. This was her way of handling a situation with aplomb.

Perhaps it was Princess de Faucigny Lucinge who was most responsible for introducing an exotic note into the twenties. Her natural individuality made it inevitable that she should shine among the unusual women of the period, and even today there are indirect signs of 'Baba' Lucinge's contributions to style or decoration.

English by birth, she had been Miss Baba d'Erlanger before her marriage. Her scarlet-haired mother was well known in England as an *avant-gardiste* of interior decoration, and the family house in Piccadilly (which had once belonged to Lord Byron) was full of witch balls, shell flowers, mother-of-pearl furniture, and startling innovations picked up for a song at the Caledonian Market. Even as a child Baba was a natural cause of wonder, though she never seemed to mind or note the fact. When she promenaded through London she was escorted, not by the typical English duenna, the 'nanny', but by a wonderful mameluke, all turban and coloured robes, who followed her footsteps like a page. As a young girl Baba wore dresses of gold tissue; later, when she married Prince Jean Louis de Faucigny Lucinge, her wedding dress was described as 'molten gold'.

Baba always looked rather like an Arab urchin, her dark, almond-shaped face betraying a light touch of melancholy. She put black paint under her eyes and grew her nails very long, enamelling them dark red. Her youth and beauty allowed her to expose her enigma even on the sunniest beach. She would wear a tarbush, or pillbox monkey hats, and pinned bunches of jewelled grapes to her bathing suit.

As a young woman, Baba Lucinge was almost inseparable from Paula Gellibrand, a great beauty, who had been discovered by Baba's mother. By nature Paula was a completely unaffected, somewhat hearty schoolgirl type, but by some freak of fortune she was endowed with an appearance of extraordinary sophistication. Her enormous blue eyes were surrounded by a halo of dark mushroom-coloured fatigue, giving her the appearance of always being heavily made up. The huge crown of her perfect egg-shaped head lent her the look of a Modigliani. Her hands were of an extraordinary flexibility and length. With her gold hair and white skin Paula Gellibrand was the perfect foil for Baba's dark Orientalism. Under the influence of Baroness d'Erlanger, Paula became even more exotic of appearance, putting vaseline on her eyelids, wearing coifs like a nurse, and, for her wedding, was dressed in the style of a nun.

Another friend of Baba Lucinge was the diminutive Madame Lilia Ralli, a Greek lady with a Parisian taste. Throughout every change of fashion she has converted the Paris dicta to her individual idiom of chic. It is not always easy to maintain an individual style once one has created it, but Madame Ralli has an unfailing sense of fashion, enormous enthusiasm, and sound theoretical sense. She seldom wears an elaborate dress, but relies for her self-adornment on elaborate hats, accessories and jewellery. She is the best example I know of the woman who is so well dressed that, for the past twenty-five years, people have not noticed what she is wearing but have known that she looks exceptionally well. Only the initiates of the highest realm of

PAVLA
GELLIBRAND . 1923.

143

fashion philosophy can appreciate the spontaneity of her natural gift and her elaborate attention to every detail of her appearance. Her sense of contrast can be judged by the fact that, although she is always changing the colour of her hair, she never wears nail polish or varnish and attempts no more than the most spasmodic or cursory indications of make-up.

Lady (Iya) Abdy invented size. She stands over six feet tall and, by wearing a cape of sable that flowed to the ground, huge felt hats, or floating velvet dresses that matched her pale trailing hair, has always done everything she could to make herself even more enormous.

Of all the exotics, one could scarcely overlook the Marquesa Casati, with her death-white face, orange hair, and black eyes, belladonna eyes that were rimmed not only with black paint but black tape as well. Yet when Luisa Amon from Milan first married Camillo Casati, a great huntsman, the Master of the Roman hounds and president of the Jockey Club in Rome, she was considered by all those who first saw her at the Meets of the Hunt to be the mousy little wife of the Master. Little did they expect the transformation that was to take place. The mousy hair burst into flames, the eyelashes spread like peacock feathers, she dressed in a style entirely of her own invention, in *incroyable* sheaths made of imitation fur, her head half hidden beneath a black lace-and-satin coal scuttle. She acquired a Tunisian slave named Garbi whom she dressed in exotic undress. She became so extravagant in her behaviour that the noblest families in Rome flocked to her house in the Via Piamenti. At a dinner given by her for Princess Lucien Murat to celebrate the canonization of Joan of Arc there was a scandal that one of the guests had cheated while gambling at cards. The Italian aristocracy were entertained in rooms in which snakes writhed on the polished stone floors. At one time she kept a large brown monkey in her salon. A friend complained, 'How can you have such a horrid smelly creature at such close quarters?' The Marquesa pulled a branch of dark-coloured lilac from a vase, poked it through the bars of the animal's gold cage. The monkey snatched at the lilac and the Marquesa triumphantly exclaimed, 'Now do you see why I have a monkey? Don't you think that

The Marquesa Casati, with apologies to Boldini, 1909

is beautiful! Isn't it like something in a Chinese painting?'

But the Marquesa Casati's taste was by no means to be ignored as merely eccentric. Though her houses were arranged less for comfort than beauty, they had influence in their emptiness, their use of alabaster—huge vases, lit within, were filled with roses (hence the alabaster lamps we see today)—and her lighting also came from behind lumps of amber or rock crystal.

At Le Vésinet, outside Paris, she bought the Palais Rose, the former home of the Comte Robert de Montesquieu. Boni de Castellane later copied this house in the Avenue Foch, and, while married to Anna Gould, gave fabulous entertainments there. The Marquesa made it into an exquisite setting for her exotic personality. Her life became a search for beauty. One day she telephoned a friend to ask if he would please go shopping with her because she felt the desire for 'something orange'. The entire day was spent in the pursuit, with the Marquesa mumbling, 'I know exactly the colour this object must be!' They looked in vain in all sorts of shops where they sell materials, jewels, lacquer (though of course never where they sell oranges) until at last the Marquesa found in an antique shop a Fabergé cigarette case of orange enamel. Then, at last satisfied, she returned home.

For street wear she had tiger-skin top hats, or huge gold paper baskets turned upside down on her head, draped with lace and worn with trailing black velvet dresses. Once she came to visit me in the country, in the dead of winter with snow on the ground, wearing an enormous cowboy hat, white flannel trousers, and gold sandals.

At fancy dress balls the Marquesa Casati excelled herself, often wearing costumes designed for her in the highest flights of Léon Bakst's fantasy. She once went to the length of gilding Garbi when he accompanied her as part of her entrance. Another appearance was made escorted by a live leopard on a chain. What might perhaps have been her most extravagant disguise never quite came off. Count Etienne de Beaumont had planned a ball, and the Marquesa Casati decided to appear as an electrically equipped Saint Sebastian. She was to wear armour pierced with hundreds of arrows, each studded with glittering

Boni de
Castellane
(after Drian)

stars that were to light up when the Marquesa appeared. On the morning of the ball, in a little side room at De Beaumont's, she had arrived with her host's permission, bringing a fleet of servants, an electrician, and stoves for boiling water to make cups of tea or coffee while the elaborate preparations for her appearance were in progress. At last, her *maquillage* complete, her hair fixed in an aureole of ringlets, the Marquesa was pulled into the tights and the armour was fixed on her with a padlock. But at the moment of being plugged in a disaster took place: the costume was short-circuited, and, instead of being lighted up with a thousand stars, the Marquesa suffered an electric shock that sent her into a backward somersault. She did not recover in time to appear at the party, leaving a note at the De Beaumont house that stated simply, '*Milles regrets.*'

But the Marquesa herself is a woman of few regrets. She never had any financial sense. When she ran short of money and a gondolier had to be paid for his services, she would hand him a pearl bracelet. Thus it is not surprising that, having run through several fortunes, she found herself stranded in a London at war with her own country, penniless but for the help of a few loyal friends. Far from the sun, the warmth, or the luxury that she knew, the Marquesa still found life full of fascination and interest. Even the squalors of poverty-struck London could not break her spirit: to this day she possesses the grand manner, though her shoes may be frayed or the lace on her hat may be torn.

Knowing the Marquesa's innate distinction, I once asked her whom she considered the best-dressed woman she had ever known. 'Cécile Sorel, without a doubt,' she replied. 'She knows more about clothes than any other living woman. She has known how to dress since the eighties. Not only does she know how to wear clothes in the grand manner, but she can take a needle and scissors and make them in the grand manner herself.'

One day during one of the gloomiest winters of the war I went to call on her to bring her to my home for luncheon and found her sitting in her room on the top floor of Byron's old house in Piccadilly, which had latterly been turned into flats. She was at a table in the middle of the room, adding kohl to her darkened eyes, wearing the same black velveteen costume that had been her uniform for the last ten years.

'Before leaving we must hide this electric stove that a friend has given me. We must lock it away so that the people down-stairs won't charge for extra electricity.' She opened a cupboard and offered me a terrifying glimpse of degradation: old artificial flowers, broken clocks, bottles of methylated spirit.

'Today is a terrible day. The devil is in everything,' she muttered as she fumbled with keys and locks.

When we arrived at my house, she relaxed in the warmth and became enthusiastic and happy as a child. 'Now let us enjoy everything. This good glass of sherry, it is so rare. This open fire, this scent of rosemary, how good it all is.' She held forth like an empress, her gestures bold and valiant. Somehow the indomitable spirit sublimated the old wastepaper basket of black satin that she wore on her head and metamorphosed the cotton rose on her shoulder into a thing of beauty. Here was a great woman, someone whose character and pluck could overcome all mediocrity and create nobility out of poverty.

In contrast to women who, like the Marquesa Casati, were anomalous to the twenties and yet a timely expression of its

148

The Jersey Lily

more bizarre aspects, Mrs Dudley Ward was, like the Duchess of Penaranda, the embodiment of the new conception of allure. Had she appeared upon the London scene some twenty years earlier, she would have been described as an undernourished messenger boy. For in the days of King Edward there were female giants on the earth: Mrs George Keppel, Lily Langtry, Maxine Elliott, and the other ladies who, a decade earlier, had sailed under the Achilles statue in Hyde Park, were imposing Boadiceas, figureheads on the prow of some Norse ship. But by the time King Edward's grandson had become the dashing Prince of Wales, the ladies who were admired had come full cycle round to diminutive proportions and were concave instead of convex.

Of them all, Mrs Dudley Ward came to be generally most admired. No one had ever looked quite like her before. In competition, even the statuesque Junos of the previous era were unable to command attention. Mrs Ward's appearance was a most felicitous combination of the attractions of an adolescent girl and a sophisticated youth of sixteen. Her sloping figure was that of a young rowing blue, her rather large hands those of the

1929

Mrs Dudley Ward

'Catcher in the Rye'. With her hair snipped in a short shingle, she dressed in natty little day suits of checks, possibly adding a huge clove carnation in her buttonhole. As she tapped the end of a gasper cigarette on a gold case before lighting it with her briquet, the gold wrist chains and bracelets would jangle, while one was reminded of a schoolboy showing a little too readily that he had mastered the grown-up practice of smoking.

But these Vesta Tilley charms were only the slightest veneer over an almost exaggerated feminine allure. In the evening the messenger boy would wear a dress of red-and-white-check gingham with a red bow in her hair, and her small daughters might well be dressed to match. Mrs Ward's questing eyes were huge, pretty periwinkles, her complexion was of pink-and-white china, and she spoke in a high-keyed voice. Whenever any man was fortunate enough to sit by her, she gave him the impression not only of being more interested in him than in anyone else in the world, but of being in need of his protection as well. Her greatest allure lay in the fact that, behind the freshness and honesty of her personality, the businesslike approach,

and the dislike of pretence, there was something a little tragic about her. The eyes had a startled fawn-like quality, and you wondered if the laughter would soon turn to fright; her voice had a plaintive note and a catch that played upon the strings of one's heart.

Mrs Dudley Ward has been the incentive for a million imitators. Especially in America has her influence been an indelible one, and the idiom has become a part of the American woman's personality. The juvenile grandmothers whose perambulator talk is given in corn-crake voices, the baby bow in the bobbed henna hair—all are travesties of this most original little figure. Mrs Ward was of such modernity that, had she not been the exceptionally intelligent and flexible human being that she is, one might have hazarded the advice that the duchess gave to Mabel in *The Ideal Husband:* 'You are remarkably modern, Mabel, a little too modern, perhaps. Nothing is so dangerous as being too modern. One is apt to grow old-fashioned quite suddenly.'

Anita Loos was another whose looks seemed surprisingly

Anita Loos, 1952

modern and, like her heroine in *Gentlemen Prefer Blondes*, Miss
Loos's appearance has gone into the annals of American history.

As a very young girl of Pocket Edition proportions, she
found herself at a disadvantage when it came to choosing
clothes for herself. In her early photographs, with the black,
shining hair dressed in heavy coils, she seems to be overwhelmed by the draped hats of velvet and sealskin, the voluminous coats, skirts, stoles, and muffs of the first moving-picture
era. But with the twenties, Anita Loos came into her own. The
new fashions gave her the opportunity to become herself. She
cut her hair as short as that of a boy in a sailor suit and went off to
buy her hats and dresses at the juvenile departments of the great
stores. Dressed as crisply and neatly as only a child at the outset
of an expedition can be, with her brilliantined fringe meticulously combed, her buckled belts and bag like a school satchel,
her Buster Brown hats and Peter Pan collars, Anita Loos became the embodiment of cuteness. She had discovered her own
grammar and syntax of fashion; and by conforming to it ever
since, her allure and chic have remained unchallenged.

Outside the coterie of these individual women who were in-
fluential in bringing out changes of fashion in the twenties,
there were in London the 'bright young things'. They danced
the Charleston, did crossword puzzles, and had extremely bad
manners, for in certain circles it was considered smart to be

rude. A number of wealthy debutantes became very aggressive, played practical jokes, and spoke their private language of eggy-peggy (pig Latin) in front of those unfortunate enough not to be allowed into their exclusive circle. If an unfavoured young man came up to talk to them, they would sit silently staring at their baffled victim and then suddenly burst into derisive laughter. They would leave the most grand and conventional dances early in the evening, to go on to night clubs. At house parties their highly powered motor cars were not infrequently driven through imposing gateways, breaking stone piers and filigree of wrought iron. One high-spirited young lady even managed to crack the bottom of an ornamental lake. Raucous, irritating, and offensive as these young people were, they were undoubtedly the spearhead of those who broke down conventions. Today well-brought-up young people do not have to lead such rigorously protected lives as they once did and are able to look after themselves with a certain independence.

In the rise of the whole new spirit of affectation and frivolity, the influence of the theatre was far from negligible. By the late twenties young women gave up speaking in mellifluous tones in favour of cigarette-throat voices, rasping and loud. Men enjoyed imitating the exaggerated, clipped manner of certain leading actors and adopted the confident manner of those who are aware of their charms. It became a fad to talk with equal authority on specialized subjects as well as on frivolous ones, to mingle cocktail chatter about great personages and events in history with jazz slang, or juxtapose the Albert Memorial and other buildings with the Latin names of plants and trees. Noël Coward's influence spread even to the outposts of Rickmansworth and Poona. Hearty naval commanders or jolly colonels acquired the 'camp' manners of calling everything from Joan of Arc to Merlin 'lots of fun', and the adjective 'terribly' peppered every sentence. All sorts of men suddenly wanted to look like Noël Coward—sleek and satiny, clipped and well groomed, with a cigarette, a telephone, or a cocktail at hand.

Gertrude Lawrence was the distaff personification of this new charm. Though not a great beauty, she used her gifts to heighten

Noël Coward in the thirties

her attractiveness and possessed the flavour and personality of the age to a high degree. She was a combination of remarkable contrasts. Her mellifluous voice was yet rather curdled. Her somewhat simian features were sunburnt. The long, loose-fitting dresses she wore suggested more than an indication of the vital, well-shaped figure beneath them: she could look remarkably provocative in a dress that covered her body almost completely. She smoked cigarettes with a nuance that implied having just come out of bed and wanting to go back into it.

The Gertrude Lawrence–Noël Coward personalities continued to dominate the theatre through the early thirties as well, in brittle comedies that caught the sophisticated spirit of the age.

In ballet, Diaghilev was still a great figure, introducing décors by Picasso, Derain, Braque and Pruna. The simplicity of Picasso's ballet designs was a complete change from the riotous innovations of Bakst. Colours became rather crude and primary, and fashion showed the influence in bright ultra-marines and whites, scarlets, and blues. Blouses were sometimes half white and half black. Ballets based on sailor themes helped to make Villefranche popular as a resort, or goaded fashionable women to dress in sailors' sweaters.

Mrs Augustus John

Young women 'interested in art' all wore their hair straight, cut sharp at the base of the neck with shears, the trilby jacket or sweater, the dark flowing skirts falling in the pleats of the dirndl, somewhere a bold touch of colour—blues, oranges and emerald greens—and sandals. These goddesses of King's Road, Chelsea, the students of the ballet in Italy, America, France and Germany, all with or without knowing it, tried to look as much as possible like Mrs Augustus John, for she it was who had invented the 'John' type.

Dorelia John may have been seen in Babylon or in early Crete, but before her in this century no woman wore those clothes that are almost Indian and yet are entirely European, that are classical and yet have abstracted something from the

gypsies. In fact no one had developed a more perfect visual expression of the art of living than Mrs Augustus John, who possesses her rare gifts to this very day. As a muse, she has been indirectly responsible for much of her husband's best work; but she is equally creative in her own right. For the last forty years she has dressed in the same manner: outside fashion, her clothes and her appearance are never dated. Today Mrs John wears the uniform of age and seems oblivious to the charm and impact of her appearance. Yet with her white hair and scarlet apron over a blue cotton dress, hugging a huge basket of fruit against her stomach as she brings it in from the orchard, she has the timelessness, the real fashion of the Bible.

It is not at all surprising that she possesses what, to me, is a beautiful house. Here is the dwelling place of an artist. It would be difficult to find one object in her house that does not fulfil its useful purpose with an inherent beauty. On her window sill a

THE JOHN
TYPE

WITH APOLOJIES TO
MR & MRS AUGUSTUS JOHN

goblet of daffodils seems to regain the pristine beauty that is lost by overfamiliarity. With Mrs John, as with all true people, the everyday triflings of life are noble: a basket of bread, a bowl of tomatoes, a bottle of wine have innate beauty. A Wills cigarette box becomes an initial part of the grandiose 'still life' of family use.

Mrs John would be the first to be shocked at my writing of her home as beautiful. 'But what nonsense!' she would say. 'It has no pretensions to beauty. It's a mess. I am too busy looking after the household—there are all the children here now—to bother about anything of that sort.' I hope she will forgive me, for if the house is untidy, the untidiness is a symbol of a lack of primness and a wholeheartedness that are typical of her generosity. There is nothing self-conscious or arranged about her: her gestures are bold ones; never two bites at a cherry, the wine is drunk to the dregs.

157

Mrs John's window sill

If any reader, intrigued by this eulogy, were to verify my enthusiasm, he might be surprised at the lack of any specific colour scheme in the John household. There is no beguiling, ready-made impact of beauty; rather, an atmosphere of beauty is sensed. No intention to decorate the house ever existed. The objects that are there were originally admired and collected for their intrinsic shape. They remain beautiful. Pictures were bought from friends in a momentary fit of zeal; books were acquired of necessity. Thus the colours have gratuitously grown side by side. Nothing is hidden; there is an honesty of life which is apparent in every detail—the vast dresser with its blue and white cups, the jars of pickled onions, the skeins of wool, the window sills lined with potted geraniums and cacti, while close to the windowpanes tits swing on a coconut shell hung from a tree. The Modigliani bust stands with a cactus pot on its head. In the corner of the entrance hall, boxes of apples and croquet mallets are spontaneously thrown together, constituting a picture of life that is full of sentiment and completely lacking in pretension.

No matter in what world a person lives, taste should never be a question of money. The palace of a millionaire, if it contains not one worn or beloved object to meet the eye, will appear lacking in soul. A home belonging to a poor person can be just as aesthetically pleasing as that of the richest man of taste.

There was nothing, for instance, in the farmhouse at Billignin, lived in by Gertrude Stein and Alice Toklas, that was not beautiful in the most simple way, yet the house had never been decorated by them. Miss Toklas admitted the house was furnished on 'spontaneity and a shoestring'. The two ladies scoured the local antique shops and with their discrimination were able to pick up furniture that was simple and rustic. A garden table made of heavy wood was carved to represent a table covered with a velvet cloth and fringe; a rocking chair served for Gertrude, and a portrait in pinpricks of Queen Victoria added charm.

Originally the building had been a manor house, surrounded by rich farms and woodland. Since it had been built in 1637, with Louis Seize additions, the rooms were well proportioned. The small dining room had crudely decorated panels 'painted in the eighteenth century'. Everywhere that the eye alighted there was something to give pleasure—an arrangement of unframed pictures, an earthenware pot of pink hibiscus picked each morning by Alice Toklas, while in the kitchen were a 'still life', baskets of herbs, a pyramid of maize, an earthenware plate, and the large wooden pepper mill that sat permanently on the kitchen table and which now, after much scrubbing and scouring, had become the warm colour of honey. Everything seemed to possess a patina that gave one's senses a delight. Everywhere was a feeling of perfection that can be acquired only by the most sophisticated people or by peasants.

Some of these subjects or people may seem to have little to do with the twenties, but all were a vital expression in that period, proving that one can often go as much against the grain as with it and still express the beauty of living.

The twenties are still close enough for the younger generation to ridicule it as a decade of delirious delinquents dancing the Charleston while the stock market crashed round them. But we are all guilty of judging another age after the fact, whereas the truth is that, as regards contemporary events, the eye is depressingly shortsighted. We condemn the Victorians for their smug bourgeois world that was only a façade covering events that led to the disaster of the First World War. We condemn the frivolities of the twenties that led somehow to the depression and economic crisis of the early thirties. But if people were clairvoyant, perhaps they could control history better than they do. Tolerance and a sense of the comic as well as the tragic ought to make us see, in the fashions and frivolities of any given epoch, the wonderful creativity that finds expression, conscious and unconscious, in clothes, songs, slang, dances, art —in short, in all that becomes history. I do not see the twenties as imbued with false nostalgia, but as a tonic period in modern life, one which is already as fixed in time as the paintings of Modigliani, the sculptures of Nadelman, or the planes of cubism that found a distant echo in the architecture of sky-scraper and 'modernism', so symbolic of the visual aspect of the age.

CHANEL
NUMBER ONE

SANDWICHED between two world wars, between Poiret's harem and Dior's New Look, two women dominated the field of *haute couture*—Schiaparelli and Chanel. The first in time and by far the more gifted was Mademoiselle Chanel, a peasant girl from Auvergne who quickly asserted her forceful and unique personality on the styles of the twenties. One can imagine her, in the small hat shop she owned, glancing round the post-war scene, dissatisfied with the musketeer hats, Directoire capes, sagging tail coats, and near hobble skirts, the remnants of a military fashion that was still in vogue, and deciding to create her own fashion. So Chanel appeared at the races in the gabardine of a young English student with a school-girl's hat on her head; at the casino her skirt was sufficiently short to give rein to her athletic, racehorse stride; at the opera she was to be seen with a waistline down to her hips. It was not long before the few women who set the styles were interested, mesmerized, and finally won over by this new personality.

Soon thereafter Chanel gave up her hat shop to enter the ruthlessly competitive field of fashion design.

The age of elaborate ornamentation was over, and an era of simplicity had begun. Chanel had literally pole-vaulted women's fashions from the nineteenth century into the twentieth. It was a far cry from Poiret's extravagant plumes and furs or Lucile's pastel-coloured chiffons to the beige uniform of knitted wool, the jerseys and short skirts with which Chanel replaced them.

She hated the way hairdressers set their clients' hair in tight waves like cart ruts, and she would take nail scissors and crop the hair of her favourites herself. She then set about concealing their breasts and buttocks. Women began more and more to look like young men, reflecting either their new emancipation or their old perversity.

Perhaps Chanel's genius lay in her intuition that ladies were tired of the finicky trimmings that had been decked upon them for decades. She guessed that women of fashion would be riding in subways and taxis and would require a new concept. Possibly she turned to nature and rediscovered, or reaffirmed, the fact that the female of the species is generally unadorned, that female birds are drab compared to the males. The trick, or the genius, was to convert this drab look into a mode of brilliant simplicity, which was exactly what Chanel did. Ruthlessly women were stripped of their finery, fitted with a tricot and skirt or a plain dress; and when they looked like Western Union messenger boys, when they had been reduced to chic poverty, then, and only then, did she drape them with costume jewellery, with great lumps of emeralds, rubies, and cascades of huge pearls.

Her way was not madness, but method. As a dress designer, she was virtually nihilistic, for behind her clothes was an implied but unexpressed philosophy: the clothes do not really matter at all, it is the way you look that counts. Thus in the twenties, fashionable women began to take on an appearance which has since become standard with the American working girl of today and which, for that matter, chic women have never quite lost.

The most important reason of all for Chanel's success was her insistence that women should look young. Previous to Chanel, clothes were designed for mature women, the social and cultural leaders of fashion. With Chanel's advent they were all designed for youth; or, if not for young women, were designed to make mature women look young. It was her belief that a good figure was more important than a pretty face; yet she claimed also that it was just as easy to dress a fat woman as a slim one.

Chanel not only invented ingenious ways of making women look twenty years younger, but she also contrived brilliant inventions for making them look expensively poor. Women would be dressed in workmen's velveteen coats with an apache hat or would wear ordinary felt overcoats. Not until the coats were taken off did one realize they were lined with sables. Chanel made dresses of sand-coloured woollen materials that had previously been used only for the somewhat sordid underclothes of men.

It was Ina Claire who, in her own feminine way, exploited the Chanel look on Broadway. She was among the first to bring real clothes into the theatrical scene. Previously actresses had worn only 'costumes'. For drawing-room comedy scenes Ina Claire would appear in pale beige kasha dresses or two-piece velveteen suits, and thereby paved the way for actresses to wear Edward Molyneux's suits on the stage.

To some extent Chanel's creativity was conditioned by theory, though never bound by it. She believed that a fashion is not for one person, nor even for a group; if a fashion is not popular with great numbers of people, it is not a fashion. Chanel herself was responsible for many 'fashions'. Few people, indeed, realize the complete extent of her personal innovations. She popularized enormous shell-rimmed spectacles. She invented backless shoes, lace dresses modelled along sports lines, evening dresses of ankle length (she maintained it was slovenly to have them longer), women's trousers cut to the calf, and many other fashions which, after twenty years and more, are still popular and may well continue for a long time. A part of the reason for the durability of her creations is their practicability: she detested lack of reason, and everything had a mathematical function. Buttons had to work properly;

pockets were put where the hands could easily go into them.

During her active period as a dressmaker Chanel often took up needle and thread herself, or would cut, fit, and invent hats in paper. She trained her mannequins with all the loving discipline of a Petipa or a Balanchine, teaching them to walk on their toes, with their pelvis thrust well forward. Cocteau has written of Monsieur Cheruit's mannequins, who were similarly trained at that time: 'Cheruit could be heard crying the whole length of the red and gold salons: "Mesdames, throw out your stomachs! Don't draw in! Bulge! Bulge! Throw out your stomachs!"'

Chanel's personality, like her designs, was something of a paradox, a mingling of the masculine and the intensely feminine. Actually the concept she had of women was entirely feminine: she wanted them to be charming and simple and natural, bemoaning the fact that the young were not sufficiently romantic. She detested affectation and believed that women should let their hair grow white if it was inclined to do so. This last opinion had such effect that many younger women went so far as to simulate, by using powder in their hair, a premature streak of white. The professions of men bored her. When Cocteau told her she had a masculine mind, she became furious and, as a gesture of defiance, put a small girl's hair ribbon round her head, knotting it in a bow on the top: a fad was created.

Though the dresses she designed seemed at times on the ascetic side, Chanel herself lived in great luxury, both materially and intellectually. Snobs and poets were her friends. Her surroundings were of Regency gilt and cocoa-coloured suède; she had Louis Quinze gold tables, brown Coromandel screens, rock crystal, and too many dark red roses.

She loved jewellery but stressed that it was to be worn as junk; i.e. regardless of its value, as something decorative or amusing, but never because it was expensive. By day, with her informal clothes, she would wear a great deal of jewellery; but at night, with her evening dresses, she wore perhaps only one bracelet. Much of Chanel's costume jewellery was copied from her own fabulous collection of flawless emeralds, rubies, pearls and diamonds.

Chanel, 1953

What was Chanel really like? Her clients couldn't know, for she made it a practice never to see or meet any of them, just as she seldom saw one of her creations after it was made. Her work was always completely impersonal, carried out in the Rue Cambon, in that large office full of embryo dresses and experimental berets.

It was always impossible to guess Chanel's age. She was dark and sunburned, with high cheekbones, an upturned nose with nostrils, as she said, 'like tunnels', brilliant black eyes like buttons, and a gash for a mouth. Her hands were delicate, of a skin with a white sheen upon it, and so strong that they could shoe a horse. She wore no red on her fingernails but reddened the tips of her toes, on the theory that feet were a dreary business and required every aid. Over her angular frame Chanel wore clothes that were congruent with what she preached and often created a fashion by an impromptu gesture. Feeling chilly one day on the late Duke of Westminster's yacht, she threw a man's blue overcoat over her shoulders. For the next generation other women did likewise. A snapshot of her at Antibes in the thirties wearing sailor trousers and a jersey, with pearls and a beret, is as alluring as any fashion invented twenty years afterwards. When Chanel rode to hounds in France, she was perfectly groomed but ruined the conventionality of her appearance by wearing all her pearls on the outside of her habit.

Many of Chanel's private dicta have entered into the unspoken rules that still govern fashion. She had an unerring sense of colour, emphasizing the use of black, which she considered extremely chic, and of white, but eschewing bright colours except in combination with a solid shade that would have a restraining effect. Pastel shades, she said, were only for redheaded women.

In the history of *haute couture* since the turn of the century, Chanel has perhaps been the most important single influence on fashion in clothes. At any earlier moment the innovations which she brought about would have been totally contrary to the spirit of the age. Yet for a great fashion designer to come into being, talent alone is not enough: the designer must have the absolute and authoritative genius to impose his or her vision of the needs of the times on the times themselves, so that fashions which a year previously would have been considered outrageous are suddenly a necessity. It is the genius who creates the need, though that need must reflect the unconscious wishes of the moment if the genius is to be accepted, at least by his contemporaries. After the war Chanel retired from the active world of fashion. The large offices in the Rue Cambon, with their beige carpets and plate-glass mirrors, were given over to the sale of her famous scents; above them in her private apartment, Chanel, with her vitality undiminished, enjoyed her luxury and the fruits of her success at leisure. Though Chanel herself echoed the theory that fashions are never revived, it is a tribute to her rare and remarkable practicality, and an anomaly in the annals of recorded fashion, that few of her innovations became dated. With each season she watched, like Nature's seeds, her past creativity flowering anew, barely hidden behind the vague alterations of less talented designers. At last she decided she must again descend into the battle and flung open the doors on to her new collection.

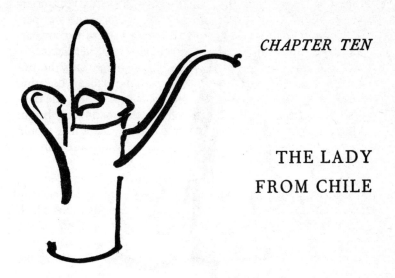

CHAPTER TEN

THE LADY
FROM CHILE

SOMEDAY, perhaps, a volume will be written about the quiet, authoritative people who, without attracting attention to themselves like noisy comets, yet, by the sheer gravitational pull of their individual choice, influence and often change the orbit of taste of a whole epoch. In literature, for instance, such persons rediscover great writers for their contemporaries; in painting, they bring forgotten artists to light; while in the world of fashion, be it clothes, interior decoration or flowers, they continually assert fresh values.

Madame Eugenia Errazuriz was such an influence. Her effect on the taste of the last fifty years has been so enormous that the whole aesthetic of modern interior decoration, and many of the concepts of simplicity which are so generally acknowledged today, can be laid at her remarkable doorstep.

Born Eugenia Huici in the small Chilean village of Huici, Madame Errazuriz' formative years and education were entrusted to the English nuns in Valparaiso. But she was destined

Madame Errazuriz as a young married woman

to leave her native country at a very early age, arriving in the
Europe of the 1880s to take up life, first in Paris and later in
London, as the wife of a rich amateur painter. An extremely
elegant woman, she always wore very high-heeled shoes and
dressed in the height of the mode. Thus garbed as a woman of
fashion, Madame Errazuriz was painted almost continually
throughout her life, inspiring such diverse artists as Picasso,
Sargent, Helleu, Chartran, Madrazo and Conder.

Eschewing the desire to become a social figure, she early
made friends among the most advanced musicians and painters.
It is said that Madame Errazuriz was the first to discover
Picasso, whom she loved throughout her life; Stravinsky was
also an early friend. Yet, for all her charm, she was extremely
vague in defining herself and was apt to be diffident when talking about personal tastes. She had little sense of money, never
knowing whether there were a hundred thousand pesetas in
the bank or none. Hence it is something of a paradox that, in
spite of the soft focus of her personality, and without being

Picasso

particularly articulate in any language, she became, by degrees, a grey eminence in the world of artists and cultivated people, who were to acknowledge themselves as her disciples. Like sunflowers turning to the sun, they looked to Madame Errazuriz for a redefinition of elegance, taste and love of the beautiful.

In common with the few rare and quiet authorities who had preceded her in the art of living, Madame Errazuriz' personality was such that her philosophy gained a wide and purifying influence. Though rich, she had grown tired of sumptuousness; having possessed everything, she decided to reduce her life to common denominators, echoing Oscar Wilde's tenet that simple things are the last refuge of complex people.

So she emptied her rooms, placing only a few pieces of furniture in them with an uncanny instinct for the dynamic symmetry of arrangement. Madame Errazuriz detested suites of furniture with sofa and identical chairs. 'Never follow suit,' she would stress. From the outset her taste was diametrically opposed to the knick-knacks, bric-a-brac, and junk of Edwardian and Victorian decoration. Bibelots were swept out as useless; frills were banished. She became the Beau Brummell of twentieth century interior decoration, allowing only things of intrinsic merit or quality to be found in her rooms. But this did not necessarily mean that they had to be of great value: more than any other woman of her generation, Madame Errazuriz appreciated the quality of individual objects, despite their category or price, and a simple wicker basket could often be found on a valuable table.

She preferred one beautiful object to a number of pretty ones. Her Paris salon had an inkwell, a blotter, a vase of fresh leaves, a flowering plant in an eighteenth-century jardiniere, a magnificent commode, and little more. There was no excess; no object was left there by chance. Each detail, on the contrary, had been selected with the greatest care, down to the ash trays that Madame Errazuriz especially felt should be the simplest, most unostentatious objects. To have an expensive ash tray on a table was, for her, as vulgar as putting out a saucer with a large cheque upon it: a plain piece of glass was all that was needed.

The abiding rules of proportion and measure were of prime importance in her estimation, and she herself always lived in beautifully constructed houses and well-proportioned rooms. Even a small apartment was obliged to have its own architectural interest.

Within such dimensions Madame Errazuriz could create her satisfying yet unadorned world. The walls of her salons were inevitably painted white; the floors had a cleanliness that comes only from soap and water.

Before the 1914 war Madame Errazuriz took a house at Biarritz which, to the amazement of her friends, she decorated like a peasant's house, whitewashing the walls and leaving the red-tiled floors carpetless but spotlessly clean. In the salon-dining room, a long wooden shelf, scrupulously scrubbed, ran the length of the wall; and on it, for decoration as well as practicality, she placed a still life of hams, huge cheeses, and loaves of bread under large glass bell jars. Her table was always set very informally, though napkins were of the heaviest linen, and

knives and forks of the best quality of French eighteenth-century silver. Picasso lived nearby and would pay spontaneous visits with a painter's smock over his bathing clothes to amuse himself by making impromptu frescoes.

In the ageing Madame Errazuriz' Paris *pavillon* (a wing of Count Etienne de Beaumont's house, which she occupied in the late twenties) the floor of the white entrance hall was always freshly scrubbed and shining. The stair railing was black, the carpet bright red, the garden table and armchair emerald green. There was a plain oak cupboard copied from an old Chinese piece. For decoration she created the strangeness of magic by the most ordinary means, using household implements that, though usually stowed away in back-hall closets, struck her as beautiful. A ladder and a coat hanger were painted grey; a wicker trunk and laundry basket stood in full view; an umbrella hung from a hook, ready for use. Often she would buy objects such as the cupboard of raw wood found at a farmers' market, because she responded to their admirable proportions. Or she might set a watering can in the hall, since it was needed to water the green plant next to it and was a thing of beauty in its own right. Garden shears or a garden basket, because of theirs, were placed in positions where they might delight the eye.

This manner of living was more purist than peasant and required both time and effort. No amount of labour was too great for Madame Errazuriz to obtain exactly what she needed, whether it was the best marmalade or the finest-quality linen. If she preferred linen rather than fine lawn for sheets, it was because linen could always be freshly scrubbed and washed. Indeed, all the objects surrounding her smelled of the pristine purity of spring water. Artificial perfumes were contrary to her tastes—she preferred eau de cologne and eau de toilette, or the fresh scent of rosemary, lavender and sweet geranium.

Her simplicity extended to food as well. Madame Errazuriz regarded as an offensive vulgarity the afternoon tea table laden with many varieties of elaborate little sugar cakes. She produced the best blends of tea and went to great lengths to have the crispest breads served with the purest farmhouse butter. Her toast was a work of art.

Once in Paris I was invited to have tea with this unusual woman. On the table before us was a simple cream-coloured Devonshire pot with a dozen white tulips rammed into it, sticking stiffly out to one side and not splayed in the manner usual to flower arrangements. I remarked on the individual boldness of the gesture. Madame Errazuriz held the pot up, and I was struck then by its beauty. She seemed amused. 'Yes,' she murmured, pausing between her words with little thoughtful noises, 'it's a beautiful pot; it *is* a beautiful pot.' The venerable hand that held the pot, her deep voice, the hesitancies—all indicated her profound and instinctive appreciation of this aesthetically satisfying object, whose crackle, colour and shape were a delight to her. She seemed, at that moment, a very earthy, direct, almost peasant woman. I felt I had gained an insight into the basis of her aesthetic philosophy.

As we sat, I made a mental inventory of the room. There were a divan and chairs upholstered in heavy indigo crash, a colour whose popular use since the turn of the century can be traced to her. In her lifetime she employed it for unlined curtains as well. Her furniture was always beautiful mahogany or fruitwood, not in the least ornate or gilded, but simple and solid English or austere Louis Seize. There were also wide Louis Seize *guéridons*, some highly polished bronzes, and curtains of clean blue and white striped linen, fresh from the wash. Abstract Picassos hung in the rooms.

In that saloon I could see the reflection of our latter-day taste for polished woods inlaid with brass, for rough cotton and linen curtains. Madame Errazuriz emphasized the beauty of poverty (not unlike Chanel's influence on the fashions of the twenties) and showed how lovely cotton linen could be. It is indeed more than probable that she was anti-silk. She disliked florists' hothouse blooms, favouring fresh garden flowers. It was also typical of her taste to prefer faïence to porcelain and glass to crystal.

Perhaps, by way of illustration, one could say that Madame Errazuriz' tendencies had a certain affinity with the Whistler-inspired appreciation for empty rooms with blue and white china and an engraving on the wall, with perhaps a Japanese screen in a corner. Doubtless her taste must have been greatly influenced by her long stay in England. It was certainly more classical than that of the decades through which she lived, and the indelible impression, though it influenced the *cognoscenti* in her own lifetime, has only latterly became apparent to many people.

Madame Errazuriz detested anything condemned to immobility. 'A house that does not alter,' she would say, 'is a dead house. One must change the furniture, or at least re-arrange it continually. This perpetual renewing is the beauty and the strength of fashion. In a house where nothing budges, the eye, too long accustomed to the same scene, ends by seeing nothing.'

To this end Eugenia Errazuriz loved bartering and exchanging objects with her friends. On one occasion Madame Errazuriz saw a beautiful eighteenth-century *bergère* chair at a Spanish inn and returned home full of excitement. 'It's the most lovely *bergère* in the whole world. I am going to sell something and buy that *bergère*, because I am very old. I am going to put it next to the window so that I can look at the world outside and never move.'

With her great-niece and great-niece's husband she went back to the inn to look at the *bergère*. It was an exquisitely bold and simple chair painted white. 'I don't like the material. If ever I get that chair, I'm going to find something blue to cover it. I *must* exchange something for that chair.'

'No,' said the husband of her great-niece. 'We will buy the chair for you!'

Delight, kisses, embraces; the chair was covered in blue and white material and placed by the window. A month later her niece came to tea and noticed the absence of the chair. Madame Errazuriz was embarrassed. 'I couldn't resist a change,' she said. 'I saw something I liked even better, so I sold the chair to Emilio Terry.'

True to her philosophy, Madame Errazuriz was a great furniture mover, one of the few (together with Drian, the painter) who had a genius for knowing exactly where to place furniture in a room. With her unerring eye for proportion she could even tell at a glance if a chandelier was hung too high or too low, according to the unwritten measure that governs such things.

Another of Madame Errazuriz' beliefs was that simplicity extended to nooks and drawers as well. 'If the kitchen is not as well kept as the salon,' she would say, 'if there are masses of old things lying about the bureau drawers, you cannot have a beautiful house. Throw out and keep throwing out: elegance means elimination.'

No photographs or miniatures stood on her tables or hung on her walls. Instead, they were fixed inside the drawers of a commode that opened on to a fascinating gallery of souvenirs of her rich and varied life, including a photograph of the portrait Sargent made of her when she arrived in London from Chile, a very young woman with a small beak of a nose and raven hair.

A gratuitous genius, Madame Errazuriz never became a professional decorator, giving advice only to relations or close friends, such as the Jaucourts, her great-niece, Madame Lopez-Wilshaw, or her nephew, Tony Gandarillas.

To these intimates she also aired her views on the subject of dressing. One day Patricia Lopez-Wilshaw (who is rightly considered to be one of the most elegant women in Paris) came to see her wearing a yellow coat and a small black hat trimmed with a yellow bow. 'That yellow bow is wrong. You must either be dressed in one colour or in many colours, but never wear a repetition of colours. You can mix colours, but it is a great fault to repeat them. And your stockings are not good—they are too thick. You must always buy the best in life; you must always try to find the best quality in the world.'

With other friends her word was often: 'Put very few things on. Don't buy five middling-good dresses; much better to have one good one from Balenciaga than a lot for the sake of variety.'

Madame Errazuriz' interior-decorating doctrines found wide acceptance and influenced many decorators, including Jean-Michel Frank. If Frank had lived, he would perhaps have been the great decorator of the future. It is he who should have decorated the United Nations Building. Better than anyone he knew how to cater to a period in which, with few domestic servants and the cost of upkeep at a premium, ingenuity must be used. Jean-Michel Frank invented new surfaces and fabrics, tables made of parchment, banquettes upholstered in sackcloth, and walls covered with great squares of raw leather. He designed low sofas and tables, even encouraging people to sit on leather floor cushions, while sheepskin or raffia were recommended carpets. He prevailed upon Giacometti to design some lamps which are among the most beautiful of modern household objects. Frank had, in general, a unique feeling for measure and correctness in his arrangements. He was that rare genius who could give elegance to modern furniture and modern décor; though even Frank never succeeded (nor has anyone since) in giving to a room decorated entirely with modern furniture a personal, individual feeling.

As an old woman, Madame Errazuriz returned to Biarritz. Always vague about money, she spent ten times more than she possessed. She now found herself in somewhat straitened circumstances, though relations and friends were always nearby to help her, while her great-nephew made certain that each day she had a quart bottle of champagne. 'Ca me donne de la vie,' she said. Each night she went to bed early and was up betimes, working barefoot in the garden from six until noon, at which time she put on a pair of high-heeled shoes. Until her death Madame Errazuriz still wore exaggeratedly high heels.

Her great-niece has described how she would go to say good night to her. Madame Errazuriz sat in bed, wearing a nightgown with full-length sleeves and a high collar fastened tight round her high neck with string. 'Don't look at the lines of my hand,' she would say as her niece kissed her hand. 'The lines are fading away. I'm so old: I know I'm not going to live long.' She had the peasant's acceptance of life and death, imbued with a deep religious faith.

During the difficult years of the Second World War, Madame Errazuriz wrote to her nephew. 'I am getting very thin, but I am not hungry. It is only age, thank God. Though I feel the

Picasso, 1946

ravages of fatigue from time to time, that is only natural and
I have no other miseries. I received a big lump of money from
Chile, and hope that if I succeed in being tidy it will see me
through to the end. I work very hard in the garden with the
wish to see it looking picturesque, and it is improving. The
plants that produce food increase. God helps the people who
have confidence in Him. That is my faith. The month of
February has been dreadful. I live in the drawing room and
even sleep in it, as it has a stove which gives real heat and the
sofa is my bed and I sleep well. How tiresome I have become
telling you about my life. Don't send me anything except some
black wool to make myself a sweater.'

About the same time she wrote a typical letter of advice to a close friend: 'I know your house will be perfect, for it will possess the three most important elements—harmony, elegance and tidiness. Nothing patched up. I would like to have seen the carpet on the floor where the bright blue chaise longue stands. Don't ever sell it. It's a beautiful object. Picasso loved it and it gives tranquillity to the other objects in the room. Put the other carpet you bought from me at the foot of the bed. How I should like to see all your things! Put all your new things in your bedroom. You already have the Picassos in your drawing room which will take your eye and make you see nothing else. Here, I have painted and washed everything in the house myself, and in the big room I put my bed just arrived from Paris from Etienne de Beaumont. The spring is so beautiful, and I love my house as it looks very clean and very poor!'

Towards the end of Madame Errazuriz' many years in France, her favourite great-niece, Madame Lopez-Wilshaw, went to stay with her in the house at Biarritz and described the old lady (with hair like white silk that she washed in rain water) wandering barefoot among the rosemary bushes and the lavender in her garden. 'Everything in Aunt Eugenia's house smelled so good, everything was so clean,' she said. 'The bathrooms had such wonderful soap, and lots of rose-geranium salts. The towels were thick, heavy ones with fringes and smelled of lavender. It was so peaceful to be with her, almost the peace of a convent. She was such a simple human being. Everything in her life had quality and simplicity—never anything complicated. On Sundays and Thursdays a French and a Spanish priest would come to luncheon. Aunt Eugenia knew the Spanish priest was somewhat of a gourmand, so she would say, "I'm going to do a special chicken for him. One must have a little vice if it gives so much pleasure and doesn't harm anyone." After lunch they talked so intelligently about all subjects, particularly about literature, music and painting.

'It was always such fun to be with Aunt Eugenia. She always looked at you with such kindness, she was so full of human sympathy. . . . We discovered we both hated the hydrangeas that grew so profusely around Biarritz, and so we decided to cut off all those horrid pink and blue heads. Aunt Eugenia said, "I didn't dare do it before, but now you're here we can do it together." ' Armed with scissors, the two women went out into the garden. ' "I particularly hate the pink ones," Aunt Eugenia said as she snipped away. "Look how much better they are just green!"'

In 1949, at the age of ninety, Madame Errazuriz realized her memory was failing. Out of discretion, and perhaps with a remnant of youthful coquettishness, she did not wish her friends or relations to see her at a disadvantage. Settling up her affairs, she gave away many presents, including her Picassos, took an aeroplane for the first time, and flew back to her native Chile. There, two years later, Madame Errazuriz was badly hurt in a motor-car accident. She did not wish to live any more; in Chile she was lonely. 'To be ninety is a nuisance. I am tired of living. It is enough.' Refusing to eat, she gave as her reason: 'I wish to help God to take me out of this life.' And so Madame Errazuriz died.

The tastes that this remarkable lady and her disciple, Jean-Michel Frank, left behind them are still being widely propagated throughout the world. In Paris, Madame Castaing is triumphantly successful with her high prices and the influence of her sober schemes of decoration whose basic values have come directly from Madame Errazuriz and which now have overwhelmed most *antiquaires* on the Left Bank.

If the lady from Chile ever had a secret, it was as simple as the fact that she was utterly individual. Only the individual taste, in the end, can truly create style or fashion, since it is not concerned with following in the wake of others. Hence, whatever an individual taste may choose, be it a step-ladder or a wicker basket, it must always be based on a deep personal choice, a spiritual need that truly assesses and gives value to that particular ladder or basket. The beauty of things is somehow transmitted through the personality of the one who chooses. It is in our selection, after all, that we betray our deepest selves, and the individualist can make us see the objects of his choice with new eyes, with *his* eyes. The sheep, who follow taste without a hope of ever achieving it, never arrive at such distinction because they do not really cultivate themselves or their potential individuality.

In the history of taste, Madame Errazuriz remains a lucid example of the personal, the only thing that ever really matters. Though her name may perhaps be forgotten in a hundred years, she is one of the not too numerous people who, even if they become historically anonymous by not having been creative artists in an enduring mould, are still true artists in terms of selecting and giving meaning to the things that make up the daily tenor of existence.

CHAPTER ELEVEN

LOW
BAROMETER

PAQUIN was dying hard. Patou, a great showman, had just displayed in his winter collection a black and yellow dress with the first long skirt that had been seen for many years. The fashionable ladies with beautiful legs went into revolt—never would they appear at such a disadvantage as to cover their legs. But six months later every woman would be entranced with the new 'slinky' look. Molyneux's showrooms were crowded to the doors with his favoured clients ordering no less than fifteen of his semi-short *dégagé* day suits or the long supple evening dresses. Gertrude Lawrence, a past mistress in the art of making clothes 'spin', was now to be his greatest advertisement. In Molyneux's polka-dotted pyjamas or white satin sheaths she would look 'divine'; but then Miss Lawrence was always a wonderful exponent for everybody connected with the making of all sorts of clothes: by wearing a mink coat over grey flannel slacks she could create an epoch.

Looking backwards, the thirties, from the point of view of

Edward Molyneux

the arts, fashion and the general course of life itself, strike one
as being perhaps the least interesting of recent decades. Heavy
wrought-iron doors, Knole sofas, their backs bound with ban-
dages of metal *galon* and their adjustable ends held insecurely
by tasselled knobs, were placed cater-corner in even the smallest
rooms. Ecclesiastical touches were brought into the homes,
with loot from churches being used in a most indiscriminate
manner. Cigarettes were kept in disembowelled books, lampshades were made of old music parchment with a scrap of *Kyrie
Eleison* on it, almost anything could be given a pseudo-antique
look by the simple expedient of applying a coat of yellow
varnish. In literature a proletarian influence reigned heavy.
Most of the young intellectuals in England found it inevitable
to be Left-wing. Many young men went off to fight in the
Spanish Civil War, and since issues were not as clear then as
they are today, youthful idealists, with the best of intentions,
made bedfellows of the Communist cause.

There were a Chicago World's Fair and a New York World's Fair, both heralding the beginning of the acceptance of modern architecture with its straight lines, plain materials and obviation of detail. Interior decorating then went 'modern' with a vengeance, but the mass-produced 'modern' furniture was to be as impersonal as anything that had previously been turned out by Grand Rapids.

From the visual viewpoint of clothes, the thirties was undoubtedly a drab period. Perhaps someone may be able to recapture the feeling of excitement that women's fashions engendered in their day. But looking at them now, one can see only an uninspired modification of the revolution of the twenties: the boyish bob had vanished, but women's breasts were still flat, and the longer skirts and slightly higher waistlines seem merely mechanical additions to the short, tubular dresses they had displaced.

There were, of course, some remarkable dressmakers working at the time, but the one who made the greatest contribution of them all was Madame Vionnet, who started her establishment in the twenties. A parrot-like little woman with a shock of white hair, Madeleine Vionnet herself wore somewhat masculine clothes and a trilby hat. Vionnet was a genius in the way she used her materials. With her scissors she changed fashion, inventing the bias cut (or the cut on the cross), which is now one of the primary principles of dressmaking. Our contemporary dressmakers would do well to study her craftsmanship, observing how she employed fabrics in ingenious ways. When the fashionable silhouette was flat, Vionnet worked in the round, evolving a harmony between the supple curves of the feminine body and the hang of drapery that was to be fluted as a Hellenic column. She made a Greek dress in a way the Greeks could never have imagined; there was nothing archaic about her lines. Everything Vionnet created had a cling or a flow, and women dressed by her were like moving sculpture. Through her use of materials she exposed the anatomy of women for the first time. Apart from the revelation of the bias cut, this designer was also responsible for the halter and cowl necklines and the handkerchief-point dress. With such innovations Vionnet revolutionized the epoch. For twenty-five years her influence on the technique of fashion has remained.

Madame Vionnet, who had once been a forewoman at the house of Callot, was never a great colourist, and her materials were nearly always of nondescript tones. She seldom resorted to trimming on her creations, nor would she ever allow padding of any sort on the hips or shoulders. Everything had to hang naturally and normally, while artifice of all sorts was discouraged. Her women, therefore, had to provide their own trimming and needed well-formed busts and hips.

Though Madame Vionnet retired from business in 1939 and considers that high fashion no longer exists as in the days she knew, she is, as the doyenne of the couture world, active behind the scenes in France today, and always at the time of the collections is in Paris to give encouragement and advice to the 'real craftsmen' of whom she has been the inspiration.

Social historians might perhaps point to the stock-market crash of 1929 as the significant epitome of a feverish, fun-struck age. Certainly, with ruined millionaires throwing themselves out of windows, it marked the end of an age of plenty and ushered in a depression that was to last for a whole era, with the advent of breadlines, the dole and a staggering economic crisis.

Women's fashions, in the name of practicability, comprised street suits of indeterminate shape and length, 'formal' pyjamas, 'tea gowns' with horse halters round the neck, and the creations, so un-Parisian in taste, of Schiaparelli.

Yet Schiaparelli was, in her own way, something of a genius. She injected a healthy note into the thirties, inventing her own particular form of ugliness and salubriously shocking a great many people. With colours that were aggressive and even upsetting, including a particular puce that she referred to as her 'shocking pink', Schiaparelli began her revolution.

Schiaparelli used rough-looking materials—oaten linens, pebbly crashes and heavy crepes—put nylon and other new materials to good purposes, and was the first to use synthetic fabrics for her dresses. Mrs Diana Vreeland of *Harper's Bazaar* once sent a Schiaparelli dress to the cleaner's. The next day she

My Aunt Jessie, 1926

Mrs Vernon Castle, 1928

Oriental teagown, 1927

Lady Diana Cooper, 1930

Paula Gellibrand, 1930

Mrs Lydig, from the portrait in alabaster by Malvina Hoffman

Madame Errazuriz, 1929

Chanel, 1953

Madame Vionnet, 1953

Greta Garbo

Christian Bérard

English beauty: the Three Graces, 1951, *The Wyndham-Quin sisters*

Christian Dior

Balenciaga

Audrey Hepburn, 1954

Mrs Vreeland, 1954

received a telephone call informing her with regret that the dress had been put into the cleaning fluid and there was nothing left of it. Mrs Vreeland, who unbelievingly insisted on seeing the remains, was told that there was literally nothing at the bottom of the pan.

Schiaparelli was an excellent editor of ideas, with many people working for her. Cocteau and Bérard gave her sketches for costumes; Jean Schlumberger applied his flair to the making of original buttons.

She was the first dressmaker to travel extensively and, wherever she went, brought back representative clothes of that country. On holiday in Switzerland, 'Schiap' would make a mental note of the ski instructors; with her return, women would be given thick jerseys with padded square shoulders. A trip to the Tyrol launched Tyrolean fashions; an Indian voyage introduced saris and gauzes; North Africa gave rise to burnooses and cord embroideries, while visits to Peru, Mexico or Russia widened the canvas of her effects. At one moment in the late thirties this capricious designer came under the surrealist influence. In her shop a shocking-pink sofa was designed like a pair of lips. Mauve lipstick was created for women, mutton chops were put on ladies' hats, and one particular headdress looked like a shoe. Schiaparelli often put women in men's coats, soldiers', sailors' and policemen's uniforms, even going so far as to introduce bus conductors' and railway porters' outfits. One suit, decorated with closed bureau drawers, was inspired by Dali. By 1938 fashion had gone into such a state of decadence that it seemed surely a last warning before the Tower of Babel fell; which, with the Second World War, it did.

Though the twenties boasted a number of striking personalities among women of leisure, their number had dwindled, or they had withdrawn from the scene, in the period that followed the great depression of 1929. One of the few outstanding beauties of the thirties was Mrs Harrison Williams, who represented the epitome of all that taste and luxury can bring to flower.

Her houses, her furniture, her jewellery, her way of life were little short of a *tour de force*. She herself was and is today a *chef-*

d'oeuvre, breathing a rarefied air of mystery, like some undine or goddess from another world who yet chooses to dress in the height of fashionable conventionality. Her clothes were always extremely feminine, soft and graceful, and I would hazard a guess that many of them had been designed by Vionnet. Mrs Harrison Williams restricted herself to pale colours that complemented her extraordinary colouring, setting off her aquamarine eyes, her short silver curling hair and very pink cheeks. Here is the kind of complexion that radiates the immaculate perfection of health, a perfection which was further emphasized by the brilliance of her eyes, the marble sheen of her shoulders, her strong and energetic hands, and the live muscular body that possesses the *élan* of a released spring.

More than any other woman, Mrs Harrison Williams also possesses the American quality of freshness. No French or South American hostess could possibly have rivalled the almost unreal perfection of crispness and newness that she created in the surroundings of her Fifth Avenue house. Everything was kept in a state of polished and dazzling cleanliness. Nothing was ever tattered, and no Ispahan carpet ever became threadbare. Her Goyas, Bouchers and Reynoldses had been tenderly relieved of years of grime and oxidization. Not a speck of dust had the opportunity of gathering on the books in the airconditioned library. English furniture and crystal candelabra were highly polished; parquet floors were waxed and shining. One even had the feeling that all the bonbons and the peppermint sweets on the dinner table were thrown out the moment the exquisite flower-strewn cloth was removed. It seemed a certainty that the jewelled gold boxes were sent off to be repolished, that the diamonds were washed along with the dog each day, and that the 'below stairs' must have boasted some great hospital sterilizer to make the glasses and porcelain shine.

Mrs Harrison Williams' flowers, especially, created an amazing impression of freshness and vigour, more so than any other person's flowers that I have ever seen. Lilies almost shrieked in their newly filled vases as they burst with joy into flower on their bold stems; the white and the pink carnations, so stout

Mona Williams
1954 -

and strong, looked as though they could never wilt; and the orchids had a metallic rigidity. Likewise, her porcelains and painted silk curtains, the pots of Fabergé flowers and her diamond-buckled satin shoes—all made their contribution to this pristine *ambiance*.

Both mistress and mansion seemed to have just stepped out of a bandbox. It was a feat that no Englishwoman could possibly have duplicated. In England there would have been a tattered cushion in a room, or a patina on the furniture. The fact that there was literally nothing, no object in any corner of Mrs Harrison Williams' house that was shabby, created a feeling of deft luxury and extravagance that was in itself quite startling.

I think it was Katherine Mansfield who, hearing the gardener raking up leaves, wrote in her notebook that 'somewhere somebody is secretly putting things in order'. In our age-old war with chaos, with the dirt and the dust that always and forever push in upon us, hoping to invade us—in that war, Mrs Harrison Williams is surely a general, and I am not being facetious in admiring a quality as evanescent, yet as important, as cleanliness. Among the few indelible impressions that the years preceding the last war have left on my mind's eye, Mrs Harrison Williams and her dazzling surroundings remain one of the most felicitous.

Altogether a different personality from Mrs Harrison Williams was Millicent Rogers. Among the poor little rich girls whose comet-like careers left streams of newspaper headlines in their wake during the twenties and the thirties, there may have been heiresses to tobacco, banks, biscuits, tinned meats, sewing machines, or five-and-ten-cent stores who were richer and more pathetic in their own right than Millicent Rogers. But none could have been more extravagant nor more extravagantly beautiful than this daughter of a Standard Oil pioneer, with her face like a lotus flower and her figure like a Chinese statuette.

The Millicent Rogers who in the forties chose to spend her last years in New Mexico had long since retired from the field of both life and fashion, leaving others to wave their banners with less flair and certainly with less originality. She had slipped unobtrusively out of a social life whose beginning would hardly have presaged the calm harbour of its later years.

For in her anarchic youth, a youth which coincided with the heyday of the twenties, Millicent Rogers had been very much involved in the social whirl. When the then Prince of Wales paid his history-making visit to America, the quixotic heiress—at the height of her strange youthfulness, with a marble complexion, pouting lips, long fingernails, and Oriental jewels setting off a short black velvet dress—was on hand to dance with him. She saw to it that anyone who observed her should never forget the occasion.

But whatever the time or place, Millicent Rogers always left her imprint upon it. One admirer has observed that he would never forget her coming along a corridor in a blue linen beach suit, passing through a shaft of sunlight that caught the red handkerchief she was holding. On another occasion he watched her make an entrance through a doorway in a magenta sequin sheath the colour of her hair. Mrs Vreeland relates the events of a coming-out ball at the Ritz Hotel in New York, where

Millicent Rogers was staying at the time. That evening the heiress had decided to play musical chairs with the prevailing fashions and kept changing her dress. Initially she wore a Patou black silk dress with bustle and train; but on the pretext of having sat on some ice cream she abandoned it for a robe of looped taffetas. The ice cream excuse gave way to spilled coffee, thus providing a further alteration, and so it went throughout the evening.

But if Millicent Rogers' exhibitionism was not easily appeased, she at any rate showed her good taste in all things. Throughout the succeeding years she could always be relied upon to make unusual surprise appearances, dressed either as Anna Karenina in sable, as a fragrant Chinese courtesan in mandarin robes, or as Gretel in Tyrolean peasant clothes made by Schiaparelli. Her originality was manifest even in the way she wore a bow or a scarf; jewellery embarked upon a whole new trend when she picked up a leaf, stuck a pin through it, and gave it to Boivin to copy in gold and diamonds.

Later she was to develop a reputation for designing jewellery herself and even in retirement in New Mexico continued her hobby of collecting silver jewellery peculiar to the South-west.

But Millicent Rogers was not content to remain a mere clothes-horse. With the passing of the years her calm, domesticated nature, her great love of her children and of relaxation and peace began to assert itself. Young or middle-aged, she remained a woman of remarkable originality, always pursuing hobbies that allowed her to express her artistic abilities. If she had not suffered from ill-health, she might have laid the ghost of her money, becoming a serious artist in one field instead of a dilettante who dissipated in a delightful way her talents, by illustrating books for her children, making acres of needlework carpets, designing jewellery and exercising her superb taste in decorating house after house, which were usually quixotically abandoned before their completion.

During one period in the thirties Millicent Rogers chose Charles James, the American dressmaker, to make all her clothes for her. Charles James is a superb tailor in satin and has affinities with the French in his master craftsmanship and attention to detail. He was naturally delighted that her orders should be so extensive, for it kept his business thriving. But after having put so much time and effort into the making of four dozen blouses which he felt were designated for the Manhattan Storage, he rebelled. When Mrs Rogers' maid telephoned for a further order, Charles James complained, 'Why, Mrs Rogers is nothing but a hoarder!'

The maid replied, 'Not a hoarder, Mr James, a collector!' True to the maid's words, in 1949 Millicent Rogers presented to the Brooklyn Museum a collection of clothes created for her by Charles James.

Dresses were not, however, the limit of this heiress's passion. Her acquisitions comprised a number of carpets, quilts, Chinese porcelains, furs by the tons, paintings, and bric-à-brac.

When Millicent Rogers retired to Taos, the courtyards of her small adobe house were painted in varying colours, while the sunlit rooms were filled with the choicest of her various possessions. Here, with her Gauguins on the wall, she sat in bed and made gold ornaments, beads and jewellery of abstract design, her tools being pumice stone and nail files. During the infrequent hours that she left this room she wore the long skirt and blouse of the Indians and went barefoot.

Throughout her life Millicent Rogers had always looked the perfect expression of her highly civilized tastes, which lent an aesthetic motive to all that she did. Within her limits she was an artist; the circumstances of her birth had allowed her free rein to create an exciting and imaginative existence for herself. Many millionaires are inevitably unpredictable, fractious or spoiled. But if it is a handicap to be born poor, it is often a greater handicap to be born with a silver spoon in one's mouth. There is nothing like wealth to create psychological problems for those who, by a freak contingency of destiny, inherit money without having done anything to achieve it. It is a tribute to Millicent Rogers' earnest nature that, after the anarchic years of her youth, she devoted herself to valuable charity work, and then, voluntarily as well as through the exigencies of health, quit the fashionable world for a last contemplation of life's quieter and richer side.

In the thirties the fashion photographers came into their own. As one of them, I must confess to having indulged myself in the generally prevailing recklessness of style. My pictures became more and more rococo and surrealist. Society women as well as mannequins were photographed in the most flamboyant Greek-tragedy poses, in ecstatic or highly mystical states, sometimes with the melodramatic air of a Lady Macbeth caught up in a cocoon of tulle. Like the souls in torments seen in Hieronymus Bosch's hell, ladies of the upper crust were to be seen in *Vogue* photographs fighting their way out of a hat box or breaking through a huge sheet of white paper or torn screen, as though emerging from a nightmare. Princesses were posed trying frantically to be seen through a plate-glass window that had been daubed with whitewash. In fact, white was the one regular keynote to these proceedings. White-on-white paper was often used as a background, with a woman in white holding a sheaf of whitened branches in front of it. Perfectly normal ladies were pictured in extremes of terror, with one arm covering the face or thrust forward in exaggerated perspective straight towards the camera.

Backgrounds were equally exaggerated and often tasteless. Badly carved cupids from junk shops on Third Avenue would be wrapped in argentine cloth or cellophane. Driftwood was supposed to bring an air of neo-romanticism to a matter-of-fact subject. Christmas paper chains were garlanded around the model's shoulders, and wooden doves, enormous paper flowers from Mexico, Chinese lanterns, doilies or cutlet frills, fly whisks, sporrans, egg beaters, or stars of all shapes found their way into our hysterical and highly ridiculous pictures.

Some of this meretricious work was inspired by a literary approach. Mannequins 'dressed to kill' would be photographed as murderesses with smoking guns, and smart witnesses appeared in the 'witness box'. I remember that George Davis would take the models, wearing clothes from Fifth Avenue, to be photographed among the sawdust and backstage trappings of the circus ring; or, wearing black satin and monkey fur, with the huge hats of a villainess of melodrama, they would be photographed against the scabrous, peeling walls of Brook-

lyn. Man Ray, Muncasi and other photographers played tricks
with elongation of the figure and with 'solarization' of the negative, all of which played havoc with the ladies' hair. No demon-
stration of madness was considered too exaggerated.

At this time, also, much unrestrained activity was afoot in
the fields of decoration. Night clubs were done up as bird
cages; baroque excesses in plasterwork were allied to the plush
luxuries of late Victorianism. Sugary magentas and pinks, together with bright yellows, were favourite colours.

Yet, in spite of much that was depressing, life in the thirties
had its highlights. Art, especially under the influence of such
painters as Dali, Picasso and Bérard, was impinging very closely
on fashion.

Even an esoteric painter such as Tchelitchew had an overt
influence. Whereas Bérard's whole idiom lent itself easily to
fashion, Tchelitchew's idiom was anti-fashion. Hence it is all
the more remarkable that his décor and costumes for Girau-
doux's *Ondine* created a vogue for fish nets, stalactites, coral
branches and driftwood. But those elements of mystery in the
theatre often became meaningless when brought into reality,
and the fish nets draped over an oak staircase in a Wiltshire
mansion seemed oddly incongruous. The influence continued
nonetheless, and photographs were taken by Hoyningen-
Huene, George Platt Lynes, Horst, Durst and myself of lost
wanderers in a Tchelitchew world of shadows. We apotheosized poverty, dragging in poor children in beggars' rags, just
as Tchelitchew had romanticized real beggars, or as Bérard had
popularized Le Nain peasants.

In the theatre the thirties did not reap a rich harvest, though
the Old Vic in London's Waterloo Road, it is true, was doing
excellent pioneer work at that time; while John Gielgud made
people appreciative of the classics, introducing Chekhov, reviving Webster, revitalizing Shakespeare, and, with his distinguished personality and voice of great range and nobility, making an ever-increasing public enjoy plays of a high quality. His
Richard of Bordeaux was a dignified success in the commercial
theatre. Yet even Gielgud lent his noble services to embellishing a play by Dodie Smith that appealed to the masses of

matinee goers, if not to more discriminating audiences. London seemed satisfied with an endless succession of drawing-room comedies and family plays based on old patterns, lacking in wit and freshness. From a visual point of view, the theatre was equally uninspiring. Only in the ballet could one find first-rate designers at work.

The New York stage had *Porgy and Bess*, Lillian Hellman's *The Children's Hour*, the early Clifford Odets, and the Group Theatre, which has latterly come under so much criticism for having been Communistic in its ideas. Musical comedy was being brought to a high degree of perfection in the thirties, and popular songs began to be more and more influenced by the growing musical sophistication in this branch of the theatre arts. But then popular music and one of the latter-day geniuses who helped to make it what it is today, Cole Porter, are well worth analysis in the light that they shed not only upon the thirties but also the succeeding eras.

One of the epigrams that people were quoting back in the early thirties is a line from Nöel Coward's play *Private Lives*, where the hero observes, 'Strange how potent cheap music is.' Popular songs, like styles in clothing, are ephemeral manifestations of the times. But it would be wrong to classify any temporal artistic expression as 'cheap'. Nobody denigrates the dresses of Poiret or Worth or Doucet: they have simply taken their place as costumes, historical pieces that reflect their time but are no longer valid, in a living sense, for our own age. So it is with popular songs: like the ironic epitaph on Keats's grave, popular songs or styles in dress are 'written on water'.

Perhaps it is precisely because of their fleeting qualities that they seem to incorporate, in their expression, a peculiarly poignant and almost tragic awareness of the unique moment in time that will never come again. There is something uncanny in the way that popular songs, especially, can quickly conjure up for us the whole emotional feeling of a decade. Like sponges, they seem to have an extraordinary capacity for absorption and can retain an ocean of memories.

Among those composers whose talents have given so much to our latter-day popular culture, perhaps no one in the first half of the twentieth century has surpassed the brilliance of achievement that Cole Porter has sustained over some twenty-five years of activity. From his songs of the twenties up to the present moment he has consistently maintained a high level of both music and lyrics. Cole Porter's advent brought a sophistication and smartness that were quite new to the realm of popular songs. With his plaintive, often minor-key airs, his dry, hard-as-dog-biscuit harmonies and staccato rhythms, he created a shock of a special and cultivated order. Like a scholar 'cutting up' or an attractive philosopher being bad, Cole Porter appeared as an *enfant terrible*, saying with charm and wit just those things that everyone secretly feared and hoped might be said.

It was this composer's success that was largely responsible for paving the way to popular appreciation of the brilliant Kurt Weill as well as a host of song writers of lesser talents. Just as, in the realms of more serious music, Stravinsky had broken new ground with his violent dissonances and made it possible for others to follow in his steps, so, too, the brilliance of Porter's lyrics set a standard that raised the level of all popular song writers. His songs are of such a quality that, if it is true about style being something enduring, the chances are good that Cole Porter's melodies will still be whistled by butcher boys long after the memory of contemporary kings, presidents, statesmen or soldiers has gone into oblivion.

In appearance this composer looks rather like a rubber imp. His thinning black hair is sleek and shining; his face is a curious theatrical rubber mask that would seem to lend itself to any sort of expression. In matters of dress he is like a tailor's window dummy, wearing natty grey flannel suits and outsized carnations in his buttonhole. When he sits, it is with his legs wide apart, trousers hitched up to avoid wrinkling. A gold-headed cane is usually held firmly in one hand, while behind the bony wrist there is always a goodly expanse of shirt cuff visible.

Cole Porter is that unique phenomenon, a one-hundred-per-cent-fashionable person. His sense of smartness seeks out the best that the contemporary world can offer him, whether it be poplin shirts or peanut butter. In jargon and argot he is always

Cole Porter 1953.

up to the minute; he reads every gossip column with the
assiduity of an Egyptologist translating the Rosetta stone. Even
his efficiency is fashionable: cigarette lighters work at the first
click, cigarette boxes are always full, head waiters are charmed
by his glib and practised way of talking to them out of the
corner of his mouth. He is a perfectionist at ordering every
thing from brook trout to Vichy water, from candied carrots
to claret or burgundy.

Going hand in hand with Cole Porter's *ne plus ultra* chic is
a rare virtue: he is loyal to his friends, whether they are themselves fashionable or no. Yet he is determined to make them
fashionable, just as everything he does himself is *comme il faut*.
In short, he is the quintessence of café society; and from this
remarkable personal reservoir he doubtless draws inspiration
for his songs.

Musically there can be no doubt that his talent is utterly first-
rate. More than any Tin Pan Alley popular composer he

has stamped the whole tone of several decades with his songs. Scarcely a cocktail bar or night club, hardly a dance hall or a juke box, but what his songs are nightly to be heard and hummed throughout the forty-eight states of America, and in England, France and Italy as well. 'What Is This Thing Called Love?', 'Night and Day', 'You Do Something to Me', 'In the Still of the Night', 'You'd Be So Nice To Come Home To'—the list of melodies is endless. He runs the gamut from the sentimental to the cynical and smart with equal ease. Typical of his cleverness are the lyrics to such songs as 'It's Delovely' or 'My Heart Belongs to Daddy', the tune that made Mary Martin a star when she sang wrapped in a mink coat.

Yet for all his cleverness, Cole Porter seems at times oddly ill at ease. He relaxes only with very simple people. There is even something tragic about him, as though behind his rubber mask another face, another personality, were waiting to be freed. The task of receiving the fleeting impressions of the age and translating them into music has perhaps prevented him from ever getting to know himself, to discover himself beneath the web of fashion that he has of necessity woven round him. Cole Porter is the paradox of all creators who work in temporal media: he combines the despair and the triumph of the Juggler of Notre Dame to himself.

Like all hard-working people, he is a serious professional who still takes piano lessons and studies musical composition. Fame is not the result of ease and facility; he has worked hard throughout the years to maintain a position as one of the few top composers in the contemporary manner. Jazz artists and jitterbugs acclaim his work, together with Park Avenue hostesses, intellectuals or anybody.

For no one is exempt from the fashionable expressions of his age. No one, indeed, but a fool could fail to be aware, for better or worse, of the picture of life offered through the various popular media. Oddly, the works of popular culture are often even more moving than those serious artistic efforts which will outlast them. That which is eternal, a Michelangelo statue or a Mozart opera, goes far beyond the nostalgia of the moment. Only in Cole Porter songs, in shoes or feathers or films, do

Greta Garbo

we find the whole expression of a moment in time that was a particular moment of our lives and is now gone forever.

In the thirties films, in fact, had kept technical pace with the other dramatic media. New stars were given the opportunity, with the advent of talking pictures, to express themselves more intimately than they could on the stage. Indeed, perhaps the most important contribution to the histrionics of the period was provided by film stars of great personality. And in particular Greta Garbo reached the height of her influence.

In the late thirties *Vanity Fair*, under the editorship of Frank Crowninshield, published a series of pictures entitled 'And Then Came Garbo'. These were comparative studies of perhaps a dozen film and stage actresses of the day, showing their appearance of a year or two previously, and juxtaposing recent photographs of the same stars that clearly showed how they were attempting to base their whole appearance on Garbo. The influence was scarcely limited to other actresses: manne-

La Dame
aux
Camélias

quins in dress shops were made to look like their Swedish prototype, and women with pretences to fashionable beauty modelled themselves along similar lines. Garbo's face was symbolized by the enigmatic clown paleness, the huge black eyelashes, and the straight blonde haircut like a medieval page's. These features gave women the discovery of a new pattern of beauty, one that was to be fully exploited for the next twenty years.

Perhaps no other person has had such an influence on the appearance of a whole generation, though in fact the owner of this face possesses other qualities that cannot be improvised or imitated. The whole secret of her appeal seems to lie in an elusive and haunting sensitivity. Refined ripples of feeling appear at the surface, coming from some deep and unknown source. Her extraordinary plastic ability suggests comparison with an undreamed-of seismographic instrument able to register the most delicate range of vibrations. The nose has the pristine sensitivity of some timid creature of the forest; her mouth combines, in a wistful, child-like ambivalence, the Greek masks of tragedy and comedy. Garbo is either very sad or fecklessly gay; and when she laughs, she proves that things metallic have a soul. Her eyes seem to offer a special compassion to each of us. Inexhaustible spiritual assets highlight the sensitivity and delicacy of these features, continually hinting at every nuance of all that she is feeling, and giving the spectator the tenuous and remarkable impression that he is witnessing the remotest depths in a human face. The rare physiognomy and personality have rightly created a legend that goes far beyond those cinematic impressions saved for posterity.

Imitations are always a far cry from the original, and especially in the case of Garbo, the poster of her face that went out to the world is in no way representative of what she was or is. Simulated soulfulness at best created a tiresome, would-be sophistication, and the carbon copies often looked more decadent than sensitive.

After having created the original expression, which to this day is still reflected in women's appearance, it has been extremely difficult for Garbo herself to sustain what was copied to the point of ridiculousness. She has been forced, out of innate taste and tact, as well as through her own introversion, to simplify her appearance, both in terms of physical characteristics as well as clothes.

Though Garbo has been credited with having little clothes sense and obviously pays no attention whatsoever to the rules of current fashion, she has an innate flair for what is fitting for her and is possessed of a great natural taste, being capable of appraising good clothes as well as of appreciating them. If she is unwilling to devote her time to becoming a well-dressed woman, she has succeeded, nevertheless, by the very simplicity of the clothes she wears, in creating a fashion for herself and, though nonconformist, has been an important factor in contributing to the tone of a whole period, innovating low-heeled shoes, hats that hide the face, stevedore jerkins and cowboy belts.

Her sartorial tastes combine those of the highwayman and Robin Hood with ancient Greece. She wears large pirate hats and romantic cavalier blouses and belts, which are always unadorned and often in off colours: dull greys and browns.

At the time of her Hollywood advent, film makers attempted to make Garbo conform to their pattern, frizzing her hair and dressing her in impossible houri trappings. But by degrees, as she gained more authority, Garbo was able to assert her instinct and bring her real beauty to the fore, which had previously been lost behind the unreal human façade that Hollywood had devised for her as another of its temptresses.

In her great heyday in the films her clothes were made with the utmost ease. She was never one to fuss or to insist upon film tests, believing that if anything looked well to the eye it would appear all right to the camera. Far from finicky about her hair styles, Garbo would proceed with the rough, sure taste of the artist: like Mrs Vernon Castle before her, she intuitively knew how she wanted to look and had no need of a mirror for approval. Her personality imposed itself on her clothes to such an extent that she could turn a tea gown into a nun's habit or an evening dress into a monk's robe. This personality aura explains why Garbo can be so readily spotted in

GRETA GARBO

a crowd: few people have so distinctive and recognizable an appearance.

It is one of the paradoxes of fashion that a woman who has not possessed an evening dress for twenty years should emerge as one of the leading influences of the style of her day. And what Garbo achieved in clothes has been reflected also in make-up. Before Garbo, faces were pink and white. But her very simple and sparing use of cosmetics completely altered the face of the fashionable woman. For a number of years she even used no lipstick or powder at all. It had been customary for stage people to use blue paint on their eyelids. But Garbo, by drawing a black line to accentuate the upper eyelashes, brought the line of the lid back into vogue. This form of make-up has been ever more used by women recently. Miss Lynn Fontanne employed it on the stage, and the fashion has now spread to everyday life.

In an extroverted age Garbo's introspectiveness has naturally led her to be utterly individual. William James mentioned somewhere that the road to discovery leads through private places. By following her own lonely path Garbo has created a style in fashion which is concerned with her individual self. Whatever she may choose, be it a pirate or hobgoblin hat or a monk's cowl, is based on a deep personal choice, a spiritual need or assessment of the hat or cowl.

In retrospect, the thirties' fashions were dull, the theatre at a low ebb, and foolishness was widespread: wholesale baroque plasterwork triumphed; Salvador Dali, on a hot summer's afternoon, read a lecture on surrealism in a diver's suit; teacups were made of fur. But brilliant personalities and brilliant artists were not lacking. Even in a low-pressure period they were able to turn water into wine, dross into gold, mutton chops into hats and meretricious material into art: the moral speaks for itself.

CHAPTER TWELVE

A VOYAGE
TO THE INTERIOR

Lady Mendl

IN the history of taste the twentieth century will undoubtedly be regarded as the most skittish, changeable, fickle and
uncertain century in both fashion and the arts. This is perhaps to be expected of an unsettled age, perhaps the most unsettled that the civilized world has yet known, for wars and
economic crises have become bigger and better with the advent
of the industrial revolution and the triumph of science and
technology. Since their renaissance, Greco-Roman forms were
valid for centuries, while furniture and styles of interior decoration remained fashionable for any number of decades. Yet
in the last fifty years forms and styles, in both the major and
the minor arts, have been in a constant state of flux. A certain
painter, decorator or colour might be in vogue for little more
than a season.

As a result of this unsettled taste interior decorators have
come into their own during the past thirty years. Their purpose,
like that of the couturier, has been to anticipate taste, to run

before it and often create it, adjusting a pelmet of a curtain or installing an ottoman with as much authority as any Parisian dressmaker. But whereas the dressmaker can create a dress that the woman, unless she is unusually skilled, is unlikely to produce herself, the interior decorator has invaded a field that any person of taste should be able to cope with. Yet if few people have the sense of authority or personal predilection to create their own home, it may perhaps be a good thing that there are guides to conduct some of us through the rapids of modern life.

Among the professions that offer women a field for creative endeavour, interior decoration has opened its arms to them ever since suffrage and emancipation. Certainly there are many men in this profession as well, but the women hold their own admirably.

Our century has produced a number of extraordinary feminine talents, both English and American, in the world of interior decoration. Certain names immediately call themselves to one's attention: Elsie de Wolfe, Syrie Maugham, Sibyl Colefax, Ruby Ross Wood, and Mrs Draper. All have left their impression on the taste of the last decades.

Throughout her very long life the relish with which Elsie de Wolfe (Lady Mendl) followed fashion and was its slave has been unequalled in our time. She was a *religieuse*: fashion was her god. A woman of unquenchable vitality, whose interests were linked with fashion in all its forms, Lady Mendl was so successful that she became a living factory of 'chic'.

After a career as a well-dressed but unsuccessful actress, the middle-aged Elsie de Wolfe changed horses in midstream and became the first great American interior decorator. It could be said that she was responsible for putting an end to Victorianism in the United States. Her pioneer efforts at decoration—the taffeta ruching, china birds and roses, Chinese wallpapers, flowered cretonnes, occasional tables and frilled lampshades—may seem today somewhat overcrowded and fussy. But one must remember that Lady Mendl was the first to battle the appallingly low level of bad taste throughout America, with the odds very much against her. Even if, as Robsjohn Gibbings

Lady Mendl
1930.

is correct in saying, she earned the dubious honour of making America antique-conscious, thus retarding modern trends and influencing manufacturers to make furniture in the Louis Seize style, yet her interiors must at first have seemed revolutionary. She was always a better decorator for women than for men; and by redecorating the great women's clubs throughout America during the boom years that preceded the economic crash of 1929, Lady Mendl awakened an appreciation for the styles of Louis Quatorze, Quinze and Seize. This activity also created the foundation of a very great personal fortune, which she spent, for the most part, on the adornment of her own houses and the entertainments she gave in them.

For a 10 per cent commission she advised multimillionaires like the late Henry Frick on the furnishing of their homes, steadfastly rejecting the heavy Italian or Spanish styles in favour of the French taste that she made fashionable.

When judging Lady Mendl's work in retrospect it must be

admitted that she did not bring any particularly original note to her lifework. At most she introduced chintz and comfort to America; later she created beige rooms with Drian screens and white flowers, or green and white rooms. Everything she sold looked as expensive as it undoubtedly was. But apart from these innovations and her introduction of leopard skin as upholstery material (and I am not sure that this did not derive from Cécile Sorel or the Marquesa Casati), lesser decorators than Lady Mendl have left a far more indelible mark.

Elsie de Wolfe passed through a number of fashion periods, yet each phase found her picking the creative vibrations of esoteric people and exploiting them commercially with great flair. This may seem strange, since she was such a very individual personality in her own life and way of living, to which she brought the ruthlessness of a company director, even planning her entertainments with an inspired perfectionism. Her businesslike attention to life's minutiae created an entirely new standard of technique, and she was seldom without a suave, efficient secretary at her side, taking down notes of any detail, however small, that could be filed for later reference. It was inscribed that Her Ladyship would not allow gladioli to be used in a vase of mixed flowers, just as three, not four, cigarettes were allotted to each place at table. She invented a cross-filing system by which she could check on the specific number of times a guest had been entertained, with full descriptions of the menu, the company invited, and the table decorations. Thus Lady Mendl could vary the pleasures of her guests on each occasion. If a hot cheese biscuit was served with the wrong dish or a cocktail was insufficiently shaken, there would more than likely be a court-martial. When a new sandwich proved to be successful, she would dictate a memorandum that it must be photographed for *Vogue*. This fetishistic concern for trivialities was to inspire the Duchess of Windsor to organize her entertainments for café society with an equal unction and determination.

The way that Elsie de Wolfe's own houses were run, lit, heated, scented, the manner in which the food was presented, were all the result of a genius for taking infinite pains. Nothing was left to chance. Only when the scene was set, the perfumes burnt in the censers, and the last candle lit was the element of spontaneity encouraged.

On her appearance, too, she lavished much fervour and fantasy. Having been at thirty a vaguely plain woman with a marmoset face and only a pair of bright brown eyes to break the anonymity, Lady Mendl improved her looks throughout the years. By special dieting, by turning somersaults and standing on her head, she maintained a svelteness of figure throughout her life. She introduced pale blue or heliotrope-coloured hair and was one of the earliest, most successful devotees of facial surgery. In later years there was much speculation about her age, for she seemed to have become ever younger and prettier; and when she was over eighty Lady Mendl came into her own as a beauty, acquiring an almost mystical look of serenity. She had discarded all the more exaggerated fantasies of fashion. She allowed her hair to turn white, wore no make-up and dressed in a simple black dress with short white gloves and a collar of pearls, she looked as she sat in her invalid chair with a leopard-skin rug wrapped round her as delightful as any of the Carmontelles hanging on the *boiseries* of her Paris drawing room.

* * * * *

The modern house that Mrs Winkie Phillipson asked Basil Ionides to help her build near Folkestone in Kent in the late twenties was somewhat more modest than Sir Philip Sassoon's *Arabian Nights* fantasy at nearby Port Lympne, but it was far wider-reaching in its effect. Mrs Phillipson had been married to a Russian who was said to have kept her under lock and key. When he died she returned to England; though she never discarded her widow's black, she married a wealthy coal merchant and proceeded to indulge her creative tastes. At first these were confined to painting flowerpots white and growing only white flowers. But soon she allowed her mania for no colour to spread indoors, and the house became 'all white'.

When Mrs Phillipson and her husband helped to set up Mrs

Mrs Syrie Maugham

Somerset Maugham as 'Syrie' in a decorating business, Mrs Phillipson suggested that Syrie's stock of oak tables and copper pots filled with Cape gooseberries should be exchanged for something a little more startling. Soon, after a few carefully placed piqures from her hostess at Folkestone, Syrie caught the 'no colour' virus and spread the disease around the world.

Mrs Maugham is a woman with flair and a strong personal taste of her own. She is also one of the most energetic women of her day. Her indefatigable strength was now given to turning the world white, not only in winter but throughout the seasons of the year. With the strength of a typhoon she blew all colour before her. For the next decade Syrie Maugham bleached, pickled or scraped every piece of furniture in sight. White sheepskin rugs were strewn on the eggshell-surfaced floors, huge white sofas were flanked with white crackled-paint tables, white peacock feathers were put in white vases against a white wall.

At first sight her own big, all-white drawing room in Chelsea produced a strange and marvellous surprise. There was something unworldly about the effect of those pristine white hydrangeas and white china against their white background. Everything was so immaculate and hygienic that Margot Oxford, who had been somewhat taken aback on entering the room, recovered herself enough to give the advice, 'Dear Mrs Maugham, what you need are a few old varnished maps on the wall'.

The innovation of the white room had thus been inaugurated in Syrie Maugham's drawing room in Chelsea. Other drawing rooms, containing wonderful museum pieces, soon followed suit. Louis Quinze commodes were bleached, and their gilt was silvered. Gilt baroque looking-glasses were covered with whitewash; white Louis Seize or Empire bits were placed in conjunction with white modern furniture. Mayfair drawing rooms looked like albino stage sets.

As with all good ideas, the white craze eventually became so much abused that one was unable to sustain a continued appreciation for the very salutary contribution that had been made. Though it may now come as a belated shock that so much good furniture was robbed of its true patina, the whiteness had nevertheless succeeded in clearing away much fustiness and darkness.

Mrs Maugham has now introduced the vivid colours of lobster salad into her own rooms while uncluttered white rooms have since taken their proper place—on sunlit promontories overlooking the sea, in California or the tropics, where they are admirably suited to their bamboo furniture, rush-matting floors, Venetian shutters or trelliswork screens.

Lady Colefax, a collector of interesting and imaginative people, lived for many years in a compact but noble Georgian dwelling—Argyll House in the King's Road, Chelsea. Here she entertained ceaselessly, peopling the delightful rooms that were decorated with all the restraint of an eighteenth-century intellectual.

Influenced in her taste by 'The Souls' (via Lady Wemyss), Lady Colefax created an atmosphere that was without any quality of pretentiousness, regardless of where she lived. A magnolia might be put in a celadon vase on a lacquer table, but there was never a clutter of *objets d'art* or a plethora of florist's flowers. She purposely avoided the inclusion of any

The late Lord Berners' house at Faringdon

grand pieces of furniture in her rooms, obtaining her effects through the use of off colours—pale almond greens, greys and opaque yellows—and an overall discretion. Everything appeared to be immaculately swept and varnished: on the well-polished oak table, the glass vases of jasmine would be freshly filled with water that was still full of oxygen bubbles. From the moment one arrived in the small panelled hall and savoured the aroma of dried rosemary burnt on a saucer, one knew one had arrived in a completely different atmosphere, refreshing as a sea change.

When in later years Lady Colefax took to decorating professionally, her individual flair was missing, and she assembled rooms that were singularly unlike her own. With a typical enthusiasm she propagated the taste revived by Edward Knoblock, the playwright, for the Regency style. Room after room would be decorated in what John Betjeman has called 'ghastly good taste': somewhat sparsely furnished, with a couple of delicate black and gold chairs, a settee, striped curtains and a colour scheme of yellow and grey. It is true that Regency, by combining lack of pretence with a restrained use of colour and

Farmingdon House

rather sparse ornamentation, is in many ways suited to the English character. Though the style has latterly taken on a somewhat gayer guise, it is still enjoying such a high popularity that continued over-use will surely begin to pall before long.

Of a similar universality has been the taste during the last thirty years for the small Palladian house. Tall Georgian proportions are now so inevitable a requirement on real estate prospectuses that we must surely be due for a change, probably to the Elizabethan manor house with its thick grey stone walls, deep-set windows and enclosed gardens.

Considered to be the best designer of modern interiors in America today, T. H. Robsjohn Gibbings is staunchly set against the mania for antiques, for European imitation and gimcrack period creations. Mr Gibbings has created many fine pieces of furniture whose craftsmanship perhaps could be compared favourably with that of the purest Chinese; he has also made excellent designs for mass production by Grand Rapids and altogether attracted many people to his unshakeable belief in modern architecture and design.

THE BEDROOM
OF THE
DUCHESS OF LERMA.

But it is doubtful if 'modern' is 'here to stay', for interior decoration, like ladies' fashions, has run a restless and ever-changing gamut since the first cave man brought a rock into his cave to sit upon; like fashion, any voyage to the interior is fraught with peril between the Scylla of antiques and the Charybdis of an operating-room sterility.

But changes in taste are no grounds for rancour, since we are all subject to them. My own former preference for the drawing-room ormolu of the French school has considerably abated in recent years, and I now find myself turning to something more stark in its simplicity. Yet it is difficult to accept the 'modern' without reservations, since so little modern furniture seems to possess individuality. An ideal tendency might perhaps be to-wards a combination of the 'modern' point of view with that of Jacobean English or of Spanish taste. Somewhat bedazzled by a surfeit of gilt glitter, I find myself more in harmony with the polished woods, as dark as plum pudding, of solid chairs which have no ornamentation and are placed against the crackled, Cornish cream richness of old panelling.

Many people are somewhat overcome by the excess of bad taste shown outside Spain and exemplified in the 'Spanish style'. I have stayed long enough in America to know that the cheapest and most vulgar decoration is vaguely classified as Spanish. Though pebble-dash walls, coarse wrought ironwork and orange light have nothing to do with the real Spain, these things have set up a certain resistance. The late Mr Hearst and others, by importing real castles from Spain, have done much to over-familiarize that which is good in Spanish decoration. Yet when the visitor to Madrid, Seville, Cordova or Toledo comes across the best the country can offer, and he sees it in its proper setting, there is nothing else in the world that can compare to it.

Among the fine homes I have been privileged to see through-out my travels in Italy, France, Spain, India, China, Germany and America, none is in nobler taste than the eighty-year-old Duchess of Lerma's palace. This venerable building outside Toledo has been given over to the nuns, and one wing has been turned into a school for children. The Duchess still retains her private quarters, but when she is not in residence, they are opened to the public together with the magnificent Lerma library.

The Duchess herself is a remarkable woman who, accus-tomed to every luxury riches can provide, has eliminated every-thing that is superfluous from her life. Her bedroom is of a monumental simplicity, decorated only by the sunlight which, filtering through the shutters on to the tall white walls, is un-ending in its variety. The bed, a giant four-poster, is up-holstered in the darkest green Genoese velvet. A writing table is covered with a cloth of the same material, and there is no ornament upon it except a massive inkpot of gold, innocent of all chasing or decoration. There are one or two stout, high-backed chairs of dark polished wood, a few rugs of superb quality on the stone floor, and possibly a Greco to be admired upon an easel.

I know of no room emanating so completely and satisfyingly the feeling of the dignity of life, except perhaps that of her maid, who sleeps in the adjoining room, a humble honeycomb cell with tall shuttered windows and a narrow but tall four-poster bed of wrought iron, its linen hangings embroidered in the most delicate red and blue needlework.

The Duchess of Lerma has a taste governed by the climate of Spain. It has the Southern character in its boldness and uncompromising use of colour; yet in its respect for form and syntax it is outside the boundaries of any country. By comparison, all other tastes seem frivolous.

The bedroom of the maid to the Duchess of Lerma

CHAPTER THIRTEEN

THE AGE
OF ANXIETY

THERE is good reason that Mr Auden, in his Baroque Eclogue, should have called the forties the 'age of anxiety'. The first half of that decade was occupied by a world war of far greater proportions than the one that preceded it, and the last half seemed already to be presaging new storm clouds for some future date.

Yet creative activity continues even in the darkest periods of history. And in both the major and the minor arts the forties were no exception. In literature the 'doubly lost generation' produced several young writers of remarkable talent; the theatre turned away from ready-made plays to embrace more poetic dramas; and influenced by T. S. Eliot, Tennessee Williams and Christopher Fry, plays took on a new vitality.

During the war no one thought much about frivolous fashion, and there were no new styles. Only those which had been left over when the war began. Perhaps the standard civilian dress for the women who took their place next to men

215

on assembly lines was the costume of men's slacks and shirts or jerseys, with coloured handkerchiefs that tied neatly around the head like a turban. Yet, even when England was under siege and France was occupied, Paris continued to show that style could still exert itself. In view of the petrol shortage, there was no more 'chic' form of transport than a bicycle, and suitable fashions in clothes had forthwith to be invented. To spite German supervision, the French fashion magazines continued publication.

There is something touching about the persistence of fashion in periods of holocaust. Paris styles during the war—short skirts and square shoulders, high wedged boots or clogs and cumbersome Breughel-like hats of velvet and barnyard feathers —seem to us now more hideously disproportionate than those of any previous period of history.

American designers tried to prove that they were independent of Paris, but evolved no significant fashion, marking time until the day when they could again receive inspiration from the accepted source. The moment war ended, Paris dressmakers knew that a sudden change, complete in its influence, was needed. Generally fashion variations occur slowly. It is only over a period of a decade that one can see the changing line and, indirectly, the changing times. But the New Look of 1947 provided a necessary and drastic metamorphosis.

There were valid reasons why many women revolted against its initial appearance. In England, for example, clothes rationing was a serious business, and the few coupons permitted for basic necessities did not contemplate such an extravagant change. Nor did the new fashion permit women simply to drop their skirts, even presuming that the hem contained enough material to allow for lengthening below the calf. The skirts of the early New Look were not only inordinately long, but also quite luxuriously voluminous: the whole silhouette had been changed. Fashionable women were overnight obliged to become ballet dancers, and for the first time in many years the curves of the feminine figure were emphasized once more.

Most women have an innate dislike of waste, and fashion changes ought, at least superficially, to justify themselves as being in some way superior to those which they replace. Nineteen-forty-seven was one of those rare moments in the chronicle of recorded fashion when women staged an abortive revolt against the tyranny of a vastly expensive change that required the complete discarding of their old wardrobes. For one brief, historical instant they came perilously close to anarchy, to realizing that fashion is *au fond* ridiculous and perverse. Many persisted in their old ways and refused to adopt the new extremes in skirt length over padded crinolines. But once again fashion succeeded and within several seasons any woman in an 'old look' dress was marked for pity and ridicule. The new silhouette that emerged with its full splendour of bust and padded hips was as intensely feminine as the styles of 1915 and in some ways bore a superficial resemblance to them. Though this New Look underwent considerable modifications, the silhouette was nevertheless to remain intact for the next five years.

Perhaps the one creative artist who represents both the triumph of individuality and, at the same time, a tragic compromise with contemporary pressure was Christian Bérard. His recent death makes it fitting to include him in a survey of the last decade, though Bérard's talents had been in full flower during the previous years as well, stimulating the thirties and even the late twenties.

In his serious work Christian Bérard limited his subject matter to the tragic world of the poor: melancholy urchins, acrobats and peasants were his favourite sitters, and he painted them with a palette of restrained colours. These canvases could have little influence on fashion, but it was Bérard's other gifts which made him such a powerful catalyst on the arts and styles of his time.

It was, more than anything else, through the medium of his very personal colour sense that Bérard's influence was most felt. Like some virulent germ, these poisonous colours attacked the beholder and created horror throughout the salons of Paris. His colours were seldom of a mood of gaiety. The wide use of black and the sombre colours of the funeral parlours (from which Bérard's mother inherited a fortune) had a lasting impression on his consciousness. He revaluated all sorts of colours and by bringing them together in unusual combinations could create an effect that was entirely his own: red seemed like blood again, a primitive yet sophisticated colour. Bérard knew how to make the best use of 'cheap' colours, and by placing a particular pastel mauve or baby pink in conjunction with a deep plum colour or dark emerald green he gave the pale shades a great force of impact. Mauve mixed with orange created a strange atmosphere. He could turn a dark red plush or an old lady's cape of moss green, both of which had hitherto been considered dowdy, into things of regal richness and grandeur.

Bérard's ballet and theatre décors, contrary to their seeming facility, were the product of long, hard work and reflected an inspired use of the stage. Here his colour scheme was given full rein, for he was able to use all forms of colour that the brightest ink or gouache could not convey. Even such a gay trifle as the ballet *Cotillon* contained a few drops of deadly poison among the colours; even here the presence of death was only partly hidden behind the dark red curtains festooned about the stage boxes of his décor.

Many times during his frantic, overcrowded life Bérard said that he would give up designing in the theatre, eschewing all his many other more frivolous activities in order to restrict himself to being a serious painter. But fashion's deadly toxin had made serious inroads, and some irresistible offer would soon beguile him back to the footlights. He would then illustrate more books, design more dress materials, handkerchiefs or scarves, or give his inimitable flourish to decorations on glass and on china. All of this work, even the most meretricious, was touched by a flicker of his genius. Indeed, though he enjoyed fashion, it never poisoned his artistic side: he was able to split his life into two separate units and in his serious paintings was all artist.

Unfortunately the sweetness of the poison usurped much of his time. Bérard worked in a torrent of enthusiasm for fashion magazines. His sketches, suggesting so much by elimination,

Christian Bérard

were far freer in line than the usual fashion plates, and he could indicate a face without delineating its features. When his drawings first appeared in *Harper's Bazaar*, William Randolph Hearst was so irritated by them that he dubbed the French painter 'Faceless Freddie'.

Faceless Freddie's influence was to extend to the far quarters of the world of advertising. Most young students tried to draw like Bérard, imitating his Japanese use of a brush dipped in India ink. But without Bérard's mastery they could not imitate their god to any degree of proficiency: Bérard defined eclecticism.

Behind Faceless Freddie's apparently facile fashion drawings was an enormous knowledge. They were the work of a man who knew architecture (he was at one time trained to be an architect to follow in his father's profession) and had an intimate friendship with all painting as well. Bérard was a connoisseur of antiques; he had a great sensuous appreciation of rich and beautiful objects. An enormous amount of time was spent in reading, and I imagine that he slept very few hours, devouring everything from Balzac to *Screenland* magazine by the light of a late lamp.

In all manifestation of the minor arts Bérard had a profound interest. He was in many ways a disciple of Beau Brummell, for though he enjoyed feathers and fashion, he indulged his taste in very broad strokes, just as Brummell had introduced many notes of simplicity into men's clothing. Bérard's settings for the stage, as well as his colour schemes, exemplified the simple and bold style. Fundamentally he was a purist.

Christian Bérard was something of an anomaly and more than a little paradoxical. He was a serious artist, yet adored the smart world, much as his literary predecessor, Marcel Proust, had before him.

For years he lived in a small bedroom several flights up in a somewhat squalid and liftless hotel. It was one of those hotels where people could sign the register (or not sign the register) and have a room for an hour. Bérard's small den had a brass bed, a chair, a table, a yellow-stained cupboard and futuristic wallpaper of magenta roses. In this room he smoked opium, painted as he sat on the bed and accumulated piles of books and magazines. To his hotel came not only engraved invitations from the *beau monde*, but the most pampered and spoilt ladies who knew that, without Bérard's approval, they stood no chance of being considered elegant.

The day arrived at last when there was so much litter that the painter was obliged to move into an apartment. Since his taste was always eagerly watched by the public, there was naturally much curiosity as to what the new apartment would be like. Bérard enjoyed keeping up the excitement of the secret. The baroque chichi or surrealist rococo had reached its fantastic peak, exemplified by Charles de Beistegui's apartment in the Champs Elysées, with its welter of glittering silver, pepermint pink, white ostrich feathers and blackamoors. Bérard's friends naturally imagined that his new apartment would even surpass this fantasy and that perhaps feathers, paper flowers and crystal chandeliers would run wild.

But they were struck dumb with surprise when they dis-

covered that Bébé had decorated his apartment with relentless
authority and formality, with all the seriousness of a master
architect. There was, indeed, no form of decoration at all. A
needlework rug, white walls and no curtains set the tone of
sober simplicity, in the middle of which was the Louis Seize
mahogany furniture: architects' desks that folded in many ingenious ways, together with pieces of cabinet-makers' triumphs
that unfolded and became something of bold, masculine simplicity. Nothing was pernickety; on the contrary, everything
was solid and severe. As decoration on the chimney piece were
two heavy terracotta dogs and a pair of stout black candlesticks.
All this was baffling to many people, and of course it was something that could not be capitalized on the American market.
The result was achieved through quality, which can never be
reproduced wholesale, for it ill lends itself to mass production.

Bérard, so indefatigable, so generous with his vitality, gave
off sparks of inspiration in every direction. It is little wonder
that he is responsible for more creative activities in the world
of décor than any other person of the last twenty years. Anyone
working in the creative arts would go to him to listen to the
thousand ideas that poured out of him; and so magnanimous
was he that he was delighted when they were able to utilize
his superfluous talents. He was amused if his work was commercialized by others. Friends would ask him to do a few
scribbles on the back of an envelope, and with this in their
pockets they embarked on the refurnishing of their houses, a
hotel, a night club or a scent shop. Dressmakers could get a
few tips from him and then make up a whole collection as a
result of half an hour spent in company with his fertile imagination. Florists were advised to include cornflowers, poppies and
marguerites among their stocks of accustomed flowers, or they
would arrange nasturtiums and sweet peas together in Bérard's
combinations of colour. He enjoyed, too, encouraging young
designers, often working behind the scenes with them until
dawn.

In Paris it was considered that a word from Bérard could
make a hat shop or break a dressmaking establishment.
Whether it was a matter of a new shop, the latest interior,

actress or play, his opinion counted for more than anyone else's. He helped to launch a friend of long standing when Christian Dior decided to go into a dressmaking business on his own. After Bérard's death it was said that Dior would not be able to exist without him. Dior's natural gift has, of course, been proved a thousand times since, but it was Bérard's whole-hearted support and enthusiasm that gave him such a send-off.

Bérard was not only a great figure, but that rare phenomenon in Paris, a man who was as well known in the highest circles of the aristocracy as in the most bohemian coteries of art. Whatever stratum of society he moved in, he always looked the same: bearded and dirty, surprising, provocative, malicious, kind, generous and with a genius that was the quintessence of Parisian taste.

Christian Bérard is dead. Apart from my personal feeling of loss for a great and dear friend, I find that Paris is a little less wonderful for me than it was when he was alive to interpret more of its diverting facets. Each time I arrived at an hotel I would telephone to him and at once find myself launched on exciting new voyages of discovery. His zest for life was un-paralleled. George Davis, who for many years was an intimate and understanding friend of Bérard, has in his possession a scrap of paper that is an extraordinary self-portrait of Bérard. It is an acrostic from an after-dinner game, on which Bérard had scribbled a significant adjective for each letter of his name:

Cruel	Brilliant
Humain	Enfantin
Rapide	Refoulé
Instructif	Aimant
Snob	Reclus
Théâtral	Dérasé
Imaginatif	
Angoissé	
Noyé	

On the day he was buried, Paris went into mourning; people from every walk of life filled the church. Bérard would have been pleased to see the care and love with which the flowers that were sent as tributes had been selected, for he himself had an extraordinary gift in creating wonderful combinations of flowers. He would select a bit of this and a sprig of that, and in an instant had made a bouquet that possessed his style, taste and natural selectivity.

One day on his way to meet Alice Toklas for luncheon Bérard, as was his wont, rushed late into a small shop near his apartment off the Place de l'Odéon, where the *patronne* was accustomed to watch while her client frantically pulled out flowers from the vases standing in the window and spontaneously created a most charming bunch of flowers. On this occasion Bérard selected several lemon-yellow carnations, one speckled red-and-white carnation, a scarlet rose, a sprig of fern, the top of a branch of apple blossoms and some purplish-black wallflowers.

When Bérard died, Alice Toklas went, quite by chance, to the same shop off the Place de l'Odéon. The *patronne* watched while she chose three yellow carnations, one speckled red-and-white carnation, a scarlet rose and a sprig of fern. Suddenly she exclaimed in astonishment that this was exactly the same combination of flowers that Monsieur Bérard had once made up. Alice Toklas was equally surprised. 'But how do you know that?' The *patronne* explained how Bérard often ran into the shop and how she was always so spellbound by the arrangements of flowers he chose that she could never forget them.

Alice Toklas replied, 'No one could bring flowers together in quite the same way that Monsieur Bérard did. You are quite right when you remember that he once made such a bouquet as this, for he gave it to me. I, too, have never forgotten it. Nothing could be more charming. And that is why I am taking these flowers to his funeral.'

* * * * *

When after the war we were asked who were the new beauties and women of great individuality, we made excuses and said that beauty needs a frame, that there were no gilded, beautifully carved frames, or that our changed life did not permit us to squander praise on mere physical perfection. Yet great physical beauty is a coin that will never go out of currency; our attitudes towards beauty may change with the four winds, but true classical perfection is always the criterion.

Today we can still discover in various strata of humanity an enormous number of flowerlike women of timeless beauty. Among them we find the South American Madame Martinez de Hoz, as flawless in her nectarine perfection as she was twenty years ago, and still moving among the horse-racing members of the *faubourg* of Paris.

A dark Brazilian with the face of a sentimental madonna painted by Murillo, Madame Martinez de Hoz is one of the rare women who have sustained the tradition of great beauty through many vicissitudes. This is particularly surprising, since few South Americans seem to withstand the onslaughts of middle age without damage. During all these years Madame de Hoz has been acclaimed by everyone. No dissenting voice has been heard; all agree she is 'a great beauty' whose particular type has never been 'out of fashion'.

Her dark, thrushlike eyes are of such brilliance, her regard so bland, and her smile so serene that one feels she is exempt from the nervous disorders of her day and must surely have been sheltered from all the disconcerting winds of life. Like all luxurious ladies, she gives the impression of being cool in summer and warm in winter.

Madame Martinez de Hoz has never struck a note of originality, would never wish to launch a fashion or make an experiment or a discovery of her own in an unknown shop. She seems, indeed, to be disinterested in the artists who create innovations. She is not interested in being anything but 'perfectly dressed', and then only for the reason that any lady as gracious as she is must be beautifully turned out. That this takes endless time and money she knows, but she is willing and able to spend the time and the money. She will buy expert advice from the greatest specialists that Paris can provide. Jewellers, dress- and hat-makers have enough respect for her innate distinction to avoid experimenting with their latest ideas, reserving for Madame de Hoz only the safest and most truly tried concoctions: they cannot afford to risk a failure. By the time this vision of perfection gives her approval to a fashion, it has already been proved impeccable, and her acceptance of it is its highest reward.

In contrast to Madame de Hoz, Alice Astor Bouverie stands, by her own choice, very much apart from the fashionable world. Indeed, she makes that world's values seem rather despicable simply by the way in which her personal style asserts itself with grace, breeding and sensibility. Though Mrs Bouverie does not play fashion's game, she has a healthy regard for convention, and her more conservative acquaintances know that she could be the most fashionable woman in London, Paris, Rome and New York if it gave her the slightest interest. She is, however, more interested in being herself and following her own sense of values, which she does with style and modesty. There is no anarchy implied in her choice of friends among true artists and valid bohemians: they are the people she finds most interesting and most rewarding; their ideas and their way of life correspond to her own. Yet she dislikes phony artistic movements, avoiding the solipsismal circles.

Alice Bouverie is one of the very few wealthy women who have used their riches in an imaginative way, and is even the more rare because she has in no way been spoilt by her possessions. If she can be more extravagant than anybody, she has at the same time a sense of money and knows how to be economical or uneconomical with the same sense of proportion. She may give large sums of money to charity or to organizations that interest her; she enjoys the fun of choosing bargains from Sunday papers and ordering from Selfridge's, Macy's or Bloomingdale's. Over the years her interest in the arts has led her to patronize painters, writers, poets and especially the ballet, which she adores, and whose catholic tastes reflect her own very catholic view of aesthetics. To all of these activities she brings a sensitivity, which is more European than that of almost any American woman.

In appearance Mrs Bouverie is rather like an Indian, with her dark olive complexion, her sad, compassionate eyes and a sweetness of expression that betokens an inward calm while all about her is rush and chaos. Although she seems fragile, with her tall, thin body and medieval slouch, she has tenacity and endurance and a violent enthusiasm that belies the outward calm. Since she refuses to be rushed, she may often be very late for appointments. On the other hand, even when she is interested in something, time means little to her. She can stay up all night and be surprised when the dawnlight peeps through the window and a breakfast tray is brought to her: in this she shows an almost childlike quality of intensity and application.

Mrs Bouverie has an unerring sense of the colours that are appropriate to her appearance; maroon and sage or dark grey are a part of her chosen range. An Eastern influence can be detected in her gold tunics and jewellery. She wears the imprint of her subtlety and discretion, so that one has to look twice to realize with what selective care she is attired. Alice Bouverie accumulates innumerable quantities of clothing but always manages to wear them sooner or later and is quite likely to appear in a peasant costume she has been hiding for fifteen years.

If at times Mrs Bouverie gives the impression of being soft, quiet-spoken, and even passive, she has a stubbornness that serves her in good stead. With her dependants, her children and lame ducks, she is always surrounded by dozens of people who rely on her to some extent. One is led to conclude that she must be more of an executive than she seems to be.

Standing outside the world of fashion, yet respected by those who are in it as well as by her more individual friends, Alice Bouverie has truly made her own style, compounded of a sense of true values and her own remarkable European sensitivity that go hand in hand with one of the least ostentatious and most honest personalities among the rich women of contemporary America.

When the Second World War was over and the manufacture of furniture, rather than armaments, was again considered, the 'modern' style had been so incorporated into daily life as to represent no longer either threat or anarchy. Picasso, Matisse or Klee had filtered down to Christmas cards and calendar repro-

Mrs Bouverie wearing Hungarian peasant costume

ductions. Eames chairs were to be found in a million New York rooms with their colour schemes of oatmeal and white and geometric-patterned curtains of tweed.

Simplicity and functionalism are fine in theory and the stripping to essentials has been a candid endeavour to use materials ingeniously and for a purpose, shying away from the cluttered and overstuffed Victorian tastes, or from neo-Romantic dreams which would be out of spirit and keeping with modern life. Even the masters of the new idiom are unable to bring an intimate or individual touch to their designs and the result is often as impersonal as the cellophane wrappings that insure the hygiene of American foodstuffs.

It is as though the soul had gone out of modern living, and the pity of it is its inevitability. In the recent past there have been wholesale periods of re-created Spanish taste, or Louis Seize taste; now we have re-created 'modern' taste, yet functionalism expresses no more charm than its ersatz predecessors. One thinks of the remark of a George Kelly character in the play *Craig's Wife*. Commenting on Harriet Craig's house, the elderly aunt observes, 'When I look at these rooms, they have the look of rooms that have died and been laid out.'

But these failures in modern interior decoration are indicative of that deeper failure in the whole range of contemporary life. We are suffering from a fatal disease which shrewd social doctors might well diagnose as the 'failure of the personal'. No panacea or penicillin has been invented in recent years to stop the tide of mass production, of cheap and vulgar imitations, of conformism, of sterile starkness, tasteless nudity, gimcrack workmanship and the mass levelling process by which any original idea or its expression is quickly distorted, beclouded, pulverized and made anonymous.

Accusing fingers have been pointed at the machine age, though to its credit technology in itself has helped to raise our standard of living and may indeed be the only remedy for the world's seemingly insoluble economic problems. Yet, if there are many complex reasons for our malady, they do seem to stem, directly or indirectly, from the forces that have created modern society. Nowadays time is considered too valuable to allow for such things as handcraft or a sense of the personal. Even the most outlying handcrafters have been corrupted. The African Negro still carves his wooden statues, and tourists may buy them, but they have little or no resemblance to the works of art fashioned by his forefathers. China is no longer made in China, tea comes in tea bags, cakes come in boxes, and French creams are made of artificial sugars, colours and flavourings.

In some aspects of modern life this synthetic tendency is barbarically amusing. Nothing is more wholesome or delicious than peasant bread prepared from unbleached flour. But in

America flours are sifted, their whole bran and kernel removed; they are washed, bleached and patted, and then are made into bread with a consistency like cotton wool and so lacking in vitamins that the United States Bureau of Standards became alarmed and suggested fortifying the very staff of life. The up-shot is that today all vitamins are taken out of flour in the milling process, and are then pumped back into the bread in the form of chemical derivatives. Surely this must stand as its own ironic commentary on our scientific age.

Yet beneath all the pressures of uniformity and depersonaliza-tion, people have a great drive for the personal. Finding little out-let in their work or the environment about them, they often turn to eccentric manifestations of behaviour. Perhaps our very crimes today are distorted personal expressions in a near-robot age.

One of the paradoxes of mass taste is its love of the indivi-dual and the way in which it destroys the individual. It was Oscar Wilde who said that each man kills the thing he loves, and our modern life offers full expression of this. Producers cry for original plays but only want to present time-tested formulae. If occasionally a unique personality rises to the top as a writer or entertainer, then the imitations come so thick and fast that their originals become *passé* and even hackneyed.

Everywhere we find that modern life is killing the goose that laid the golden egg. The golden egg was the stark beauty of individuality, and the goose was the social conditions that allowed for it. Caught in a vice-like grip by forces that have grown almost beyond his control, modern man's individuality is being snowed under by the machine-made conformism of present-day existence. Without having struck a direct blow at the West, Communism must secretly be delighted with the depersonalizing forces in our Western society, for it is exactly that which, by violence, they have imposed on millions of others. Happily, we of the West have clung to democratic in-stitutions; a few of us can still be personal and eccentric if we choose; and, above all, we can fight the tentacles of the impersonal wherever they clutch at us, we can continue to express the joy and the beauty of individual taste that selects, sifts and creates the only values worth living for.

Whenever one surveys one's immediate time, it always becomes difficult to analyse the trends. Looking back today at the political events of the thirties, we begin to see their inevitable pattern, just as the styles of the thirties emerge with a certain clarity. But the forties are only just past, and it is difficult to drawn an empirical formula for the styles of that decade or for its social and political meanings. Apart from revolutionary changes in women's fashions, the forties brought the culmination of many great scientific innovations. If one were to make a graph of man's scientific advancement in the last fifty years, the line would rise slowly until the end of the nineteenth century, then would skyrocket into the stratosphere. Had I been born in 1800, the change by 1850 would not have seemed so very great. But from those Edwardian ladies in their landaus to jet-propelled aeroplanes and atomic bombs is an incredible technological leap. We have geared ourselves psychologically for the most rapid and radical changes, and today accept the altered pace of life.

CHAPTER FOURTEEN

CABBAGES,
KINGS AND
FOREIGNERS

The Duchess of Kent

SINCE royalty by its very definition is above the crowd, it stands to reason that the fashions of kings and queens should be individual and unique, abiding by their own rigid laws and prohibiting imitation by the lower classes. In the Middle Ages, for example, only the queens and princesses were allowed to wear veils of a length extending to their feet. There was a time, also, when the styles of royalty were extravagant to the point of fantasy: Richard II had elaborate coats costing upwards of seven thousand pounds. Marie Antoinette, who delighted in being the leader of fashion, was responsible for seventeen fashion changes in women's hats between 1784 and 1786. It was the French Revolution that inhibited arbitrary and fickle behaviour, especially in masculine attire. By the time Queen Victoria had ascended to the throne, royalty was beginning to conform to conservative bourgeois patterns.

Queen Alexandra probably started the modern tradition that British royalty can wear anything. During her husband King

Edward's reign she would wear spangled or jewelled and bead-embroidered coats in the daytime, an innovation which has now become an accepted royal habit. Or she might wear half-length jackets covered with purple or mauve sequins and garnished with a Toby frill collar of tulle. These were clothes which most women would have worn at night, but the fact that she wore them during the day removed her from reality and only helped to increase the aura of distance that one associates with the court.

Though royalty is no longer the arbiter of fashion in the democratic countries, its influence is still felt today in certain European kingdoms, notably in Great Britain. British royalty generally has clothes that are best seen from a distance, and it has become virtually an established tradition that female members of the royal family should wear pastel colours. It was not uncommon to catch a glimpse of the late Queen Mary wearing sweet-pea colours on an afternoon's outing to Earl's Court, or to see the Queen Mother Elizabeth wearing a pale blue outfit at a morning rally of the Victoria League.

Queen Mary wore almost the same style for the last forty years of her life: beaded evening dress, tailored coat and skirt, long-toed shoes and rolled parasol, with a large toque perched high on the tall dressing of hair and taking the place of a crown. As Janet Flanner wrote, 'She has resisted hints from dressmakers, worn her skirts long when skirts were rising, raised hers slightly when it was too late; her hats, during her super-sensitive sartorial twenties, caused them pain. Today, she satisfies everyone, even her family. She looks like herself, with the elegant eccentricities—the umbrella or parasol, the hydrangea-coloured town suits, the light lizard slippers, the tiptilted toque—of a wealthy, white-haired *grande dame* who has grown into the mature style she set herself too young.' Queen Mary thus created an appearance for herself that served as an all-weather model, good for rain or shine. Wherever one saw her, everything about her neat silhouette was as compact and tidy as a ranunculus. You knew that you were in the presence of royalty; and, with true *noblesse oblige*, she was always reliable in her appearance, never letting you down, but turning up

Queen Alexandra

regularly with mechanical precision upon any occasion, however small.

Almost as individual as her late mother-in-law, Queen Elizabeth, the Queen Mother, has also created her own mode of dress. By day she appears incandescent in pale hues of an immaculate powder quality. At night she appears with all the unreality of a spangled fairy doll on top of a Christmas tree. The effect she creates, wearing a huge crinoline and a diadem in her hair, is dazzling in its effect upon her devoted but dazed beholders. The Queen Mother has been particularly successful in wearing an impressive amount of jewellery during the daytime. Fortunately her daughter, Queen Elizabeth, has adopted the same picturesque styles for her evening appearances, and, with her immaculate pink-and-white complexion, the sparkles of diamond and spangled tulle give the effect of sunlight at early dawn on a snow scene.

Royalty must dress for the crowds. Of first consideration is

the fact that they are to be seen. For this reason off-the-face hats are worn; while, if possible, height is added so that those at the back of a crowd can catch even a glimpse of a felt halo or an aigrette and not be disappointed. The Duchess of Kent, who perhaps has a more Parisian dress sense than any other member of the English royal family, has learned to apply the rules dictated by the massed crowds. But years ago, as a young bride, she stirred up criticism by appearing in a carriage at the Jubilee celebrations of her parents-in-law wearing an enormous cartwheel hat of champagne colour. Unfortunately the hat hid half her face and had to be held on to with one hand. She soon learnt, however, to appreciate the requisite demands of the public, and since then her appearances in a succession of toques and feathered boaters have caused the delighted crowds to acclaim her resemblance to her great-aunt Queen Alexandra.

It is an irony of modern man's development that in fashion

he has gone against nature, adopting for himself the drabness which, in all lower forms of life, has been relegated to the female of the species.

This has not always been historically true, however. Until almost the end of the eighteenth century men's fashions were as extensive as women's: gentlemen employed cosmetics, wore wigs and decked themselves out with paste and lace. Even today, among primitive tribes, it is the male who has the prerogative of wearing the feathers and the paint. Why, then, has the appearance of the male become so drab in modern Western society? Why should men have adopted a standard uniform which changes little with the passing of the decades, whereas women's dress oscillates to extremes within the space of even a few years?

The French Revolution dealt a severe blow to men's fashions from which they have never quite recovered. During the Reign of Terror many noblemen adopted the garb of the citizens, which was in contrast to the frills, ruffles and satin pants of the aristocrats. The changes that came about as a result of those years made it impractical and even bad taste for men to vaunt their economic status in terms of dress. Women, on the contrary, were soon to find more leisure and cheaper materials as a result of the industrial revolution. Their increasing emancipation also allowed them to assert their femininity in a broader sense than they had hitherto been accustomed to. Fashions were thus no longer confined to ladies of the highest social status.

Many other forces caused male clothing to be reduced to a standard formula which has altered little in the last hundred and more years. Beau Brummell exerted such a powerful influence on men's appearance that the best of male satorial fashions today are derived straight from his innovations.

Like many historical personalities, Beau Brummell has been high misrepresented, even vilified. His name has become synonymous with the effete and the ornate in male attire. But if Beau Brummell spent nine hours a day in the preparation of his toilet, sent his laundry to France or wiped his razor on pages from first editions of the classics, he was also, paradoxically, an important enough personage to alter the whole history of men's clothing. One has only to compare the portraits of the beginning of the eighteenth century with those of a lifetime later to see the result of his authoritative imposition of a new style of dress.

In fact, far from being a dandy, Brummell stood for the absolute simplification of men's tastes. Until his day men wore powdered wigs, brocade coats with lace ruffs and collars, diamond buttons, silk embroidered waistcoats and satin breeches. Suddenly Beau Brummell stressed simplicity as the only word in good taste. He wore navy-blue cloth suits with the severest of striped waistcoats. The 'Beau' despised silk, preferring linen and the best-quality serge cloths; his ties were of linen, his shirts and handkerchiefs of lawn. Instead of having his carriage upholstered with silk quilting, he chose the most refined whipcord, and a sparse little carpet on the carriage floor instead of the usual fur rug. Footmen's clothes and the wonderfully tailored overcoats worn by the brigade of guards, with their long but ample line, are today in the tradition Brummell created.

In his own house, like Madame Errazuriz a hundred years later, Brummell chose exquisitely simple furniture, avoiding display with the exception of a few fine gold snuffboxes. A reflection of his tastes in interior decoration can be seen today in London clubs like White's or Boodle's, where the decoration of beautifully proportioned rooms is limited to Hogarth engravings in frames on the walls and solid mahogany furniture upholstered in leather.

In our own time the Savile Row tailors and their conservative Boston counterparts have kept alive the traditions of Beau Brummell, to whom Peter Quennell attributes 'that indefinable air of greatness which belongs to the natural leader, the born creator'. It is generally acknowledged that London is the men's fashion centre of the world, a status which may be explained by the British love and care for tradition, as reflected in the suits cut by Scholte, shoes by Lobb and hats by Lock—all showing the measured thought that has been given to them.

Not only did Brummell create today's taste in men's clothes, but his genius is also being expressed in the general appearance of women. For some time now women have been wearing grey flannel suits, navy-blue or black tailor-mades, white linen collars, spruce gloves and well-cut, polished shoes—all in the Brummell tradition.

Whether tradition in men's clothes will ever change radically seems doubtful. Yet a certain amount of alteration has made steady progress. The summer popularity of the French Riviera in the twenties gave birth to a new wardrobe of *plage* outfits. Sun-bathing spread in popularity, and with it came short trousers and gymnasium vests. Today it is a common sight on a summer's day even in England to see workmen with naked torsos at work in the fields or on the roadside. But twenty years ago a child could have been arrested by an inspector on the beach for not wearing a top to his bathing costume. America has influenced many facets of men's clothing and is responsible for the widespread use of the moccasin shoe, crepe soles, the dinner jacket worn in preference to the tail coat and a bolder use of colour. Some of the sports clothes, the cool seersucker suits and bathing trunks surpass those of other countries.

Even in England variations on men's clothes have been effected in the last twenty years. The upper classes, especially in the heyday of the twenties, were responsible for a number of fads. University aesthetes of twenty-five years ago wore, for the first time, turtle-necked sweaters and beige-grey flannel trousers cut so wide that they flapped at each step and were called Oxford bags. Double-breasted jackets with tight-fitting sleeves became popular for day suits. Ultimately dinner jackets were cut in this style and worn with a dark red carnation in the lapel.

Together with these changes in dress went a change in manner. The clipped habit of speech spread. It became extremely smart to turn the toes slightly inward. The generation of Oxford graduates that produced Evelyn Waugh and Harold Acton has affected a whole manner of speech which is precise and precious, yet has been employed by many strata of society. Even the Colonel Blimps adopted over-used, effete turns of phrase, together with such expressions as 'madly' and 'divine' and 'too'. People often remarked, 'How terribly unfunny!' or 'How terribly exciting!' Ordinarily unpretentious men and women became very self-conscious about the use of language, of the play on words, and started to italicize certain phrases by their inflections. 'Darling' became more of a commonplace than a term of endearment. Among those who influenced phraseology, Sir Philip Sassoon was outstanding. When he spoke, he emphasized every single syllable with a trip-hammer tongue: 'My de-ah, I could-dern't be more sorry, but I was rat-tling about like dice in a box.' It was he who coined the currently popular 'I could-dern't care less' or 'I could-dern't agree more'.

Few individual men have influenced fashion since Beau Brummell, for ridicule or scorn often reward those who turn off the modern highway of conservatism. Certain politicians, until recently, with their tall hats, cravats, eyeglasses and orchid buttonholes, dressed for their roles in Parliament. Today, with the exception of Sir Winston Churchill, whose wardrobe has a distinction that belongs to an earlier age, even politicians look disappointingly like the rest of us. The late Lord Ribblesdale with his gigantic height and picturesque Victorianism, and the diminutive Mr Berry Wall, one of the last of the Edwardian

Lord Ribblesdale

dandies, were stubborn exceptions to the rule that men's clothes should be inconspicuous and successfully ignored the general tendency towards anonymity. Perhaps only those in positions of power or who possess great social prestige can flout fashion successfully. The Duke of Windsor, when he was Prince of Wales, defied convention. He wore straw hats instead of the customary Englishman's felt hat in summer, loud checks and suède shoes, and resented stiffly starched shirts for evening. With a real *goût de scandale* he would appear at a formal reception in lounge clothes. If the ordinary man today were to appear in some of the unorthodox hats and highly coloured tweeds that the Prince modelled he would doubtless become an object of ridicule.

If every muscular movement of the body is the result of thought, then people may well think themselves into different sizes and shapes. Just as the latter-day breeding of roses affects

Mr Berry
Wall
Edwardian Dandy
1937

the size and shape of the petals and the colour of the bloom,
so, too, women have been fat or slim, hyperthyroid or splenetic,
sallow or pink-cheeked, slouched or erect, according to the
prevalent notions of beauty. I know little about the theory of
genetics, whereby a change affected in a living organism is
transmitted from generation to generation; but these outward
physical changes seem to last as long as the current notion of
beauty dictates.

At the end of the last century women thought of themselves
in terms of being well covered: they wished to have a wonderful
décolletage and would have been ashamed of hollows in the neck
as deep as salt cellars. But nowadays ladies are so intent on
being thin that a scraggy *décolletage* has become inevitable.

Not only have they made themselves half the weight they
were three or four decades ago, but they have also thought
themselves into entirely different contours. With whalebone
corsets that ruthlessly laced the human figure into an hour-

glass shape, Victorian waistlines became as small as sixteen inches. But though a small waistline was essential, the flesh above and below had to be full, of a Renoir-like voluptuousness. The mature women were handsome, the younger ones demurely pretty; nowadays women are neither demurely pretty nor handsome. Those fabulous professional beauties for whom people stood on their chairs in the park were Juno-like goddesses with great, carved features, chiselled nostrils, and prognathous jaws—a type that today would be considered too monumental for the average man's taste. Men have come to accept as a premise women who look more like young boys, with thin flat hips, who have even adopted blue denims, blouses and short skirts and haircuts. Women, likewise, have accepted a lankier male to take to their breasts with a pitying, motherly interest.

Our pace of life has quickened so that women's features now reflect the frenzied, insecure age in which they live. Women's eyes used to be wistful. Today few possess serene eyes; they do not mind creases in their brows and often wear a frown on their foreheads. Young girls are proud of their high cheekbones and a flat hollow in their cheeks, whereas fifty years ago cheeks were fully rounded. Latterly the rather prehensile mouths have replaced the rosebud of yesterday. Whereas make-up was used only by *cocottes* in the Victorian and Edwardian heydays (ladies used to slap their cheeks and bite their lips before entering a ballroom to obtain a higher colour), any woman without lipstick today appears anaemic. Hair dyeing has become so general that it is not kept a guarded secret. Eyebrows, instead of being arched or wearing the old-fashioned startled look or the look of pained surprise, are slightly raised towards the outer edges, even acquiring a mongolian look. After twenty years of eyebrow plucking, eyebrows do not grow as thickly as they did. So that Elizabeth Taylor's naturally heavy black eyebrows have brought her as much fame as her acting talent. Audrey Hepburn increases the contours of her eyebrows with paint. The result is admired today, but an earlier generation would have cried out in horror 'Why, it is George Robey.'

Perhaps women's hands have changed more than any other

feature. Thirty years ago pudgy little hands with dimples and pointed fingers were admired. Today the joints of the fingers are clearly discernible, and dactylar reactions are more nervous, highly strung, like those little wooden hammers that appear if the corresponding piano key is struck. When a woman holds her handbag it is with her thumb sticking out at a tangent. Thirty years ago the thumb would not have been noticed, for it was discreetly hidden, with the purse held daintily by the tips of the fingers, the little finger crooked like a handle.

It would be difficult to trace the causes of some of these physiological transformations. Easiest to understand is that changes in weight are undoubtedly a result of modern diet. Science has taught us much about balanced meals, starchy foods and over-eating. At Victorian dinners nearly everyone overate. But the present generation eats less because it has come to think of eating less. Vitamin discoveries and various diets have also influenced the slimmer contours of today.

Even the appearance of food itself has changed: it is now considered old-fashioned to garnish and over-decorate a dish. Escoffier's famous cookbook seems appallingly rich and heavy to us: who today would want or could possibly afford to spend five hours on one sauce? Courses are fewer, their colours less vivid and their serving less elaborate.

But if we have become healthier through our more scientific regimes, stance and posture have both deteriorated. Henry James could write of his turn-of-the-century Madame de Vionnet that 'she was the kind of woman who could put her elbows on the table between courses and still appear graceful'. But the habit of slouching, lying on sofas with legs tucked beneath, or sitting on the floor has become general; and few women, once addicted to these habits, are able to break with them. The result is that they now have a total inability to sit up straight, have become hunchbacks with a tendency to rheumatism.

Ever since the Boston Tea Party, America and England, mutually interdependent in worldly affairs, have been travelling on their separate paths and their cultures have become strikingly different. In one sense this difference has a healthy effect on the fashions of both countries, but they still cling to certain prized idiosyncrasies. Perhaps no two peoples of the Western world misunderstood each other's tastes so much as the British and the Americans, who guard their habits with a staunch, national pride.

It seems to me that in America materials are always pristine, shirts are newly ironed, collars starched and dresses have the air of being fresh from the seamstress's needle. Surface qualities and packaging are always appetizing. By the time the first crispness has worn off, objects are taken away to the incinerator; rarely in America is one allowed to see something in its decline.

One has, indeed, in America, the notion that objects are whisked away before scratches, wear and tear, or mildew are allowed to blemish the patina of life.

Englishwomen, by contrast, appreciate something with a patina on it. In certain well-regulated houses in Britain oak tables are polished every day, until years of care give them the deep, nut-coloured sheen and the rich quality that can come from age alone. Americans create objects with a ready-made finish or eggshell patina, and from that moment onwards the *dégringolade* begins.

At its truest the taste exhibited by Englishwomen has a certain 'literary' quality: almost, one might say, a Virginia Woolf appreciation for clothes that possess the association of ideas. They are less interested in the outward appearance of the merchandise and scarcely think of an object in terms of the silk paper surrounding it, nor of the allure of its newness. Old things have a certain romantic quality about them, and Englishwomen of sensibility appreciate this. Far from preferring a trim, neat look, they incline more towards the picturesque. They appreciate well-tailored suits, but they like hats to have brims: they love picture hats. Other penchants are sashes and waistbands, possibly with roses tucked into them; they are also fond of gloves, not necessarily new, even old garden gloves. This constitutes a sort of romantic garden-party way of dressing that is perhaps more nostalgic than applicable today. Likewise, in the gardens that they love and where they work so earnestly, they prefer the rustic interpretation of their taste rather than blue jeans and a more utilitarian approach and will wear a garden hat with a huge brim not merely because it keeps the sun off, but also because of the sympathetic and romantic mood it creates.

But if English ladies like to wear clothes that suggest a mood and create an atmosphere for them, one has a very contrary impression of American clothes: they seem to have come out of a refrigerator, and, like American bread or butter or foodstuffs in general, are often wrapped in cellophane.

Climate no doubt affects costume as much as any other factor. Englishwomen have always worn shawls and always will wear them, which may perhaps be attributed to inclement weather and draughts. Not so long ago, when Paris innovated shawls once again, an American editor of a fashion magazine remarked, 'Heavens, Englishwomen have only just got out of shawls, and now they'll get back into them!'

French or Italian tastes are again a whole law unto themselves. But since France is the acknowledged centre of Western fashion, its taste is naturally quickly absorbed by other nations and does not for long remain insular. Yet many French innovations are too fleeting to have a serious appeal outside that country.

Italian taste has had a wider influence than its quiet approach would indicate. The elasticity of the Italian temperament, combined with thousands of years of invaders, can readily absorb all outside influences and yet rise above them and conquer with its own individual expression. The Italians have always been great craftsmen, ever since the first architects, landscape gardeners and cabinet-makers were imported to England as far back as the Elizabethan age. Today, in Italian fashions, we recognize the same quality in their suits, their coats, their shoes and their sandals, and they quietly set a standard for others to follow.

Typical of the taste of Italian women are the picture dresses, the semi-dirndl skirts, the long earrings and sandals. Black has always been a favourite colour among Latin people, and both the Italians and the Spanish have periodically re-emphasized funereal values of colour. Equally assertive, however, is the Italian taste for harsh colours and vivid stripes, which on that peninsula are worn with a sophisticated insouciance.

In many ways France, Italy, and even to some extent England, have resisted the pressures of a technological society and realized that the way of life exemplified by America, for all its value in raising the general standard of living and promoting a luxury for the many that was never before possible, still carries with it a deadly virus: the virus of standardization. For Americans this argument may not count for very much, particularly at a time when Western unity is essential. But if we value that which Western individuality has produced in the past, we may well have to pause to examine the conscious or unconscious extent of our own betrayal. No one can blame America for perfecting a science that has given much to the world and has helped in such a degree to alleviate the human condition. But we can all seriously appraise the vices as well as the virtues inherent in new trends of living, and must fight to preserve, or incorporate in the new, the cultural values of generations of Western life. Our ancestors would have wanted us to do no less.

CHAPTER FIFTEEN

KING PINS
AND NEEDLES

FRANCE is proud of the talents of her artists, whether they be great sculptors, cooks or dressmakers. The artist is pampered and spoilt and protected against so many of the obstacles which, particularly in England, assail him and obstruct the execution of an inspiration. In England today the mere effort of living partakes of much creative ability. In France the artist is a sacred monster, a being apart; his energy is left unimpaired for his creative work, and there are many who are willing and proud to help him, to carry a bag, to prepare his evening meal, to transport his work to headquarters.

Typical of the reverence in which the talented are esteemed in France is Christian Dior, who is treated as the national asset which he undoubtedly is. Nancy Mitford tells how, soon after Dior had opened his own dressmaking establishment, she was sitting in a taxi, on her way to a dress fitting at Dior's, when the driver turned round in his seat and announced proudly, 'At last we have another dressmaker to rival Monsieur Balenciaga!'

Monsieur Balenciaga's 'rival' has passed into legend since

247

Nancy Mitford's taxi ride. The name of Christian Dior, the Watteau of contemporary dressmakers, has become among women in every country of the Western world a byword for chic: but little is known about the man himself.

In appearance Dior is like a bland country curate made out of pink marzipan. His apparent composure is a deception that belies an innate nervousness and tension, which result in almost total prostration after each new collection has been created. After the openings Dior looks to his country house at Milly for salvation. There he can rest between bouts in one of the world's most arduous and competitive professions, puttering in the garden, sometimes making an excursion to the local antique shop to bring back a bit of Sèvres china or the chair that he has long been promising himself: but his purse strings are carefully guarded by his secretary.

Dior enjoys the trimmings of life. A bourgeois with his feet well planted in the soil of reality, he has remained as modest as a sugar violet in spite of eulogies that have been heaped upon him. His egglike head may sway from side to side, but it will never be turned by success. Dior does not make the mistake of believing in his own publicity, though when he arrived in New York he received as much newspaper space as Winston Churchill. He is grateful that when fashion tires of him (and even the greatest can hold the throne for no more than several decades) he has been lucky and wise enough to save a nest egg on which to retire to his farm and cultivate his gardens.

There is a wide basis for Christian Dior's great reputation. After a gloomy interval of war he brought back to fashion an air of excitement that it had been missing for too many years. Far from being a flash in the pan, Dior's initial success was founded on a talent for the fresh and the unexpected that has been sustained through each succeeding collection. He seems to possess an inexhaustible vitality and zest, infusing his work with a radiating vigour. To see a collection of Dior's dresses filing past gives one the pleasure of watching a romantic and spectacular pageant. With an impeccable taste, a highly civilized sensitivity, and a respect for tradition that shows itself in a predilection for the half-forgotten, Dior creates a brilliant nos-

talgia. He can effect a mood by his personal colour sense alone and has put his authentic stamp on certain shades of lily-of-the-valley, leaf green, grey-yellow, pale apricot-rose or nacreous grey-greens. From this spectrum he creates his reverie, making a rhapsody out of flower-strewn chiffon, while even the most useful of his day suits evokes a certain empathy.

When he was young, he never thought he would be a dress-maker. 'Naturally,' he says, 'I was impressed by women's ap-pearance. Like all children, I inevitably looked at an elegant lady with admiration.' He distantly recalls the fur wraps, the para-dise feathers and amber necklaces, the Boldini-like gestures, but he explains he would have been greatly surprised if some-one had predicted that one day he would spend his time study-ing the complex details of fabrics, drapery and the intricacies of cut.

It was chance and necessity that led Dior to create his initial sketches in 1935. He had just recovered from a long illness, and his finances had taken a turn for the worse. For the first time in his life Christian Dior had to think seriously about a career. Previously he had led the leisurely life of a dilettante, had developed his aesthetic tastes, dabbled in the arts, had known a number of painters and musicians, and had even run a picture gallery to 'sell the paintings of my friends'. But though of Norman stock, Dior had never developed a practical sense, and the gallery failed.

Jean Ozenne, a friend of Dior's, suggested that he try his hand at designing clothes, Dior attempted some first sketches, and although the draughtsmanship was groggy he submitted them to a large dressmaking house. To his astonishment, they were accepted, but he realized there was a long row to be hoed. Dior made hundreds and hundreds of drawings, stubbornly and patiently attempted to learn, to understand and to intuit. After two years of labour and research, working night and day, he had finally attained his end; he had become a good dress designer.

During those early years Dior kept a sharp eye on the work of other designers. 'Nothing is ever invented,' he readily admits. 'You always start from something. It is certainly Molyneux's style that has most influenced me.' He also admired Chanel, who 'with a black sweater and ten rows of pearls' had revolutionized fashion.

Later, when he became involved with matters of technique, Madeleine Vionnet's dresses proved a valuable lesson. The more he learned the trade, the more he understood how exceptional and admirable she was. 'No one,' Dior asserts, 'has ever carried the art of dressmaking farther than Vionnet.'

By degrees a number of well-known dress houses bought Dior's sketches, though he often said that their finished products were much better than his originals. Janette Colombier, working for Marie Alphonsine, said to him one day, 'Seriously, you don't pay enough attention to the back or the sides of your dresses! You may be satisfied if they seem all right from the front, but my clients look at themselves from every angle.' Such experiences were invaluable to Dior.

The New Look

He was then asked to submit sketches for the fashion pages of *Figaro*, and there his work began to appear regularly. In 1937 Dior met Robert Piguet, who asked him to take a job as '*modeliste*'.

Dior spent two years at Piguet's, until the advent of the war. Here he considers the most valuable thing he learned was 'how to suppress'. Piguet knew that elegance lay in simplicity, and he taught this lesson to Dior.

Piguet was amused at Dior's concern for technique and *coupes savantes*. Today Dior feels that Piguet had no right to criticize, and emphasizes that it is only through technique that fashion can be profoundly modified.

During the German occupation of France, Dior spent a long time in Provence, marking time. For two years, like many others, he returned to the earth, got up with the birds, and cultivated his garden. He continued, however, to sketch for *Figaro* and finally was able to return to Paris, where he worked as *modeliste* for Lucien Lelong.

At Lelong's, Dior learned the importance of what he today considers to be the essential thing in dressmaking: the eccentricities and behaviour of different dressmaking fabrics. 'With the same idea and the same fabric,' Dior admonishes, 'a dress can be a success or a perfect failure.' A knowledge of how to direct the natural flow of the cloth is imperative; and a good dressmaker always submits to the natural bent of wool, organdy, velvet or whatever material he happens to be working with.

At Lelong's, Dior, together with Pierre Balmain, shared the responsibilities of creating Lelong's collections. The two dress designers were friendly enough, though Balmain was ambitious and dreamed of opening his own establishment. His reveries were catching, and Dior began dimly to entertain similar notions.

After the liberation of France, Balmain opened his own successful dressmaking house. Dior, whose timidity had led him to believe he would work for Lelong for ever, became more and more dissatisfied and felt ever less free. Though his friendship with Lelong was great, he had no choice but ultimately to leave and create his own headquarters.

On the eve of the New Look, Dior maintains that he had no idea he was about to start a revolution. He could scarcely foresee the reception that would be accorded to him, having merely done his best according to his beliefs. No doubt many women all over the Western world, plagued by clothing rationing and high cost of living, cursed him for what they considered wanton fantasy. But to Dior, the image of the wilfully spiteful designer is pure legend. It was the times, as much as his own ingenuity, that launched fashions on a more feminine trend, and he feels he was merely the instrument by which to express what the ladies unconsciously felt.

A few designers have the gift of expressing themselves in words, and Dior is one of these exceptions. He is something of a philosopher in his own right, and his observations about fashion and the present epoch are shrewd and just. It is his firm belief that 'dressmaking is, in the machine age, one of the last refuges for the human, the personal and the inimitable'. He regards the exercising of his profession as a 'sort of fight against

the demoralizing and mediocre influences of our time'.

In answer to the inevitable question as to whether there is a logic to fashion, Dior will reply affirmatively. He points out that each age seeks its image, the mirror of that image being the mirror of truth. The long skirts and bouffant thighs of his New Look were merely an expression of what his intuition told him was needed. 'By being natural and sincere,' Dior says, 'one often creates revolutions without having sought them.' Thus the styles of the twenties showed the influence of machines, as did Léger's paintings of the same period. But today, Dior feels, the robot woman makes us afraid. Our contemporary problems have brought us face to face with an uncultured and hostile world, have forced us to take stock of our traditions and our culture and to reaffirm human values. That is why the mode in women's dress has become increasingly feminine.

Dior is perhaps the last of the great couturiers, fighting valiantly to maintain creative values in a sombre epoch of history. He believes that luxury is as essential as anything which the West prizes. 'Everything that goes beyond the simple fact of food, clothing and shelter is luxury. Our civilization is a luxury, and it is that we are defending.' These words seem to echo those of another brilliant dressmaker, Mainbocher, when he says: 'I do not consider dressmaking an art, but it is as important as cooking or living.' In the face of impossible odds, Christian Dior continues to create, refusing to throw up the sponge. 'Things are always falling apart,' he sighs. 'Our simple duty is not to yield, but to be an example, to *create* in spite of everything.'

Create he does, and always with a practical mind. To the ladies who think that dressmakers are expressing wanton personal taste, Dior replies sharply, 'I risk the salary of nine hundred persons in making a collection.' Knowing this, he can never do anything wilful or perverse. No matter how much a collection may seem to be a free expression of the dress designer's fancy, it has all been carefully thought out and executed with as much precision as a master chess game. Each dressmaker strives to interpret, through the personal prism of himself, the mass taste of the moment, anticipating that taste before it has even taken form. Dior stresses that 'the atmosphere of the times is an essentially unknowable element, but it is very important'. The success of a play, a party, a political event, an exhibition, a king's visit—all of these things can explain and even predict a fashion.

It is inconceivable to Dior that anyone could believe the principal designers plot together to decide what the following season's collection will be. 'How could you imagine personalities so totally different,' Dior asks, 'using working methods so diverse, and then bending to a common rule and taking a decision so far in advance?' This, he claims, would be to deny the very essence of fashion and dressmaking. On the contrary, the dressmakers work in great and indispensable secrecy. The spirit of novelty is the very spirit of fashion itself. And for inspiration the dress designer either travels, withdraws to his country house or 'just feels fabrics'.

Yet each season there is a spirit of fashion. Dior maintains this spirit is created by the public, though the public may be unaware of it. The atmosphere of the moment, the choices made by the fashion magazines, the successes of the previous season—all these things have influence. Wittily Dior turns an epigram: 'The couturier proposes, but the ladies dispose.' It amuses him to observe that the same models are always taken up by the different fashion magazines; and then, modified, amplified, deformed or exaggerated, these models become everybody's fashion the following season. Once the mode is thus propagated and has become so widespread that it affects everyone, it ceases to be timely and is already *passé*.

In this analysis of fashion Dior is possibly exercising professional discretion. Actually dressmakers have often accused one another of stealing ideas and are frequently at needle points with one another. They are apt to hate their genus and seldom meet one another, for jealousy, envy and rivalry consume them. With few exceptions they are a tiresome, unreliable brood. Almost all inarticulate, they have never invented their own vocabulary, and their abuse of the French words *chic* and *élégant* have almost robbed these adjectives of their significance. Dressmakers will describe a dress or a coat as a 'little nothing';

and it is their cousin, the *vendeuse*, who has created the cliché, 'But, modom, it is so much "you".'

Only the 'hands' have their language, the language of the pins. Like tramps who chalk good or bad signs on walls so that others may benefit from the luck of a night's lodging and a gift of bread or, conversely, may avoid angry dogs and strict police; or like hotel porters who, by their manner of pasting the labels on departing travellers' trunks, inform others of the likelihood of tips, so, too, the *ouvriers* can give their initiates the instructions for a certain garment in the making and, no doubt, with the help of a few extra pins, also provide a character sketch of its prospective owner.

Yet Dior's analysis of the way in which the spirit of the new fashion spreads is accurate. It is perfectly understandable that different dressmakers can pick up the same message from the jungle drums of fashion, just as Indian tribes far up the Amazon will know of the advent of a white explorer weeks before he arrives at their village. In this case the fact that the skirt will be raised four inches is signalled by jungle wireless and appears simultaneously in the following season's collections of different dressmakers.

Little does the woman of fashion realize all that goes into the making of a collection. A year previous to any given season, fabrics have already begun to be woven in Lyons, in Northern France, in Switzerland, in Milan, and on the farthest isles of Scotland. Sometimes the dress houses suggest certain colours or weaves to the fabric makers. Dior himself tells a charming story about visiting Madame Brossin de Mere in Switzerland. 'How I would love it,' he exclaimed, 'if you could create a fabric like those roofs!' The roofs in question were of scalloped grey slate. Three months later Madame Brossin brought Dior a delightful embroidered organdy covered with his roofs.

After the weaving of the stuffs, the salesmen, like Chinese illusionists, come to the great house and spread out, fanwise, bolts of dazzling materials and colours. It is, Dior says, 'like a fireworks display'. Unconsciously the dress designer begins to discover his favourites, but only after his choices have been made does he perceive the dominating colours which will turn

out to be next season's 'fashionable' ones.

Though Dior is, at first, almost drowned in a sea of fabrics, he must resist temptation and set aside those which are too impractical. It is then that he begins to think of the possible dresses that can be made.

A collection, Dior says, is made up of few ideas, a dozen at most. This seems paradoxical, coming from a man whose fecundity seems to dazzle the fashion world with every season. But, he admits, one must know how to vary the ideas, how to adapt and impose them on the public.

Once his final sketches are finished, they become blueprints for the ultimate creations. His three collaborators, the Mesdames Bricard, Marguerite and Raymonde, take over. The ateliers are set in operation, and under the hawklike eyes of Dior and the three fates, the collection must be finished in six or seven weeks, with not a minute to spare. 'There is no doubt,' says Dior, 'that any object created by a man's hand expresses something, and, above all, the personality of he who made it. It is the same in dressmaking.' What Dior did not add is that dressmaking, like the theatre, is a collective art; many hands work towards one final expression, which must yet be that of the playwright or the designer himself.

Once the dresses have been made, there follow showings, first for the Press, then for the buyers. The curtain of grey satin opens, the first mannequin enters the room, and the excitement of an opening begins. Each model has a name and a number which are announced in English and French by a female barker. Unlike the Press, the buyers must pay a fee to see the collection, though this fee is an advance on what they may later prudently purchase. The sum is asked to compensate for their photographic eyes, which are often capable of copying the ideas of certain dresses. Many buyers, of course, are eminently ethical and have a respect for the couturier's work; they know that that work represents time, labour, money and love. But others, though they often buy certain models, will rape and tear seams, altering to suit their fancy. To protect themselves as much as possible, the dressmakers 'filter' those buyers who are allowed to see the collection. This may seem humiliating, but everything is done to avoid copying. And copying, for Dior, is tantamount to stealing: however much of an honour it may be to the dressmaker, it costs him money. He is still badly protected against this organized pillage and must do his best to circumvent it.

Dior, like any dressmaker of note, has, of course, his special clients, women of means who order their dresses from him alone. Dior humorously divides them into various categories: the woman who is insane for dresses; the woman who is never contented; the woman who does not know what she wants; and the perfect client, who knows what she wants and how much she can pay for it.

Dior stresses that, though the average person regards the professions that cater to ladies' fashions as compounded on insanity, perversity, pipe dreams, squandered money and just plain silliness, they are in reality, behind their façades of perfumes, of organdy and mannequins, commercial enterprises where the least yard of mousseline becomes a figure on a page, where the collections of each season become the francs and the sous of hundreds of employees who cater to that amorphous monster, the general public of women.

In the world of present-day dressmakers, Balenciaga stands apart, like some Elizabethan malcontent meditating upon the foibles and follies of fashion, yet committed to acting and creating in the very world which he regards with a classical Spanish eye. He is so much the opposite of a Christian Dior that they might well be placed at the far ends of the dressmaking world; yet each has a respect for the work of the other, and each is unquestionably a genius of contemporary style. If Dior is the Watteau of dressmaking—full of nuances, chic, delicate and timely—then Balenciaga is fashion's Picasso. For like that painter, underneath all his experiments with the modern, Balenciaga has a deep respect for tradition and a pure classic line. All artists who, apart from their unique personal gift, are also mediums transmitting the message of the art of the past inevitably are timely as well as timeless.

Unlike Dior, Balenciaga knew, even as a small boy, that he wanted to be a dressmaker. But though he pursued his vocation for many years, it was only in 1938, at the age of forty-two, that his star rose, calm and faithful as the Dog Star itself, over the skies of Paris fashion. Success came late, perhaps too late, to Balenciaga, though it may well be that this very tardiness of recognition accounts for his unique place in contemporary fashion. Balenciaga belongs to no clique, plays nobody's game but his own, steadfastly refuses to commercialize either himself or his talents, pays little attention to the seasonal changes of styles and pursues a solitary creation of values which have won him the respect, admiration and patronage of those who know modern fashion intimately and can recognize his unusual genius.

Born in a small fishing village on the Basque coast of Spain, Balenciaga's personality gave early evidence that he was destined for a career other than that which his background might ordinarily have dictated. His father was captain of a pleasure boat, catering to the simple outings of simple people. He could not help being amazed by the son who, at a tender age, showed little inclination to swim and fish or lead the life of the peasant children. Balenciaga preferred, on the contrary, to 'sew like the women'. His father threw up his hands in horror; but his mother, sensing perhaps the future that was already being prepared within him, protected the boy and allowed him to continue with his hobby.

In the small Spanish community there was little opportunity for an embryo dressmaker to see any fine ladies of the outside world. The one exception, perhaps, was an elderly marquesa, a former great beauty who owned the large house on the hill and whom the dreamy Balenciaga could admire from a distance in church, or fleetingly when she passed in a carriage. One Sunday morning, among the crowd that poured out from the church following Mass, Balenciaga watched the ageing Marquesa descend the worn stone steps, wearing a *tailleur* of white tussore and a straw hat enveloped in a maroon veil that tied under her chin in a bow. Unable to restrain his admiration, the youth murmured aloud, 'How elegant you are!'

The Marquesa paused and looked intensely at the boy in the hard Spanish sunlight. Surprised at such a remark from what was evidently a peasant boy, she must have found her curiosity piqued, and began to ply Balenciaga with questions. She quickly discovered his interest in sewing and his nascent aesthetic abilities which were fervent and manifest, however mawkish their expression might be. As a result of this meeting the Marquesa decided, shortly afterwards, to bestow upon Balenciaga the great honour of allowing him to copy her Drecoll suit. She gave the boy a bolt of material and lent him the original creation that he had admired so much.

The young Balenciaga was petrified and in a state of great elation at the same time. The prospect of copying a suit by Drecoll was a rare one; but supposing he should ruin the Marquesa's expensive material? With fear and trembling he executed his copy, and the Marquesa paid the crowning tribute to him of wearing it. Balenciaga admits today that the copy was no great shakes; but it marked a conspicuous beginning and

gave him the confidence and growing sense of ambition which he needed.

The following year the young dressmaker, scrubbed and shining and fortified by a modest sum of money in his pocket, went off to Paris for an *Arabian Nights* visit during which he watched the collections of Doucet, Drecoll and Worth, where he sat rapt in wonder. When his money ran out, Balenciaga returned home, happy in the conviction that he would become a great couturier. But the Basque Dick Whittington had a long and hard road to travel before he was to become the lord mayor of contemporary fashions.

Luck has played a great part in the career of this Spanish genius. Balenciaga has always been clever enough to seize his opportunity when it presented itself. He knew how to ride the tide that comes in the affairs of men, and in this was served well by his direct simplicity of spirit. It is not often reflected upon that only complicated people are unable to collect their win-

Balenciaga 1953.

nings when the wheel of fortune stops at their number. But Balenciaga was not complicated in that sense: he knew how to claim what was rightfully his.

He started his first dressmaking establishment in San Sebastian on a ridiculously small sum and with pathetically limited materials. It took many years of hard work to compensate for his background, his early lack of opportunities and education. Slowly Balenciaga acquired what his native intelligence needed; eagerly he seized his luck as it presented itself to him. And in 1936, past forty years old, he set up shop in Paris on ten thousand pounds of capital. Perhaps the difficulties of commercial success had held him back for too long; his success had come, but it was as ashes in his mouth and could not be like the heady wine of a youthful acclaim.

Today Balenciaga is a man of fifty-seven but appears much younger than his age. He has tired, yet bright eyes, and it is only when he fishes out a pair of rimmed spectacles that you realize he is myopic. His nose is beaked and Spanish, and his thin mouth has a slightly humorous, faintly sardonic smile that suggests a long-buried bitterness or an ironic awareness of human nature. In spite of the aloof pride written in its lines, the whole expression of the face is intensely human. His personality is somewhat suggestive of the bird kingdom. He is a natural phenomenon, yet there is a fleeting quality about him in repose, like a composed bird standing on one leg. Balenciaga is as we see him when he comes down from a branch to ruffle his feathers before returning to a solitary perch.

True to his appearance, the great dressmaker avoids publicity and the attentions and claims of worldly women. He has no ambition to enlarge his kingdom. He enjoys life as only simple people can, and because of that simplicity he seems utterly rare and fascinating in the world of artifice in which he works. If his pride is softened, it is because it is attuned to the exigencies of the world: he has known hard knocks and has triumphed over them.

In his work Balenciaga shows the refinement of France and the strength of Spain. His dresses have elegance and solidity: like their maker, they can mingle with kings and keep the common touch. Balenciaga does not provide any startling changes. His is a slow and carefully worked out development. Whereas Dior's dresses are most ingeniously and beautifully evolved from sketches, Balenciaga uses fabrics like a sculptor working in marble. He can rip a suit apart with his thumbs and remake or alter his vision in terms of practical, at-hand dressmaking. It is even possible that he makes no sketches at all, relying entirely on the picture in his mind's eye.

Again, by contrast with Dior, Balenciaga's dresses alter little with each season. His pendulum is more measured. Yet, paradoxically, his styles are nearly always several years ahead of existing fashions. He is a real leader, and his dresses never go out of fashion, for they are based on a strong foundation. Other dressmakers may enjoy the trimmings of life; but Balenciaga, dour, Spanish and ascetic, is a master architect, working along enduring lines.

In contrast to more feminine creations, this Spanish dressmaker's work is altogether bolder, less compromising and more masculine. If one looks at the art of dressmaking and strips it to its essentials, considering it in its simplest terms, then one must concede that Balenciaga is indeed today's Titan among couturiers. His touch has the rugged, peasant-like sureness of the great artist.

He is always certain of his effects. If he prescribes a short black sack of a dress for a beautiful or an ugly woman, if he sends her out with a flue brush sticking out at an unexpected angle from her pillbox hat, then his judgment must be respected.

And respected it is. Like pilots who trust the complicated instruments on their dashboards to bring them through a difficult stretch of navigation, many women believe utterly in Balenciaga's bold but unfailing talent and find themselves steered from danger to safety in the currents and eddies of contemporary fashions. His black woollen costumes, ceremonial sheaths of Byzantine embroidery and extravaganzas of jet should be enshrined side by side with the peasant clothes, the sacrificial vestments and ceremonial robes to be found in our national museums, for they form a part of contemporary fashion history.

Balenciaga will talk volubly, but he is fundamentally reticent. He has few but firm maxims, one of his tenets being that no dressmaker can make a woman chic if she is not chic herself. Nor does he believe in the chic that comes from following the mode of the moment. If a woman is *courci*—an untranslatable Spanish word which might best be described as 'dowdy smart' —if she has a matching bag, dress and handkerchief, she may achieve a smart vulgarity, which is scarcely what is desired.

Balenciaga also believes that a lady of fashion cannot be elegant unless she patronizes a single dressmaker. And that dressmaker, to be true to himself, must remove himself from the constant flurries and competitive chirpings that flourish in the forest of the Place Vendôme.

If asked what constitutes a distinguished woman, Balenciaga will slyly quote Dali: 'A distinguished lady always has a disagreeable air.' He makes a distinction, however, between distinguished and glamorous: it is his belief that the glamorous

BALENCIAGA
1952:

cocottes of yesterday have become respectable and are today's distinguished ladies.

But for Balenciaga life has irrevocably changed. Women no longer have the time, the same leisure to seem as beautiful as they did in the early years of this century. We live in a different world. One age ended with the First World War—an age of elegance, presided over by Worth and Doucet. After that there was an age of chic, created, Balenciaga maintains, by Cheruit, who asserted not so much of a style as a certain piquancy and suppleness that made for chic. And still another age ended with the Second World War.

Yet, like Dior, Balenciaga believes that the couturier must go in the direction that the times dictate. The dressmaker cannot do battle with his age but must rather allow his expression to find its appeal through the temporal mode. He must sense what is needed and how women are to look at a given moment. Balenciaga himself always makes a collection by considering that which is indispensable and not that which he would like to give. Yet somehow his creations always pass through the filter of a strong, unyielding Spanish personality, which brilliantly creates a solidity out of the fleeting and makes an enduring quality out of some temporal phase.

Balenciaga does not try to follow the new season's fashion, nor does he know what it is. He attempts, at best, to feel what a woman should look like at a given moment. In this attitude one senses perhaps that a Dior feels more impelled to observe the line of the mode from previous seasons and from other indications, rather than turn his back upon it and create a new expression. Balenciaga may be more conservative, but in the end he is oddly more daring than many of his French rivals.

Sadly, this Spanish genius points out that modern women find it difficult to become refined when they are in too much of a hurry. Yet in their favour he discovers that many modern women are aware of the dangers of being chi-chi or extravagant. They have no time to be chi-chi.

Always Balenciaga will return to his basic assertion, emphasizing that a couturier cannot make the inner spirit of a woman but can only create the outward clotheshorse. The woman herself must have an inner quality that makes her wear her clothes well. As illustration, Balenciaga points out that you may put the same dress on two different women, and one will be vulgar while the other will achieve distinction.

Balenciaga does not believe that women should vary their clothing often in order to be well dressed. Men, by contrast, wear the same several suits most of the time, yet they can and do manage to look elegant.

If one could say that fashion is a serial story that never ends, then the good designer must invent new plot developments to continue the tale, and all good dressmaking must conform to the fictional pattern of fashion's evolution and continuation. Balenciaga does not believe in the eternal novelty of the new, as so many fashion maniacs do. Quite the contrary: his plot developments must be integral with what has gone before, must stem from characters of fashion itself. Though he will sometimes make concessions, he never alters his basic thought.

As an example of this, a year or so ago, when collection buyers complained to Balenciaga that certain of his clothes were much too loose, he adjusted and made alterations, changing the over-filled, untight look, but he did not for a moment give up his basic conceptions.

Balenciaga's colour sense is so refined, sharpened to such a remarkable degree, that he can unerringly scan four hundred colours and choose the right one for his purpose. It is Balenciaga's belief that a dressmaker must be virtually scientific in the choice of the colours that support his inspiration.

Behind his casual remarks about women, fashion and the modern world, one senses a firm but vital thread of pessimism. This may, indeed, be the basis of Balenciaga's unique creative abilities. For that which is rooted in pessimism can never die. Though he believes that a grand way of life has disappeared forever, and though the money and splendour that created the atmosphere of a fabulous heyday of fashions are irrecoverably

gone, yet, like Dior, Balenciaga adjusts himself to the age and goes on creating what the age must have to reflect its true image of itself. Proud, Spanish, classical, he is a strange rock to be found in the middle of the changing sea of fashion, and one which will endure long after the capricious waves of the moment have done their best to dislodge him.

Apart from the several reigning dressmakers who occupy the central throne, there are grouped about them, as for a photographic sitting, the creators of accessory fashions; and, still close to the throne, are the blood relations connected by the ties of *Vogue, Harper's Bazaar, Femina, Mademoiselle* and the dozen-odd magazines whose important business it is to promulgate the modes of the moment. The feminine genii among these magazine editors are known, not perhaps by the person in the street, but by those whose relationships have ever involved them with the inner circles of fashion. Mrs Edna Woolman Chase and Mrs Carmel Snow for years have been seen in the front row at fashion openings, holding key positions as promoters through whose activities the changing trends and rulers are made familiar to the anonymous majority of women who accept, whether willingly or grudgingly, the dictates of the moment.

Mrs Edna Woolman Chase, more than anyone else, is a veritable fashion institution. Only recently, when *Vogue* magazine filed a court suit against a modelling school that, having no connection with the Condé-Nast enterprises, was taking *Vogue's* name in vain, Mrs Chase testified as a witness and told the startled judge, in answer to his question, that she had worked for *Vogue* since 1895. The magistrate lowered his glasses, peered over the top of his desk at her, and then murmured, 'That is a very remarkable fact.' In the span of these fifty-odd years of tenure with *Vogue* Mrs Chase has both directly and indirectly exerted a tremendous influence on changing methods of promotion and presentation, and the innovations that could be laid at her doorstep are without number. In spirit and character Edna Woolman Chase is a bountiful woman with valuable homely qualities, a warm heart, and a fighting spirit that has often waged war against both chi-chi and the destructive persons or tendencies that have sometimes attempted to sabotage the principles she believes in. Now in her late seventies, she still takes an active interest in the magazine she has so courageously served in the course of its half century of life.

Mrs Carmel Snow of *Harper's Bazaar* served her apprenticeship with *Vogue* and the Condé-Nast publications, an apprenticeship for which she is always deeply grateful. Like a good vintage wine, Mrs Snow becomes mellower and finer with each passing year. Today, with pale mauve hair and carnation cheeks, she is the rich fulfilment of the qualities she possessed at the beginning to make her an inevitable key woman. Mrs Snow combines an Irish temperament with (and she has no French blood in her) a French intuition. Guided by her unerring instinct, she seeks and finds the tendencies of contemporary fashions before they have even made themselves apparent to many a professional eye. So attuned is Carmel Snow to her atmosphere that she often anticipates what other people are about to suggest, and can telepathically finish thoughts and sentences for them. Keenly appreciative and endowed with a quick intelligence, this director of *Harper's Bazaar* will yet readily depreciate herself, insisting that she is illiterate and uneducated. But her literacy is that of her profession, and her education is the result of the French instincts that she has brought to bear in a world whose needs are too ruthlessly immediate to permit inefficiency. In that, Mrs Snow has no cause for worry: her agile mind, like a salamander darting out its tongue to capture a fly, seizes impressions on the wing and incorporates them in a magazine whose consistent high standards have been an index for achievement to others.

Madame Marie-Louise Bousquet, the French editor of *Harper's Bazaar*, is like that magic ingredient which the Chinese have used for centuries to flavour soups and sauces. Without her, the world of fashion would lose an integral part of its mind and heart. Though she moves in an environment which has its silly and brittle aspects, Marie-Louise Bousquet has never lost her sense of true human values nor her high aesthetic appreciation. She understands artists' problems and life's cruelties; she has a great literary sense, inherited, perhaps, from her husband and the literary salons they promoted together during his lifetime. To fashion, Marie-Louise Bousquet is a brilliant asset, not merely because she is present at the birth of the new in the minor and major arts, but because she is often the midwife herself. This great French lady is an inspiration to those who come to her with creative problems, a sort of fairy godmother. Beneath the outward trappings of her fashionable clothes, her institutional Thursday-afternoon salons, and her own inward suspicion that she has, perhaps, sold her soul in order to earn a living in a world of transient values—beneath all this, Marie-Louise Bousquet is tragically individual, hewn out of granite qualities that endure and persist. In spite of her bad arthritis and a game leg, she is never rattled, putters about in her little car, and seems to be everywhere, posing hands on feverish brows, promoting kindness, friendships, helping to launch talent, and, in general, serving as the brilliant Florence Nightingale of fashion which she doubtless is.

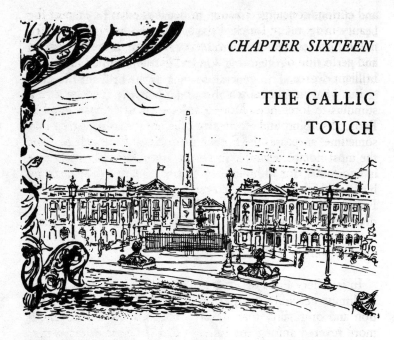

CHAPTER SIXTEEN

THE GALLIC TOUCH

REFERRING to our aesthetic and spiritual heritage from the golden age of Plato and Phidias, Shelley once said that we are all Greeks. It might equally well be said, 'We are all Frenchmen.' For nearly three hundred years France has maintained a unique position as the centre of Western culture, fostering both the major and the minor arts with an instinct, a flair and a creativeness that are distinctly recognizable as 'the Gallic touch'. In poetry and perfumes, dressmaking and drama, interiors and ideas, the French seem to be continually effervescing with inspiration.

It is no accident that they are past masters at the art of living. A truly civilized people does not scorn the minor arts, for it knows how important the manifestations of living can be, even when embodied in a less permanent form of expression than marble or indelible ink. France can rightly be as proud of the talents of her jewel makers or decorators as of a Stendhal or a Rodin. The porter who opens the gates and the good-natured and curious concierge knitting in her lodge have a respect for beauty in its many forms. Possibly for this very reason fifty million Frenchmen have maintained the lead in the refinement and perfection of the minor arts and have developed them to a brilliant degree.

But whatever the causes of the phenomenon, it has proved a stimulus to foreigners. More than one expatriot has settled in Paris, absorbing and expressing this ability to a degree that sometimes surpasses the French themselves. Picasso is perhaps the most notable example in recent times. His debt to France is enormous, for although we know him to be Spanish by birth and character his cultural roots are unquestionably French. Yet there are other endeavours than in the fields of dressmaking at which the French, or the 'naturalized' French, are equally adept, and they are as widely disparate as the making of jewellery and interior decoration.

In jewellery Paris designers, typified in the designs of Jean Schlumberger and the Duke of Verdura, show more imagination and originality than in any other capital. Yet no one is more revered among the initiates for her extraordinary taste than the talented Jeanne Toussaint. In the course of the last three decades this birdlike little woman, with a beak of a nose, an exquisitely pretty mouth that hints of her sensitivity, and with chinchilla-coloured hair worn in the bobbed wisps of the twenties, has designed jewellery for the firm of Cartier. Her influence has encompassed the earth. She might have been an architect or a sculptor, an actress or a wonderful cook, but she has brought her original gifts to the handling of jewels. As a result of this love for strange settings and juxtapositions of stones, unique jewellery, never before seen, has made its appearance in the world of fashion.

Madame Toussaint can unite different elements with an utterly fresh approach, yet her work is still bounded by the classical. Her sense of equilibrium and proportion is so strong that anything she creates represents safely good taste. For this artist, the stone itself is irrelevant: she does not consider it a jewel, a bijou, until it has been wonderfully set and presented.

She is more interested in working with the less expensive stones, and with yellow sapphires, tourmalines, amethysts, coral and aquamarines creates colour combinations that have hitherto existed only in the jewels from India. Madame Toussaint can take First Empire tiaras, bracelets or brooches from their heavy gold settings and make parures of a filigree lightness, with wonderfully mixed colours.

Her jewel-maker's touch is a light one. Continuing in the vein of eighteenth-century brooches (with bunches of diamond flowers quivering on their taut wires), she has made diamonds flexible, hanging them in little fringes, stalactites or tassels, creating chains of diamonds that are as supple as the beads of a rosary.

The Toussaint gift springs from an unswerving, granite-hard instinct, allied with irrevocable powers of decision. She knows exactly what she wants and, if she is convinced that one of her ideas is good, can never be influenced by any opposition nor swayed by any theory of public taste. This extraordinary independence insures the originality that is eventually claimed by the public.

Madame Toussaint's apartment, to which only a few enlightened souls are invited, reveals another aspect of her very sensitive but rugged feminine taste. No colour schemes assail the eye, nothing is blatant, no feature stands out; yet everything is calculated down to the smallest detail. Hers is a quiet authority that takes one into its confidence by degrees; one must seek out the details of a harmonious whole. This apartment is like a secret that only a few are privileged to share with its owner.

The arrangement of these almost empty *boiseried* rooms is modern in spirit, yet the furniture consists of the most rare and wonderful eighteenth century pieces. On the parquet floor polished like glass is an antique vase of stone filled with the heads of white lilac, a table of exquisite charm and proportions is graced with a fragment of a Greek sculpture, one stalwart lily sprouts from a Chinese pot on a shelf, while the head of a Buddha on a column casts its carefully arranged shadow on to a curved screen. An enormous divan, upholstered in white satin, is strewn with a rug of pale-coloured fur and cushions

Madame Toussaint, 1953

of champagne-coloured velvet. Madame Toussaint's wonderful canopied bed is hung with a heavy satin that is neither white
nor blue nor grey, but is all these colours, and of a consistency
that combines the richness of Devonshire cream with the
rigidity of metal. This apartment is purity itself, the millionaire's equivalent to the extreme simplicity of the cottage room
with a cane chair and a pot of geraniums. Being the combination of an artist's and a collector's sensibility, the result is
highly intellectual. In her jewellery Madame Toussaint reveals
her voluptuous sensibility, and in the superb quality of the
wine and food over which she presides. They are the gourmet's
delight, revealing this unusual creator's awareness that man
does not live by thought alone.

Madame Toussaint is a typical example of the catholic taste
of the French. A jeweller by vocation, she demonstrates her
skill in these allied arts of living. One marvels, indeed, that
the French have been able to maintain such standards of creati-

vity in the difficulties of a post-war world. Most western European capitals, even at this late date, are far from recuperated in their manifestations of luxury.

Marie Laure de Noailles, the remarkable wife of the Vicomte Charles de Noailles, has been for the past thirty years probably the most dedicated and energetic patron of art in all Paris. In her enormous house in the Place des Etats Unis at almost any time of every day she can be seen bird-brighteyed, ivory complexioned, her dark hair worn in Medusa-like curls, giggling or holding forth in mellifluous tones in the centre of a group of musicians, poets, painters, and not only those who have already made their name; many an embryonic star has had his course made less difficult by the encouragement and help of this most genuine devotee of beauty in its differing forms. Just as she mixes artists from many worlds so is her house a receptacle for their works; a concerto dedicated to her lies specially bound on a piano, and on the panelled or the leather-covered walls of her rooms the great masters of the Flemish school hang in perfect harmony next to exponents of Dadaism or Surrealism. Madame de Noailles has a gift for fusing all the elements of art, and her Goyas, Delacroix, Juan Gris, Max Ernsts, early bronzes and gilt unicorns become part of her provocative, sometimes sensational, and always abundantly vital personality.

Perhaps the most difficult aspect of luxury to keep alive today is the large-scale decoration of private houses. Yet this enterprise still flourishes in Paris, where in spite of perpetual economic upheavals a handful of *régisseurs* seem to have large enough coffers to bring about great wonders of building and ornamentation.

Happily, there is no lack of craftsmen as well. Perhaps only France can today boast of skilled workers who excel at eighteenth-century carving or are willing to apply a hundred coats of paint before they have acquired the exact tonality that is required. Such men are artists in their own right, appreciative of various nuances, and they applaud rather than condemn the master's aesthetic integrity when he refuses to accept a second best as substitute, tenaciously clinging to his ideals of perfection.

Of all cities, contemporary Paris still boasts those survivors

Arturo Lopez-Wilshaw, 1954

of the seventeenth, eighteenth and nineteenth centuries—the rich patrons who are themselves dilettante architects, capable of producing results alone or hand in hand with their own architect. The Vicomte Charles de Noailles and Monsieur Charles de Beistegui, for example, work with Emilio Terry, a wealthy South American architect of consummate skill and taste, who has a reverence for the Greek simplicities. Arturo Lopez-Wilshaw, in conjunction with Paul Rodocanachi, built additions to the Rodocanachi house at Neuilly. Together they created a miniature Versailles. Since Mr Rodocanachi's death Mr Lopez-Wilshaw has worked with Georges Geffroy, who has a practical sense, an uncanny taste in *objets d'art*, and a flair for discovering the rarest pieces of furniture.

Since Mr Lopez-Wilshaw is, I believe, a South American of great wealth, he has been able to devote much of his time to the search for unique pieces, and his knowledge has become infallible. If his taste treads little new ground in its grandeur of style and perfection of theatrical effect, it at least continues to keep open the path trodden by Largillière and Cécile Sorel in the style of Louis Quatorze. To look at the house in Neuilly, one can hardly believe this transformation scene is of recent development. The very fact that contemporary workmen have been trained to work in shell decoration and are quite capable of duplicating a ballroom with eighteenth-century *rocaille* is in itself an astonishing feat. Likewise, the yacht in which Mr and Mrs Lopez-Wilshaw sail the Mediterranean Sea, with its ormolu, *chinoiserie* and its furniture, the work of *maîtres ébénistes*, must be unique in the history of navigation.

Mr Geoffroy has also had a helping hand as adviser and sleuth in the imaginative metamorphosis that has recently taken place in the apartment of young Baron de Rédé at the beautiful Hôtel Lambert, which was built on the Isle Saint-Louis in 1640 by Le Vau, the King's architect. Voltaire observed that 'it is the house of a sovereign who would like to be a philosopher'.

In his principal apartments the note of splendour is given the slightly wry expression of today.

In the Gallery of Hercules (whose ceiling was painted by Lebrun before Versailles had even been started) innumerable balls and fêtes have been given since its walls of gilded stucco were completed by Van Obstal. It can never be seen to better advantage than today, with its powder-blue chairs, monumental sculpture and candelabra, and the dinner table set in all its splendour for fifty covers. When the frail and good-looking young Baron entertains, dozens of chefs in their tall white hats can be seen through a window as the guests mount, from the Court of Honour, the stone staircase. On these occasions the Meissen porcelain is in use, orchids and yellow roses are sprayed with artificial dew, and at intervals footmen rush forward over the parquet with the next course of the Lucullan banquet. The effect is far from suggesting that the assembled guests are living in the century of the average man.

In Paris, also, the American-born Princess Chavchavadze has a knack of making a splendid setting for herself. Her houses, of similar appearances, contain her opulent collection of French and Russian pieces. But she brings such discretion and taste to

M. le Baron de Rédé, Palais Lambert

assembling a room, as well as adding the comforts of England and America, that the general effect is neither overpowering nor vulgar in its richness, conveying rather an impression of warmth and cosiness.

In England the taste of the *élite* is more rugged. Attentions to detail are more cursory. Yet, whereas present-day difficulties preclude the spending of vast sums on interior alterations, gardens are cultivated with more relish than ever.

Among those who energetically flout all contemporary obstacles or disparagements, Mrs Nancy Tree (who is somewhat of an exception to the rule, bringing an indefatigable eye to detail) has a talent for sprucing up a stately but shabby home and making a grand house appear less grand. She has an adequate reverence for tradition, observes the rules of style and proportion, and manifests a healthy disregard for the sanctity of 'important' furniture. Unless it can be used as grist to her particularly effervescing mill and be integrated with a liveable, gay and pretty ensemble, she will have no scruples about changing its colour or discarding it. Her love of colour, her flower sense, and her feeling for comfort have brought a welcome American touch to many an English house sorely in need of such ministrations.

Since the war Paris has given rise to one particular kind of interior decorating taste that has not yet infiltrated into England or America. It is even doubtful whether such a taste could flourish outside France, for it is the height of super-sophistication. The aim of those who have acquired this predilection is to assume character rather than an effect that is pleasing to the eye; and the character must be of a stolid nature. Certain objects and colours are given prominence because, while they might seem ugly from one point of view, they have the virtue of being able to evoke the period of security enjoyed from 1860 to 1900. The general intention is thus a slightly cynical reversion to a period when the general level of taste was admittedly bad, 'flair' was unknown, and artistry denied. In those days of Victorian France, the gardener had charge of indoor floral arrangements and the butler was responsible for the look of the dining table. Comfort was cushioned (often on leather cushions), curtains were chosen primarily to keep out the chill of winter, and carpets were likewise selected for their effect of warmth.

This taste is epitomized with certain piccalilli-coloured or pale soup-green majolica pots of the nineteenth century and plates representing a sunflower or pansy, baked into a heavy ochre or restrained mauve. It is a cult for the sobriety of the nineties, when nobody thought in terms of decoration, except to believe that clear colours were lacking in reserve and that it was unrewarding to follow carefully the earlier traditional styles of former periods. Individuality found expression in the stuffed animal's head hanging in the hall, a trophy of some

Louise de Vilmorin

personal hunting expedition. Or private taste might at best be reflected in the silver-rimmed drinking cup that had been converted from the horn of a favourite old heifer.

In its most advanced terms this revived aesthetic is to be found in the house of the family of seed merchants, the Vilmorins. The three Vilmorin brothers and their sister, the writer and poet Louise de Vilmorin, indefatigable detectives of objects that express their particular brand of beauty, have created a dun-coloured world at Verrières, their seventeenth-century house outside Paris. Verrières is so *raffiné* and *recherché* that, by comparison, it makes grandiose taste seem somewhat conventional. The Vilmorin atmosphere is one of poetic perversity combined with a well-to-do nostalgia for the joys and the unhappiness of the day nursery and the schoolroom of forgotten foggy days. Each of the rooms has its own calculated atmosphere: some are consciously lowering in their effect, some fraught with a particular form of melancholy; but none is spontaneous, brightly coloured or gay.

Verrières is the house of memories of a united and strangely original family. Each brother has his own highly developed ego, yet none of them is ever in disagreement with each other or with their adoring and adored but egocentric sister. It is the house of people of high sensitivity—a mansion of botanists, a fortress calculated to give its occupants the maximum feeling of security, moral comfort and invulnerability.

The ordinary person would not consider Verrières at all out of the ordinary. But for others it is unique. Louise Vilmorin regards it as a house which, decorated in a mixture of styles of the Second Empire, 1860, 1914 and 1925, succeeds in being the most luxurious expression of poverty. Everything at Verrières is significant. The sister says in explanation: 'It means that we still love and revere our grandmother and could never treat her house in a way she would not have liked. It means, "How can we throw out that ugly table of Father's when we remember so well his sitting against the lamp which made a halo round his head and cast a shadow on that green tablecloth?" It means a brother taking his sister by the hand and saying, "Do you remember when we bought that china donkey carrying those flower containers?" Every room is haunted with souvenirs that mean so much. The silver filigree duck from Yugoslavia means a day of rain, or sunlight, or how you cried.'

Like memory itself, the house has little colour; it is a house in daguerreotype, with walls ·the colour of egg shells, pale brown or blue or pale green, illuminated by old electric light fixtures that provide a gentle, warm golden glow. The vases of *tutti flori* might have been made by Fantin Latour. There are rich but subdued colourings for the plush cushions and the carpeted sofas. Often the family conducts *La Veillée* sitting in rows in the living room, with the three brothers and sister, their wives and children (ranging from thirteen to twenty-five) watching their father play solitaire. The scene might have been painted by the Victorian Guernotte or Béraud, whose exquisite conversation pieces hang upon the walls.

Among the naturalized Parisian decorators, Charles de Beistegui, a Spaniard who spends part of the year in Paris, London, New York or Venice, is a rare phenomenon in our time. He is a

Charles de Beistegui

man of fashion with an artistic integrity, a knowledge of architecture, furniture, *objets d'art* and a seemingly endless fortune with which to indulge his talent for assembling luxurious houses. Wherever he may be, he is perpetually adding to his collection.

In the thirties De Beistegui indulged himself in the frivolities of baroque decoration with as much enjoyment as anyone in his world. His rooftop apartment in the Champs Elysées was a dazzling hodgepodge of Napoleon III, Le Corbusier modernism, mechanism and surrealism. Not since Louis of Bavaria had there been so many candelabra in one room; Catherine of Russia never had so many gold boxes on one table. Certainly never before had anyone seen the like of De Beistegui's terrace. After mounting a white spiral staircase, the visitor pressed an electric button that caused a glass wall to roll back. Thus was revealed a terrace that overlooked the traffic and the lights of the Champs Elysées. It was furnished with Louis Quinze furniture that had been painted white and placed on a grass carpet open to the sky. In this fantastic apartment, mirrors, in all their narcissistic forms, were used for decoration: on the top of the long dining table, for festoons of stylized drapery shrouding windows or doorways.

A giant statue of a Negress with shoots of ostrich feathers on her turbaned head stood like a Saxe figurine between a phalanx of crystal girandoles. A baroque rocking horse, harnessed with precious jewels, pranced among obelisks of porphyry. The effect upon the visitor must have been like that on the very young and impressionable Cinderella when arriving at the Prince's ball.

As in every interior De Beistegui created, his aim was achieved with this fantasy. Yet this was a phase that did not give De Beistegui opportunity to show his real flair. As soon as blackamoors, baroque festoons of mirror curtains and plaster arabesques started to find their way into less exclusive surroundings, his taste revolted against theatrical 'chi-chi' and the pink-and-white flamboyancy by which he had been influenced. He discarded them overnight.

Charles de Beistegui is a *pasticheur par excellence*, his forte being the re-creation of an atmosphere of any specific place or age. More often than not, his intention is to produce character rather than to create loveliness. Instead of a cretonne gracefully strewn with sweet peas, he will prefer a chintz of tight-packed bunches of stiff violets to go into a bedroom with a viridian green carpet. His choice of Paisley-covered walls with travelling-rug curtains and black woollen loose covers, his adept use

of mouldy strawberry, mustard and chutney colours are intended less to compliment the eye than to create a desired emotional effect of Victorian stability and heavy comfort. Charles
de Beistegui strikingly reveals how atmosphere can be created
by the choice of certain colours. His colour sense is highly cultivated and always some years in advance of the public. Today
he prefers sombre colours—blue-greens, slate greys, royal blue,
mud, deep crimson and black. When he uses pale blue, it is as
an exclamation mark in the melancholy surroundings.

De Beistegui's taste is essentially masculine: bold, uncom-
promising, sometimes even slightly acrid. When he hangs the
walls of a drawing room with a Philippe de Lasalle silk that
has been woven for him from the loom originally set for Marie
Antoinette, the result is a room very obviously decorated with
a man's restraint, though women may certainly look their best
in it. Flowers do not play an important part in De Beistegui's
rooms and are rarely seen, except on the patterns of silks, china
or chintzes. Nor do these rooms rely on 'finishing touches':
they are as complete in the morning as when lit for a party.

Charles de Beistegui's love of the English taste dates from
his years at Oxford University. He has always been impressed
by the comfort and luxury of the grand Victorian house in the
English countryside, with the boiling-hot water in a brass jug
wrapped in a linen towel on the washstand, and the folding
mahogany steps, covered with carpeting, that lead up to the
high brass bed with its mahogany-encased chamber pot underneath. The carpeted bathrooms furnished with pictures, the
huge bathtub framed in wood, the vast Turkish towel placed
in readiness on the wickerwork chair, the heavily studded
green baize doors leading to the servants' quarters, and the
'silver' room where the family plate was on display behind the
grained wood doors of the cupboards—all these aspects of the
large country house have always had an undying fascination
for him. He is obsessed by the old houses that bear traces of
the tastes and habits of successive generations, and he has succeeded in re-creating this effect at Groussay, his country house
outside Paris. Here he has mixed the styles of the seventeenth
and eighteenth centuries with those of the Empire, Second

Empire and Restoration. The vast library with circular mahogany staircases leading to the gallery two stories high, the
billiard room and the bedrooms done up in chintz and tartan
create an atmosphere of Czarist Russia and late Victorian
England.

For many years now Charles de Beistegui's science and talent
as a decorator have been celebrated, and it is undoubtedly he
who has been the instigator of the current renewal in France of
'le goût anglais'. De Beistegui never asks advice of others; his
opinions are firm and independent. Yet his imagination allows
him to renew ceaselessly the schemes and the discoveries which
give life and variety to all his houses. Charles de Beistegui has
never been interested in decorating professionally, but to prove
that he can make a delightful setting without spending large
sums of money he transformed an apartment in the New York
hotel in which he spent one winter by the most simple and
effective means.

Perhaps some of De Beistegui's decorating is cold, without
soul or heart, and one suspects that he possesses a secret disregard for quality. He possesses much magnificent furniture
signed by the great cabinet-makers of France, but for a certain
position in some room he often prefers to make a large, bad
table rather than buy a good one. He will happily mix imitation
classical statuary with the superb ormolu and mahogany of
Roentgen; paintings seem to be decoration and not art when
hung on the walls of his room.

As the years pass, his taste becomes more classical. Perhaps
in order to protect himself he now chooses a scheme of decoration that it is impossible to copy. His Paris apartment in
the Rue de Constantine is furnished with audacious sumptuousness that could be seen today almost nowhere else except
in a museum. The *grand salon*, with red, black and blue as its
key colours, with a painted *trompe-l'oeil* ceiling twenty-four
feet above, has six tall windows hung with black fringed curtains. The sculpture and furniture are of gigantic proportions.
The dining room has a more simple and poetical atmosphere,
with its pale grey walls around a green-velvet-covered table set
out with a Saxe service of the eighteenth century. Its high-

backed leather chairs and its elongated emptiness are based on the picture where the young Mozart plays the clavichord during the *thé à l'anglaise* at the Prince de Conti's.

Likewise, his decoration of the magnificent Palazzo Labbia in Venice is devoid of frivolity and is decorated on a grandiose scale worthy of the palace's vast stone proportions and the Tiepolo frescoes.

A faddist with unlimited energy, Charles de Beistegui avoids mere reconstitutions of exact past styles and epochs. His imagination is so rich that his imitators can never keep up with him or guess what he will make fashionable tomorrow. He is always so busy with his newest schemes of building and interior decoration that one wonders when he himself has time to enjoy the results of his genius. At the moment he is building two vast wings on to Groussay: one to contain a chapel to be decorated in the Gothic style and a ballroom based on the engravings of Abraham Bosse, and the other to contain a Louis Treize theatre in which specially commissioned operas and ballets are to be performed on gala occasions.

Charles de Beistegui's penthouse, 1930

CHAPTER SEVENTEEN

VARIETY
SHOW

ONE could easily develop a monist theory of fashion, for its expression invades all aspects of man's social life. One finds the same changes and laws in the most serious as well as the most frivolous aspects of human endeavour. Literature, for example, is as subject to fashion's laws as the line of a dress; parties or flowers or scents are subject to variations depending upon the needs of man's environment. If these diverse themes coalesce in this chapter, it is not because they are related to each other in any direct organic way, but rather because they reflect the same continuum of change that rides through any given age and are, indeed, related in the sense that they often express, in their different media, the tone of an epoch.

Scientists tell us that 80 per cent of our senses are visual, the other 20 per cent being divided among taste, touch, hearing and smelling. Though it is the one among his five senses that man could most do without, the sense of smell is, in its own delightful way, one of the rarest gifts that he possesses. Each day flowers, lemons, soap, herbs, foods, oils, medicines and perfumes assault our nostrils with a never-ending variety of impressions. Not all are pleasant: some are rancid, sour, dank, sickening; some, on the other hand, are titillating, pungent, aromatic and heart-warming. From the range of pleasant smells man has chosen, in the course of civilization, to learn to extract their essences and make scents from them.

No doubt the art of perfume making goes back to the earliest civilizations. Greece and Egypt, Cleopatra and Poppaea, all had their salves and incenses, their bath oils and perfumes. Ambergris has been known since the Phoenicians, and a stranded whale with its natural cargo of ambergris has in centuries past been the occasion of a gold rush to the beach.

It is perhaps seldom considered that the tastes in scents of various ages are continually changing just as much as clothing styles or any other expression of fashion alters, to express a new attitude towards our changing surroundings.

During the late Victorian and Edwardian ages, perfumes, in contrast to manners and literature, were direct and solid in their appeal. Heliotrope, rose and lilac odours were especial favourites. Even today the tradition of classical English scents continues to range through the lavenders, rosemary and sweet geranium smells, and all the herbs that Cardinal Wolsey ever plucked as he wandered in his garden at Hampton Court.

At the beginning of the First World War, when Paul Poiret's lampshade ladies and the Russian Ballet made exoticism fashionable, perfumes began to become heavy, musk-like and Eastern. This tradition of Oriental scents continued until the 1920s: it was considered exciting for women to leave a heady trail of sandalwood or Japanese scent in their wake.

Early in the twenties a revolution took place in both the manufacture of perfumes and the manufacturers themselves. Dressmakers had started to invade the field of scent, and soon Chanel, Lanvin and others began to create perfumes in their own names.

The revolution also affected the chemical composition of

scents. Previous to the twentieth century's discovery and perfection of synthetic compounds, perfumes had been made from ambergris, flowers, herbs and leaf oils, their essences extracted with alcohols according to certain formulae that had been developed over hundreds of years. But the great age of organic chemistry had begun with coal-tar dyes and was soon to flood the scent and the food market with synthetic perfumes, synthetic vanilla, synthetic fruit flavours and ersatz colours. Even chemists will admit that there is a difference between the synthetic and the natural product. Scientists can manufacture in a test tube the smell and the taste of vanilla or of pineapple and pear: but in nature, the esters which impart their smell and their flavour to these fruits, or the vanillin in the vanilla bean, are delicately manufactured and mixed with other components. Natural growth and sunlight have made all the difference, just as hothouse flowers seldom possess the qualities of those that grow in summer.

So it is with perfumes. Few synthetic perfumes can rival the smell of carnation spice and other direct Edwardian scents; nor can modern bath oils or toilet waters compete with what James Joyce would have called the 'limony-limony' smell of lemon verbana. Even the most respectable dressmakers have been guilty in the last twenty years of selling almost consistently synthetic products. These perfumes doubtless reflected a new preference, a trend towards lighter, fruitier smells; yet many people with a highly developed sense of smell complained that they were not true perfumes. Of course a high standard of excellence went into the making of Patou's Joy and Amour-Amour, Worth's Dans la Nuit, or the products of Lelong and Molyneux. But somehow the best of these artificial scents seems something less than a true product of nature captured in a bottle.

With Chanel and her world-famous No. 5 perfume, the art of scents had been completely altered. Since No. 5, all luxury perfumes have been only variations on the essential fruit-and-flower quality. This quality, as with all synthetic perfumes, has perhaps a slightly cloying effect; and to me, none of these has ever achieved the lightness of the classical English scents.

Just as it would be difficult to trace the origin of fashions in dress, so, too, the fashion in perfumes is equally elusive. Women seek, unconsciously perhaps, to create certain atmospheric impressions; and today the perfumers attempt to interpret the atmosphere of the moment, emphasizing simplicity or sophistication as the occasion demands.

Perhaps in no other fashion enterprise do names and institutions have such a rise and fall. Famous names in perfumes change continually. In the twenties Coty and Houbigant were the reigning kings; Chypre of Coty was a typical perfume of that period. Guerlain brought in again scents with more than a whiff of spice during the thirties, and in many instances these have persisted to this day, just as the classic English scents, Green Lime, Floris' Lemon Verbena, Sweet Geranium and others have continued to be appreciated.

After the last war, perfumes changed once more, becoming even more like fresh fruit and much lighter than ever before.

What is the reason for woman wishing, by wearing perfume, to hide her natural human fragrance? Perhaps it is for the same profound reasons that made people take up the fig leaf to alter their nudity—not from shame, but for the beauty of decoration and the myriad psychological benefits of such embellishment. Perfume is ornament, just as clothing is ornament. But if clothing is also a necessary protection against climatic changes, then perfume is a complete luxury, a useless but delightful expression of man's aesthetic sense.

To speak of scents is indirectly to speak of flowers. The average person often does not realize how much taste in flowers or plants, both potted and cut, changes with the years.

He might even be more surprised to discover the extent to which man has altered the biology of the vegetable kingdom in his pursuit of a changing aesthetic.

At the beginning of the century flower arrangements were given little consideration. Flowers as symbols of festivity were in the hands of the caterer or the nurseryman. Gardeners brought their potted plants indoors, placing them near the Nottingham lace curtains or in the fireplace. Full-grown rambler-rose trees, palms and white spiky spiraea in blue and white pots created an atmosphere of festivity. Carnations were placed in silver, trumpet-shaped vases and splayed out like a fountain or a fireworks display.

In general colours were segregated. The Edwardian age was an age of pastel colours, and there was a particular variety of pale salmon pink and apricot-coloured rose which was a great favourite. New roses—Gloire de Dijon, La France and the Mesdames Butterfly, Abel Chatenay and Frau Carl Drushki —were hybridized. These were so revealing of the style of their epoch and the elegance of their day that they remain among the most beautiful of all roses.

Bridal bouquets and court bouquets became enormous. Cart-wheels of carnations and asparagus fern would have additional cascades of carnations hanging from ribbons and loops of tulle. At a wedding at which I appeared as a page, carrying a white Directoire stick with a bouquet on its top, the bridesmaids carried vast bouquets of outsize marguerites mixed with wired cabbage roses.

As the Edwardian age progressed, flowers were still seldom mixed together in many colours, though two-colour schemes— pink and mauve, for example—became permissible, and the enormous silver or glass epergnes on the dining table now boasted asparagus fern among the roses, carnations or sweet peas, while fronds of smilax trailed in arabesques on to the white, starched damask table-cloth. In the drawing room vases of separate coloured sweet peas were dotted with gypsophila or a cloud of babies'-breath. Actresses in drawing-room come-dies were invariably seen arranging wire-stemmed roses while they awaited their fiancés. This activity was stereotyped, and

they all walked to and from a vase, cocking their heads to one side before gliding forward to add a single bloom to the confection. But in *La Dame aux Camélias*, Sarah Bernhardt arranged a huge vase of flowers without once looking at them, accomplishing the gesture with such apparent artistry that when she affixed the final touch there was a spontaneous burst of applause from the audience.

A later innovation consisted of mixing cut flowers with the leaves of some other variety of plant or flower, and magnolia or rhododendron leaves were interspersed with irises or rose-coloured tulips with laurel leaves.

By the twenties, multicoloured tulips were thrust into accumulator jars, for colours were no longer restricted and massed together. Perhaps owing to the Italianate vogue among interior decorators, madonna lilies assumed a Mayfair air, and they too were jammed into fish tanks and jars in the gold and black drawing rooms.

Then came the white period. Those who had white rooms considered white flowers a desideratum. The craze for pristine whiteness became so exaggerated that even the green leaves had to be peeled off the branches of white lilacs and peonies. This stripping process, though a lengthy one, produced its surprising metamorphoses, and a bunch of syringa denuded of its leaves became something finely carved out of Japanese ivory.

It was Mrs Constance Spry who carried the art of Western flower arranging to a point of sophistication that it had previously attained only in the Orient. Even the great Dutch

painters of the sixteenth century did not concoct more elaborate still lifes than Mrs Spry. She would erect great scaffolds of lilies and grasses, or combine orchids with vegetable leaves, dried corn sheaves or bunches of grapes. For winter she would create remarkable arrangements of dried plants and vegetables. She saved pampas grass, honesty and thistles, and ransacked the hedges for old man's beard to give further variety to her ingenious displays.

Mrs Spry had undoubted taste and a love of flowers; but, like so many ideas that became commercialized, her influence was soon overdone. One can see the results of her shop off Bond Street and her Park Avenue emporium at the annual flower show in almost any great city today. Emphasis in floral arrangements is once more inclined towards the exotic, with Oriental-looking branches bursting from an alabaster vase or some gnarled tree bark. Helen Hokinson ladies sit proudly beneath an arrangement of twigs and driftwood (with one cactus flower on which a butterfly is pinned) that has gained them a blue-ribbon prize or at least an 'honourable mention'.

Modern bridal bouquets appear to have gone as far from nature as can be, with sprays of white butterfly orchids, their stems bound with ribbon, or tulips with their petals turned back, looking like a completely different flower. Perhaps flowers, like women's hair, should be arranged quickly and without fuss. A dozen tulips shoved into a vase with one gesture and never arranged individually seem often more beautiful than premeditated efforts.

In Paris, where artificial flowers are works of art, the great florists make their real flowers seem artificial, and at Lachaume and the other florists' whose names are sprinkled through the pages of Proust, flowers out of season have been cultivated to change little throughout the season or throughout the years. The sprays of peach blossom, the delicate fronds of lilac, the long-stemmed red roses, and the giant chrysanthemums today stand in the same vases and positions as they have for the last fifty years. Likewise that unique shop, Solomon's, opposite the Ritz Hotel in London, which unfortunately was a victim of the last war, never altered its arrangements from one year to the next, and the gardenias in cotton wool, the lilies of the valley and the violets were left to speak for themselves. The flower decorations of Goodyear have always remained charmingly nostalgic.

The breeding of flowers reflects the taste of an age. An enormous advance has been effected in later years in the size, colour and forms of the new dahlias. Yet the latest roses are mostly without scent, modernistic in petal formation and often aggressive in their shot colouring of yellow, flame or orange. They reflect the bad taste of the cinema, as do the flame-coloured gladioli splayed out in the cream-coloured urn in the hotel lobby.

The plants that are brought indoors also become subject to the vagaries of taste and environment. From the magnificent fuchsias and 'French' lavenders of the turn of the century, we have turned to the more 'modern' green leaves of the philodendrons, Mexican breadfruits and the ficus plants. In America we find that peperomias, diefienbachias and amarylli are hardy enough to breathe even in the dry atmosphere of the most over-heated apartments.

Under Victorian and Edwardian moons women wore corsages of dark red roses combined with lilies of the valley or gardenias. Today any corsage with wires and ribbons is considered in execrable taste. At most a woman can now wear a single gardenia or three carnations clumped together. Even men's 'buttonholes' have almost disappeared or, on the rare occasions when they are seen, have been simplified. Formerly a piece of maidenhair fern could be seen with a rose; nowdays, if any flower is worn at all, it is only a cornflower, or perhaps a clove carnation, without the addition of its grey, spiky foliage. And only stationmasters are forgiven a rose in the lapel.

But regardless of change, flowers are still intricately linked with humanity, serving at weddings, funerals, festivities, in interior decoration and for man's delight. Falling under fashion's rule, they become popular and then obsolete. Yet the moss rose or the striped tulip, though dropped for a season, will inevitably return to popularity again; while the wild flowers of the field, like people in far provinces who have no need of fashion, continue to propagate whether or not we consider them beautiful.

* * * * *

Sir Max Beerbohm has told us that to offer hospitality, or to accept it, is an instinct man has only acquired in the long course of his self-development. Lions, he points out, do not ask one another to their lairs, nor do birds keep open nests; when you give your dog a bone he does not run out and share it with another, nor does your cat insist of having a circle of friends round her saucer of milk.

Perhaps some caveman with too much bison in his larder, inviting his neighbours to a meal, was the inventor of parties. Perhaps pride and egotism were not unmixed in his motives as is the case with so many other hosts, for the hospitable instinct is never entirely altruistic, but if the aim of parties is that they should be enjoyed, give happiness to the guests, and even take them out of an ordinarily humdrum world into a more exciting sphere, then it is a sound one. Behaviour at parties is permissibly unorthodox; from whence, no doubt, springs the

Lady de Grey.

notion of wine as an incentive for more highly keyed behaviour. But the forms of entertainment change according to each epoch.

Certainly during the glittering Edwardian period a ball was more an exclusive event than an opportunity for fun. Either you were a part of the glorious circle or you were not, and woe betide you if you were one of the goats. For there were no charity dances where you could pay a guinea to hobnob with a duchess, and you had to make the best of dining and dancing at the Carlton Hotel, or the Savoy; the nightclub was unknown.

The imposing Lady Ripon (later Lady de Grey) was responsible for bringing about many changes in the social scene at the beginning of this century. Immensely tall and handsome, with the profile of a parrot, a china complexion and always dressed in the height of elegance, with enormous grace and a flair for music and an appreciation for the arts, Lady Ripon was that rare phenomenon, an intimate of 'Marlborough House circles', a great patrician who numbered among her friends not only the Prince of Wales, and his intimates, but most of the well-known painters, writers and poets of the day together with virtually all the great singers from Covent Garden Opera. By being the first to mix her guests from divergent worlds she created what was later to be known as the 'intelligentsia'. To the large room at Coombe, her country house on Kingston Hill, audaciously frescoed for the times by the Spanish painter, Sert, came a hotchpotch of interesting people whom she mixed with audacity and dash. It was not surprising for Nijinsky to sit next to Queen Alexandra at Sunday luncheon, or for Jean de Reszke to spend the weekend there, among the French tapestries and Jacob chairs, in company with King Edward. By inviting Chaliapin or Caruso to sing, or Pavlova to dance her Bacchanale on her lawn at a garden party, Lady Ripon interpolated the 'divertissement' as part of an 'occasion'. Artists were thereafter paid enormous sums for a few minutes entertainment with which to give cachet to an 'At Home'.

During even the worst years of the First World War, in order to boost morale and give a 'good time' to those back on leave in 'Blighty', a more impromptu form of party was given almost every night of the week, but the aftermath of war

brought about a revolution in entertaining; with the introduction of 'tango teas', cocktails and nightclubs, formality was
dead.

Among the less conventional society hostesses of the
twenties and thirties, Mrs Benjamin Guinness, Mrs Richard
Guinness and Mrs Syrie Somerset Maugham mingled artists,
writers and royalty in their large houses which, with Ambrose
and his orchestra playing 'Time on my Hands', acquired the
sophisticated atmosphere of a sublimated Embassy Club. These
ladies also started the fashion of serving breakfast foods at a
long buffet; haddock, kippers, scrambled eggs, kedgerees and
bacon appeared side by side with oysters and caviare, super-
seding those suppers where silver dishes of vol-au-vents or
stuffed quails were placed on the circular supper tables, together with pink shaded candles.

In London during the twenties, Miss Ponsonby (now
Loelia, Duchess of Westminster) was one of the instigators of
a new type of gala. She lived with her parents in St James's
Palace (where her father held a position close to the King), and
preferred less conventional parties to those attended by other
courtiers and their folk. Miss Ponsonby would, on an impulse,
arrange a last minute party and ask her friends to contribute
an essential ingredient: some benevolent godfather would
supply a band, other guests provided supper, all brought
champagne. Nancy Mitford, and a bevy of new personalities
just down from Oxford, Lord Kinross, Evelyn Waugh, Harold
Acton and Oliver Messel, were the nucleus of a group who
were either of the aristocracy or entertained the aristocracy by
their talents. They had a splendid zest for life and an ability
for expressing that zest. Friends provided impromptu cabarets
with their imitations and impersonations; elaborate and ingenious treasure hunts were organized, and hoax picture-
exhibitions were arranged. The spirit of masquerade reached
new heights, and almost every night there was some excuse for
putting on fancy dress. When others began, in a less imaginative, though wilder fashion, to emulate them, the 'bright
young things' began to receive unfavourable publicity, and
their 'bottle parties' fell into disrepute.

In New York where each separate 'world', as in Italy, though not in France, lives without contamination from any other, Mr Condé Nast, with an elaborate penthouse on Fifth Avenue, invited stars from every hierarchy; and they came to his bidding. The boom of the twenties produced some fabulous New York nights. Whole hotels were taken and decorated to represent a circus; debutantes came out in the Ritz Hotel to the tune of 'Button Up Your Overcoat' and twenty-five thousand dollars. Under a Palm Beach moon, good-time hostesses had their one moment of glory, vanishing, like the ephemerae they were, overnight in the stock market crash.

Mrs Corrigan, a rich woman from Cleveland, Ohio (who was never received by the society of her home town), conquered London society with her parties which had a calculated spontaneity about them; the most eminent or fashionable guests somehow were generally those fortunate enough to win the tombola prizes of gold cigarette cases, and an air of informality was created by the assembled company sitting on the floor while headline artists, receiving more for their ten minutes' turn than they would for performing weekly at the Palace or at Covent Garden, gave an all-star cabaret. Finally, to spare her guests nothing, Mrs Corrigan, amid a rolling of drums, would stand on her henna-coloured head.

The Californian, Miss Elsa Maxwell, operating first in Paris and then after a long interval migrating back to New York, would take over an entire nightclub for an evening. She created her own 'international set', which developed into what is now termed Café Society, and included, as well as persons of social stature, a mingling of celebrities from the cinema or the minor arts. But Miss Maxwell's real ambition is never satisfied until she has made the most distinguished people appear undistinguished. To this purpose she invented many clever 'stunt' parties at which members of the aristocracy of Italy, France and England, together with politicians and statesmen, were knocked off their pedestals. At her first pompous party in London, she made her self-assured guests sit on the floor and blow a feather off a sheet. One of her most publicized evenings was a 'farmyard' affair, where the sophisticated friends appeared as rustics, and milked an artificial cow for champagne. Since Elsa Maxwell has more character and intelligence than many of her guests, she succeeds in her objective. The pictures that inevitably appear after each party make her victims appear wonderfully foolish.

The thirties also produced parties whose aims were perhaps more elevated; their design was to create beauty. In 1928, Mr and Mrs Cole Porter gave a red and white gala in the impressive Palazzo Rizzonico in Venice, where the guests were supplied with costumes of red and white paper that had been produced for the occasion in Milan. Acrobats in red and white performed on wires strung across the courtyard of their Palazzo.

The Sicilian, Duc de Verdura, made his international guests travel all the way to his baroque Palazzo in Palermo to appear in fancy dress costume of the Empire period.

Baron Nicholas de Gunzberg gave a lyrical *fête champêtre* on an island in the Seine embellished with haystacks, cart loads of marguerites and flocks of beribboned sheep. When the then Princess Marina of Greece, and other guests, in crinolines and straw hats, arrived in boats, they created an exquisite picture by Winterhalter.

Perhaps this type of festivity culminated in Charles Beistigui's celebration of the anniversary of the building of his Palazzo Labbia in Venice during the summer of 1951. Its purpose was to create a fête at which Antony and Cleopatra, as painted by Tiepolo on the walls of his great hall, were to receive the Emperor of China and his Court, the Ambassadors from Turkey, Persia and Russia, and the guests from contemporary literature, painting and history. No anachronism was tolerated in the candlelit scene. The flowers and all the arrangements were taken from documents of the eighteenth century; since the guests were asked to arrive in gondolas rather than in motor launches, the scenes outside as well as inside the palace, with the gay Venetian crowds and the flickering lanterns, gave the impression of a Canaletto come to life.

Most recently the Marquis de Cuevas gave a highly organized and elaborate festivity in Biarritz. This brought him more newspaper space than any of his ballet seasons.

Lady Diana Cooper recently remarked that in the days when she came out, attempts other than to call in the florist to provide extra flowers and potted plants, were never made to beautify the setting for a ball. A recent development in creating a gala atmosphere is to cajole some expert such as Oliver Messel, Felix Harbord, the late Rex Whistler or M. Boudin of Jansen in Paris, to create a special décor for the occasion. Sometimes an elaborate fairy story ballroom will appear, mushroom fashion, on the lawns, but the lovely scene, made for one night to fête a foreign royalty or President, to launch a debutante or some less worthy social career, with its heavy construction of wood and plaster hung with silk and tapestries, ornamented with specially created sculptures, garlanded with fruit and flowers, unlike the mushroom, has taken many weeks to come into being.

But these elaborate parties are rare. Grand and magnanimous displays can only be given by those who are endowed with the world's riches. In our age of discretion gestures of splendour seem a little embarrassing, but we should remember that art and culture flourished under the Medicis, Queen Elizabeth and Louis XIV, and at other times when there have been those with the taste, leisure and interest to make the gestures of magnificence. For those of us who have never known the 'grand days' there can still be a great deal of enjoyment to be found when we decide to participate, either as host or guest, on an altogether less elaborate scale; if today we rely less on wired carnations and *vol-au-vents* than on good talk, wit, an interesting exchange of ideas and impressions, there is still the element of the unexpected, the vividly coloured, the exciting, about seeing our friends in the heightened atmosphere of a party.

CHAPTER EIGHTEEN

THE VELVET
GLOVE

AMONG the many remarkable women who have affected
the life and times of the past fifty years, there are some
who defy classification, either because they cannot be
linked to a definite profession or because they go so far beyond
their professions in the expression of personality that it would
be unfair to limit them in that way. Yet all have been tre-
mendously important figures in influencing the multiple aspects
of fashion as expressed in their changing environments. Some
of them have died; all have brought their unique gifts to several
or more decades, and those who still hold the fort give promise
of influencing many more years as well. These pages are devoted to them, Americans and English alike, in the hope that
these verbal sketches convey the indefinable charm of these unusual personalities.

One of the first women ever to wear a short skirt was the
ultra-stylish Phillis Boyd. But it is not merely for introducing

a fashion note such as this that Phillis de Janzé's name should be toasted in memory. She was in many ways a remarkable personality.

A granddaughter of the beautiful Mrs Jordan and William IV, she had inherited artistic ability, charm and distinction, together with a beauty that was haunting and mysterious. She had the face of a puma, an extraordinary lithe line to her strong column-like neck, and the fastidious walk of a crane. It was extraordinary that England could produce something so essentially exotic as this Slavic-looking creature. With her pale complexion, knobbly features, nose of a pugilistic cherub, full cherry lips and huge, pale aquamarine eyes—eyes rimmed with a sharp line of black, as though from a fine mapping pen dipped in India ink—it was little wonder that Lady de Grey should sail up to her and say, 'You *are* like Nijinsky.' But Phillis' reply was typically surprising. 'I am, ain't I,' she laughed.

Henry Lamb, the painter, has said that any beauty whom he admires must have a boat-shaped face; that is, that the widest part of the face must be across the high cheekbones, curving down to the small prow of the oval chin. Here, in Phillis, and *in excelsis*, was Lamb's boat. Her skull was rounded in a rather flat curve. Her hair was like a quarter of a yard of nut-brown satin, or like an exquisite wig that was a size too small and had

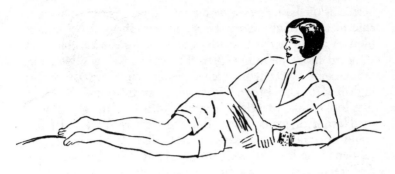

Phillis de Janzé

slipped a fraction out of position, so that the parting ran at an oblique angle. To see Phillis de Janzé turn her head, laugh and swing her dangling earrings from side to side was to marvel at a complete work of art. She could have been produced only in a period of the highest civilization.

But nature alone had not created this phenomenon. Phillis, as a result of her artistry, had helped to make her own appearance the *tour de force* that it became, though as soon as she had finished the creation she forgot about it. There was nothing self-conscious about her: her frankness and sense of reality belied the innate exoticism. She had a carefree, coltish quality that was as refreshing as her waterfalls of laughter.

She might have been part of a sultan's harem, or a court beauty at the time of Charles I. But it happened that she suited the silhouettes of the twenties so perfectly one did not know if it was she who had invented them or they that had invented her. The truth was both Phillis de Janzé and the twenties made a unique combination.

After her marriage to the Vicomte de Janzé in 1922, Phillis lived in Normandy, irritating her English friends by alluding to France as '*mon pays*'. She migrated to Paris, exchanged the somewhat picturesque type of dressing that she had adopted as a young art student for the ultra-smart suits from the house of Patou, for whom she now worked, and was highly publicized as the best-dressed woman in France. She gave an extra chic to the straight short skirts and the long-waisted jumper blouses and was the first to wear a baby's cap on her sleek shingled head, tied under her chin with a velvet shoestring. With her exaggeratedly arched instep she wore impossibly high-heeled shoes of red leather with a strap around the ankles that looked like bracelets or reminded one of the shoes worn by Harriet of match fame. But the lady with the boat face could not take clothes seriously. She left Patou, she left her husband, she left France; the only thing she didn't leave was the French taste that she brought with her when she settled in England.

As a young girl Phillis had shown promise as a draughtsman at the Slade School and could perhaps have developed into another Gwen John. But she was content to make her life a work of art and cultivated a gift of unending leisure in which to enjoy the Regency rooms she had arranged for herself in London. Here she read eighteenth- and nineteenth-century books on travel, or sat, wrapped in a shawl, under the fig tree in her small garden, writing long descriptive letters to a friend abroad or working on an extraordinary piece of Persian needlework embroidery. Phillis received friends from all walks of life and always had time to devote to them and to her lovers.

For Phillis de Janzé was always in love and always had a posse of ardent lovers around her. She lived for and by her amours. She would provide them, at any time of the day or night, with a sympathetic haven, sitting cross-legged on the floor while they ate boiled eggs, oysters or foie gras and drank burgundy, listening to her clipped, rather precious voice as she beguiled them with fascinating stories told in the coarsest language. Phillis could be Hogarthian in her manner, and when she flew into a rage became the original shrew.

As the years passed, her interests became ever more absorbing and varied, allowing little time to bother about her appearance, though she always chose her things, whether from a barrow or from Woolworth's, with the touch of the connoisseur. She was wonderfully oblivious to the squalors and mediocrities of life. The look of the twenties gave way to a more barbaric or 'artistic' appearance, with gipsy skirts and black blouses; she grew her hair so that it fell in fronds around her sturdy neck. To see her shopping at Fortnum and Mason with her maid, friend and companion, both wearing identical hats, was like coming across a figure out of mythology, a goddess living in disguise, or a supernatural spirit with her Pekingese dog as her familiar.

If she had not been racked at an early age by an unknown illness, Phillis de Janzé would doubtless have been another Lady Hester Stanhope. For she became an ardent traveller, journeying in great discomfort to the most unlikely parts of the globe. She would go for a summer holiday to Haiti, and in Arabia fell in love with a pasha.

But though her friends mourn her loss and are regretful that Phillis de Janzé was not able to continue her activities into middle age (and there is no question but that she would realistically have faced up to and adapted herself to any change of conditions), there can only be rejoicing that her life was so complete. By living as she did, she fulfilled herself. It was irrelevant for her to leave a portfolio of drawings as a legacy: her contribution to her time was herself. Phillis de Janzé was her own finite expression. It is people such as she who, though not public characters and unknown to the masses, nevertheless have enormous influence on their devoted friends and disciples, possessing in themselves the rare seed that sows itself in unlikely places, there to blossom and enrich the world for those who come after.

* * * * *

Lady Juliet Duff has for many years held a unique position behind the scenes of the London theatre. She has remained completely stage-struck, counting among her friends all sorts of lights from the theatre, big and small, high and low. Their regard for her is mutual. Many successful playwrights who know little of the mentality of the real aristocracy but try nevertheless to evoke 'high life' explain that their duchess or *grande dame* is 'Let's face it, really Juliet'.

Among Lady Juliet's theatrical friends few are capable of assessing her real worth. The majority can appreciate only in a vague way her good manners and taste. Often when a point is raised in the discussion of a new production with the management and producer concerning a phrase, a girandole, a window seat, or whether a room should be built in a certain style, the criterion is always, 'Would it be like this at Juliet's?' With questions of etiquette and behaviour she is apt to receive a telephone call from the provinces (where the latest play is being tried out prior to coming to London) at any time of the day or night for advice on some particular point. Actors, authors and producers alike know she will throw herself into their problems with such conscientiousness that she is likely to follow up her verbal advice with a telegram or will personally motor for miles to beg, borrow or steal the requisite gold wastepaper basket.

Lady Juliet Duff not only inherited many beautiful Fabergé objects and French eighteenth-century pictures from her mother, Lady de Grey (the Duchesse de Guermantes of London), but also possesses her mother's graceful gift of striking a happy note between grandeur and cosiness.

Her rooms never sacrifice comfort for effect. Far from being stage sets, they are the living emanation of their occupant's interests and tastes. The upholstered easy chairs, shoulder-high screens of striped silk or white and gold crackled painted bookcases, which in a decorator's house would be considered impermissible, her china owl of a lamp, her blunt-pencil drawings by relations, her calendars from Tattersall's or the late Queen Mary, her snapshots in *passe-partout* frames, and her sewing baskets—all of these details give extra charm to a room that boasts magnificent Jacob chairs with rams' heads and a remarkable Oudry swan sitting on two eggs as it is being frightened by a ferocious dog in a flash of lightning. Her other pictures are a jumble of Eve Kirk, Tchelitchew and John drawings, together with Boilly and a contemporary portrait of Madame de Pompadour's dog.

Lady Juliet is continually altering the arrangement of her

Lady Juliet Duff at Bulbridge, 1953

furniture. After driving a hundred miles from London to arrive home late at night, she will suddenly say before going to bed, 'I see now that desk should be moved over there.' Sleep forgotten, she then starts to reorganize the drawing room completely, to the surprise of the household next morning. The heavier the furniture, the more she is inspired to use her imagination and strength. Each new scheme seems more comfortable and pleasing to the eye than the last.

Lady Juliet's colour sense is restrained to such a degree that only when a room is assembled does it come to life. The patterns of pea-soup green, dull rose and grey seem dull and lifeless in the hand, but in her rooms they create a harmonious ambiance.

Although she has carried out her mother's dictum that every room ought to contain at least one shabby object and *une note de rouge* (Edwardian ladies were very fond of sprinkling their sentences with French phrases), Lady Juliet herself has few theories about decoration. Like manners, she considers it best not to think too much about it, though her instinct is remarkably firm, and she seldom listens to advice, even of those whose taste she most admires. One feels that if interior decoration had never been invented, Lady Juliet's house would always be the same. Her talent is natural and unconscious of others. Every room is recognizably her own, with its particular landmarks: the table covered in the French fashion with a rather shabby circular cloth of brocade, cluttered with bibelots; a brass model of the Eiffel Tower from the exhibition of 1870; a plaster cast of Coquelin as Cyrano, Titania's flowers in pots, or enamel frames by Fabergé containing infinitesimal snapshots of Queen Alexandra and her sisters.

Lady Juliet Duff's combinations of flowers, grasses and herbs, picked from her garden, are always natural and unsnobbish. She never makes flowers appear grand or expensive, and no field grass is considered too plebeian to be part of a grandiose 'still life' in her drawing room. Somehow she lifts those coarse, and to me quite horrid, Poulsen roses, or such flowering shrubs as weigela, privet, choisya and ceanothus, to her own heights of grandeur.

Among the women whose vocations involve them with the world of fashion, none is more strikingly individual than Mrs Vreeland of the American *Harper's Bazaar*. She is indeed such a powerful personality in her own right, and so little dependent on the fashion world for her terms of appeal, that many of her friends never think of her in connection with printer's ink. Outside business hours Mrs Vreeland talks neither about her work nor the worlds with which it is involved; she seems totally unaffected by the more fatal aspects of fashion, its determined snobbery, its ruthless pursuit of the new for its own sake. The lures of cocktail parties and celebrities have little interest for her, and they certainly offer no competition to the husband and two grown sons with whom she spends the majority of her leisure hours.

Yet in the world of fashion the name of Diana Vreeland brings a smile of warmth to the lips of all and sundry. Though she has no married daughter in Provence to write to, Mrs Vreeland is unquestionably the Madame de Sévigné of fashion's court: witty, brilliant, intensely human, gifted like Madame de Sévigné with a superb flair for anecdotes that she communicates verbally rather than in epistles, Mrs Vreeland is more of a connoisseur of fashion than anyone I know and possesses both the seriousness and the humanism that are necessary for making her own tolerant moral judgments about the behaviour of the world in which she is involved.

To the observer Diana Vreeland's physical appearance is like an authoritative crane; and though, unlike that bird, she always stands upon two feet, she can and does give the marvellous illusion of balancing upon one. With her pelvis thrust boldly forward to an astonishing degree, and the torso above it sloping backwards at a forty-five degree angle, Mrs Vreeland invites comparison to the medieval slouch, and indeed wants only the hennin and the veil hanging from her head in order to be catapulted backwards in time some six hundred years. Students of posture could no doubt find a certain affinity between the medieval stance and that of the twenties. It may well be, as I suspect, that Mrs Vreeland matriculated in that Great Gatsby era when ladies willed their bodies to look as much like cooked asparagus as possible, taking the form of whatever sofa or chair they sat in. But whereas the posture of the twenties could be unattractive, it looks good on Diana Vreeland.

Above her small-boned, beautiful body, with its feet like the bound feet of Chinese ladies, Mrs Vreeland's head sits independently on top of a narrow neck and smiles at you. Everything about her features is animated by amused interest: her nose, as broad as an Indian's, is boldly assertive; her eyes twinkle; her mouth emits the most amazingly aggressive and masculine laugh, a red laugh that is taken up by her cheeks, expertly rouged with an art which has gone out of style and of which she is one of the few remaining masters. Surrounding these features like a metallic skullcap is her navy-blue hair, which she wears lacquered back from her face. Diana Vreeland has, in fact, a fetish about hairlines and believes that, together with hands, they are the secret of elegance.

Mrs Vreeland has an almost Chinese appearance, with her black tunics and plethora of gold jewellery, although Truman Capote said that her style is based on high-yellow chic. Combined with this compact, fresh-as-a-bandbox appearance and a walk like a rope unwinding, Diana Vreeland's personality is apt to prove a little startling to those who meet her for the first time. She bounces with a life that is utterly natural to her. Her resonant voice covers the gamut from an emphatic whisper to an equally emphatic and almost Rabelaisian roar. The total effect is almost Falstaffian, more remarkable precisely because it issues from a slim wisp of a body. Yet there is not the slightest trace of vulgarity in her positive, booming vivacity. She is totally free of any affectation and so perfect in her manners and her intense human consideration for others that she could never be found guilty of violating even the most subtle of the rules that govern human intercourse.

The terms of Mrs Vreeland's human appeal are liberally peppered with an astonishing slang. One would think that she spent hours in ambiguous Times Square drugstores or Fifty-second Street night clubs, absorbing the highly coloured range of pimentoed expressions that are an integral part of her linguistic repertoire. Nor is her slang ever out of date. She will

Mrs Vreeland, 1954

innovate expressions long before they have become popularly known. This gamey speech, combined with her personality, inevitably sends her friends off into gales of laughter at almost every sentence.

Mrs Vreeland's hours between the office and dinner are often given to massages, facial treatment and dress fittings, as well as to doctors, osteopaths and chiropractors, for she is a complete believer in modern medical science. At the cocktail hour in her apartment she will probably serve tea and genuine madeleines which are made by her cook, while dinner visitors may always expect the unexpected almond in the cake, or bits of orange rind in the orange compôte.

The visitor is ushered into her apartment from the hallway of a rather anonymous building, but her quarters are far from anonymous. The living room is completely personal. Over her desk is a bulletin board on which she pins newspaper clippings, postcards and pictures; very much in the Cocteau tradition, though the effect is as clean and immaculate as Diana Vreeland herself. The room is lined with long, low banquettes covered with blue-and-white cotton fabric and loaded with cushions of scarlet cloth. Large bowls of pearl chips contain paper white narcissi in bloom, though their scent can scarcely account for the fragrance that fills the room and comes from the Guerlain atomizer burning in discreet, unseen depths of the apartment. Her taste, as exemplified by the objects in the room and the paintings and drawings on the walls, is all-embracing. Piero della Francesca rubs shoulders with drawings by Christian Bérard, while gold-mesh fish paperweights curve their tails on her desk. Among her drawings is a wonderful early sketch of her by Augustus John, showing the Modigliani eyelids and the generously large nose that almost quivers with the sensitive vibrations of her personality. Bookshelves are filled not only with art books but with assortments of shells or curious pieces of glass or china which have caught her fancy. It is a full room, almost a Victorianly stuffed room, but it does not seem so, for every last shell is polished, and there is not a speck of dust to cry accusation.

These surroundings reflect Diana Vreeland's haphazard genius. She has educated herself to be a very remarkable piece of civilization and embodies knowledge of European tastes, together with a great appreciation for literature and architecture. She is an aesthete without being either a snob or an intellectual. It is completely refreshing.

But Diana Vreeland has always had an original character and natural flair. If she is not a beautiful woman, she has certainly made herself an arresting one. So arresting is she that, indeed, it is not uncommon for her to leave the room for a moment to have a Vitamin B_1 injection and then return nonchalantly a moment later, taking up the conversation where she left off. This is all part of her scientific way of preserving inspiration, so that when you do see her she is always, like an athlete, at her best, talking as one would write a poem, allying her verbal brilliance with the novelist's true gift of description and a tremendous sledge-hammer emphasis that takes the form of repeating phrases with a Claudel-like incantation. But she knows that all her great personalities are excessive, and her own excess is as completely natural as that of a great actress. Everything that has cropped up along the line has been absorbed by her, until she is like a fine tea mixture of orange pekoe and pekoe. There is nothing artificial about her; she will never lead you off the scent and has no desire for pretence. She has wisdom and a hard philosophical core, has become cultivated through her enthusiasms, acquiring the exact poetic approach. But for all her remarkable human talent, Diana Vreeland is no egoist. She has an enormous respect for other people's work, for their personalities and needs. In this she manifests a genuine human warmth which is neither prying nor curious, but desirous of being helpful. If she senses that a friend is in inner or outer trouble, she will telephone on an instinct, just to announce that she is there.

Altogether she is one of the most remarkable creatures who has lived and worked in the zany confines of the fashion world. A combination of Madame de Sévigné and Falstaff, Mrs Vreeland graces that world with her presence, as unique a presence as it has ever boasted.

In a book that pretends to give any indication of the people who have influenced the taste of their time it would be an omission if no mention was made of Lady Cunard. Not that she has had many disciples or successful imitators, for Lady Cunard was unique. But in her own individual way she did more to generate an interest in the major and minor arts than perhaps any governmental body. The newspapers wrote of her as 'society hostess, friend of royalty, statesmen and men of letters, enthusiast for music, great spendthrift'. These phrases seem so remote in connection with the real Lady Cunard. She was a hostess, yes; leader of fashion, yes; a music lover and devotee of the fine arts. But other people have filled these roles with a greater weight and power. Her distinction is that she possessed so deft a lightness of touch and such remarkable originality.

Lady Cunard appears in many contemporary memoirs, and when she died in 1948 some of her literary friends tried their

Lady Cunard
at the Dorchester Hotel
London. 1941.

best to evoke her special flavour in their obituaries. Although
her personality was so vivid that no one who had met her for
more than a few moments could ever forget her, and all who
came within the orbit of her charm were fascinated, she somehow defied definition. As a brilliantly witty conversationalist,
she knew the value of surprise, and it is perhaps due to her
frankness and unconventionality that one can now say almost
anything to anybody. That she moved in the conventional
world of society and made that world bow to her idiom was
her triumph, for she was essentially a *fantaisiste*. Although she
respected their strict attention to rules, she herself paid little
attention to them. When she played the game of society, she
was like a great comedienne; yet Lady Cunard was too sincere
and genuine a person to be an actress for long.

Born Maud Burke, she came to Europe from San Francisco
via New York, where she lived with a French grandmother.
Her first ten years in England were spent as the wife of the

middle-aged and fox-hunting Sir Bache Cunard, who maintained an enormous house, Neville Holt, in Leicestershire. The hardest-bitten members of the hunt asked in voices of horror, 'Who is that extraordinary young woman that comes to the meet covered with turquoises?' But Lady Cunard showed little reciprocal interest in the horsey set and spent her time reading Shakespeare and Balzac. From earliest childhood she had been a consummate bookworm and was thoroughly grounded in the Greek and Latin classics. Indeed, for most of her life she read until four or five in the morning, and her literary memory was such that she never forgot a book once she had finished it. The characters she became acquainted with in books were as real to her, if not more so, than those she met in life.

By degrees she came to know artists, musicians and intellectuals, inviting them to Neville Holt. But Lady Cunard was not really happy until she had left the country and settled in a house in London, where she soon created a stronghold for the social world that impinged upon the intelligentsia. She became a sprightly critic, speaking with a delicate touch but much authority upon a diversity of subjects. George Moore was her inseparable friend. Together with literature, music became her passion. The best artists of the day were bidden to perform for her, and her friend, Sir Thomas Beecham, relied upon her encouragement for the survival of opera in England. Enormous sums of her own fortune were spent to launch a further season, while she tirelessly bludgeoned her rich but vandalistic friends into subscribing for boxes at Covent Garden, and in a subtle way she influenced and educated those in high positions who were flattered into feeling they were the means whereby the arts could be more widely appreciated.

Lady Cunard's appearance was a *tour de force*. Her nose was beaked and her chin recessed; none of her features was regular. Yet by the way she presented herself she overcame all physical obstacles and succeeded in looking the embodiment of her own charming wit and gaiety. Her skin was incandescently white. Her cheeks, unlike those of other fashionable ladies of the last thirty years, were always rouged bright carnation pink. Added to these were cerise lips and hair as pale yellow and fluffy as the feathers of a day-old chick. Lady Cunard's legs had the fragility of a sparrow's, and for shoes she must have taken a smaller size than Cinderella. Her gesticulations were bold yet gracious. Though in later years she was twisted with rheumatism, the hands remained always so expressive.

Lady Cunard dressed in the height of the latest fashion, choosing the most exaggerated garments. But she wore them with a certain amusement and was aware that they had little affinity with her. She once described to me, in uproarious detail, a mad Poiret dress she had worn. 'Would you believe it,' she said, almost overcome by her own warm chortles that sounded like mice in the wainscoting, 'it had two trains edged with sable. And, if you please, it was called *Tramcar*.' Somehow she gave to her clothes a 'brio' that took one back to the delights of the most impressionable moments of childhood.

I feel very privileged that for nearly twenty years I was a friend of hers. I never ceased to admire her originality and fantasy, her courage and lack of self-consciousness and wit. In France, Italy, Germany, America, I was to see Lady Cunard in many varied and sometimes tragic circumstances. At other times they have been curiously comic. On one occasion I rescued her from a circus roundabout that revolved too fast for her fancy, and in another setting picked her up covered with the contents of a pail of milk after she had been bunted by a cow. I have known as much enjoyment in her company as with any single person and would often say to myself while in her presence, 'At this moment I am happy.' Like others, I felt she had a unique sympathy for me and my problems, and she understood all that was passing through my mind sometimes even better than I knew myself. Her real warmth and sympathy endeared her to her friends and made her a touching and vulnerable person. For artists and younger people she radiated a glow of appreciation.

When I first knew Lady Cunard she was living in a large house in Grosvenor Square, decorated in the French eighteenth-century taste with a drawing room rather unsuitably hung with Marie Laurencins in looking-glass frames. Her luncheon or dinner guests would be assembled in a small downstairs bou-

doir, eyeing one another somewhat coldly as they waited for
their hostess to appear. Emerald, as she had become, considering the name more euphonious than Maud—Emerald Cunard
was invariably late. She would sometimes come downstairs in
an extremely peppery temper. 'Oh, everything's gone wrong.
Why doesn't the footman open the windows and attend to the
fire?' She would struggle with the cords of the window and
manipulate the poker in a most ineffectual way. Then suddenly
she would right herself. A smile would creep over her face and
she would chuckle at her own absurdity. Or she would come
into the room with, 'My maid's furious at me for coming down.
She says I'm not properly dressed and she hasn't had time to
straighten my eyelashes.'

Then she would introduce her guests to each other. 'Do you
mean to say you don't know the Ambassador? Why, Mr Ambassador, this is little Sheila: we all know little Sheila.' (Lady
Milbanke would smile like a Lely court beauty.) 'And here's
little Poppy. Everyone loves little Poppy, everyone's crazy
about little Poppy.' With her upturned palm pointing towards
an elderly gentleman of somewhat formidable appearance she
would say, 'This is Lord Berners, a saucy fellow.' As soon as
the introductions were over she would forthwith commit herself to create an entertainment at which the most widely
opposed people, linked together in a bond of admiration for
their most surprising hostess, would talk sympathetically to
one another.

Lady Cunard's genius shone in the manner in which she
presided over the small, circular, green-painted dining table.
She would bring out the latent qualities in each of her guests
and was past mistress at the art of giving the field to anyone
with something interesting to say, just as she would abruptly
snatch it from them when they showed signs of becoming
bores. If she herself performed, it was a virtuoso indulging in
persiflage or heroics. She was brilliant in her sense of timing.
The inflections in her husky little voice were so varied, her
gestures so telling, her chuckles so effective, and her confiding
manner so mock-sincere that one knew one was present at a
unique occasion.

319

Lady Cunard made many enemies. There were certain people whom she could not appreciate. Perhaps she would not have succeeded in establishing herself among the more rigorously formal society of the Edwardians, but she brought a lightness and originality to even the conventional circles of the late Georgian period. There is a story that when the Duchess of York became Queen of England she sighed, 'I'm afraid even now we shall never be included in Lady Cunard's set. You see, she has so often said that Bertie and I are not fashionable.'

With the Second World War, Emerald Cunard's world collapsed. The Grosvenor Square house was empty, the footmen were called up, the Marie Laurencins sent to the sale room. Emerald, after an unfortunate visit to America, where she hated, and was hated by, all but a few devoted and loyal friends, came back to live in two rooms of the Dorchester Hotel. Society as she had known it no longer existed; her finances were said to be somewhat rickety, and she told her friends how impossible it was for her to economize. Even under these straitened circumstances she managed to present herself, paradoxically enough, at her peak. Never before had she seemed so fully integrated as a personality; never did she appear to her friends wiser, kinder and more understanding. Although, living in a large hotel, she was immune from the more rigorous restrictions of rationing and queueing, yet she reacted like a sensitive barometer to the changes that were taking place outside her ivory tower. She moved with the times to such a degree that she labelled as 'dated' much younger people whose point of view had not become adapted to the changing world.

But however much the world changed, Lady Cunard's intense interest in people always illuminated her life. She was a real collector of personalities; not, like other hostesses, with the intention of being the first to show them off, but out of a profound sympathy. She would discover people of merit—an unknown painter, a promising politician. A brilliant talent scout, she would rout out the author of some play she had seen in the small basement of an arts society production in the purlieus of London, to give him help and encouragement. Emerald Cunard could never become old.

Lady Cunard From the etching by Rzewuski 1929.

Her sitting room at the Dorchester was an oasis of civilization in the barbaric wastes of war. A lift would take one from
a dreary world beneath to the seventh floor. On arrival at
Room 707, one was enchanted by the sight of an array of cherry-
coloured chairs, boule furniture, desks ornamented with ormolu figures, and, among the *objets d'art* and most exquisite of
all, Emerald, like a fantastic canary bird, holding forth on some
strange topic with tremendous vivacity, reviving everyone
around her by the originality of her provocative mind.

Sometimes during the middle of the night I would be
awakened by the telephone. Oblivious of the fact that other
people were asleep, Emerald would be at her most conversa-
tionally inspired. After lying laughing at her in the dark, I
would switch on the light in order to make a note of some enchanting or inspiring remark, but without her vocal inflection
and out of context the pencilled quotations seemed lifeless next
morning. Yet perhaps a little of her can be seen through the

321

following excerpts which I have picked at random from diaries.

In a 'stage confidence' tone she would relate the latest scandal: 'I don't know her, of course, but my doctor does. Doctors know everybody. A lot of people say she's very common, but I don't know about that. Nowadays all that sort of thing is changed. It's the Duke that's now considered beyond the pale, and this particular Duke has made the terrible mistake of falling in love. Well, he couldn't help that, poor fellow, but I think perhaps he shouldn't have told his wife about it. He did, and the shock was a little bit too much for her and she died from it, and people didn't like that. The poor man's been dreadfully criticized.'

Without her sweetness, her edicts might have seemed a little hard. But she would raise a tremendous laugh when, in shocked seriousness, she would confide to the whole dinner table: 'Babies are a terrible lot of trouble! Babies are terrible!' or, 'Husbands can't love wives; no, that is not possible!' or, 'Boys must not marry girls!'

Although Emerald was a fantastic, she often brought others down to reality. One day Sir Thomas Beecham was holding forth. 'A cello,' he said, 'cannot be listened to by itself for more than a minute, or else you want to murder the man who plays it, and after ten minutes you do. murder him.'

Lady Cunard asked, 'Yes, and what does all that mean?'

When interrupted by the telephone, Emerald would pick up the receiver and say impatiently, 'Yes, yes, who is it? Not that I care.' Sometimes she was a character from Oscar Wilde, asking, 'You are not going to offend me by offering me champagne, are you? What I want is water. It is so difficult to get water. Water is so scarce in London.' Or when genuinely admiring some stranger: 'Isn't her hair lovely? Such a beautiful colour. It takes a little dye to make that effect.' When looking at pictures in a small gallery off Bond Street, she said to the salesman in a horrified voice, 'Oh no, you must not show me anything Dutch. Don't you dare show me anything Dutch. I can't bear anything Dutch!'

When towards the end of her life things might have been considered difficult for Lady Cunard, she had few regrets. 'I know I should look after my affairs, but I don't and it's terrible. My house is burned and it should have been insured and it wasn't and it's all my own fault and it's terrible but we won't think about it.'

Sometimes she would say in a frivolous manner something that meant more to her than she realized: 'Maternity is a strong natural instinct and I abhor nature. I believe in art.' She made her life a work of art that was as delicate, witty, gay, sensitive and eloquent as herself.

When Emerald became ill, the bodily aches and pains to which she was not accustomed baffled and lowered her vitality. She felt life was leaving her. At a small dinner party in her room she told her friends she did not think she could survive another three months; and since the world was becoming so ugly and life unlike everything she considered it should represent, she was not sorry to go. Thereupon Emerald Cunard raised a glass of champagne and said, 'I drink to my death.'

Reared in the Edwardian school by a remarkable mother, Lady Diana Cooper is one of the few living aristocrats who can violate all the rules and still keep her balance on the pedestal of *noblesse oblige*. Her roots are so deeply embedded in tradition that, like some incredible plant, she thrives in an atmosphere of bohemianism without ever departing from her origins. English tradition is behind her whether she is cohorting with theatrical people or the highest society.

One-time ambassadress to France, Lady Diana has never allowed herself to become conventional: she mingles with commoners and keeps the royal touch. Her station is such that she might conceivably have married the Prince of Wales, but chose to marry Alfred Duff Cooper, later Lord Norwich, whose recent and premature death brought to an end one of the happiest and most stimulating partnerships.

Like most complex people, Lady Diana has many facets. She gives the impression that she bathes only in asses' milk and has been pampered since birth by attendant slaves. But nothing could be further from the truth: her looks belie her character, for she is the complete opposite of this superficial

Lady Diana Cooper - 1953 -
Norah.

appearance, being a woman of quick intelligence, tremendous courage, and great loyalty. Her rigid Edwardian training has left her with a cast-iron discipline that never rusts. She can set herself the most difficult tasks, flagellating herself in her endeavours. She never allows herself to look fatigued, can drive five hundred miles in a motor-car and be the life and soul of the party on arrival. Her mind, likewise, is constantly exercised through the reading and analysis of books, a pastime which she often carried on aloud with her husband. And though she staunchly affirms that she is not *avant-garde* and that her appreciation stops with Cézanne, she maintains a lively interest in new art and artists.

This discipline reflects, too, in her sense of obligation to others and, combined with her aristocratic grace, it renders her capable of great empathy and concentration where people are concerned. Often she will help her friends without ever letting them know that she has done so.

Having been born a blonde, Lady Diana accentuates her pastel beauty by wearing the pale colours with which her mother taught her to compliment her natural opalescence, and the result is a luminosity that creates the effect of all the lights being turned on when she enters a room. Yet Lady Diana thinks of herself as a brunette and possesses many of the gipsy's bohemian traits. Little wonder, then, that the public has always had the wrong impression of her. It cannot believe that any great beauty should be so without airs and graces, and mistakes her naturalism for affectation.

From a spartan upbringing, Lady Diana has now, of her own volition, turned to the life of a Boy Scout at holiday camp. Like a sailor, she can tie every sort of knot and is executive in all manner of ways. When the car breaks down, it is Lady Diana who mends the punctured tyre. She can wallpaper a room and sew muslin curtains, knows how to do everything from embarking upon carving a ham and making cheeses to wiring a bouquet of lilies of the valley. In addition to this impromptu virtuosity, she will never accept a negative answer. She seldom stops working and allows herself very few hours of sleep each night. However late to bed, Lady Diana is on the

Lady Diana Cooper

job early in the morning, often bringing a cup of tea to wake members of the household who have early trains to catch.

Lady Diana's appearance is always romantic or picaresque, and her styles have changed only in detail during the years that she has remained one of England's great beauties. She has clothed herself in a series of costumes that range from those of an apotheosized cowboy, a highwayman, or a sublimated peasant with dirndl skirt and sandals. With head tied in a chiffon scarf she is like a nun in a coif. In a yachting cap Lady Diana is a young naval commander in an operetta, while oyster-coloured satin metamorphoses her into a court lady of Charles II.

When on rare occasions Lady Diana conforms to the dictates of fashionable dressmakers, appearing in the latest Paris dress, she is less effective than when she improvises out of her own imagination and her own wardrobe, creating costumes for all and every occasion, from buying vegetables in a Venetian market to attending a ball at Buckingham Palace. Her treasure chest doubtless contains corduroy trousers, large pink chiffon handkerchiefs or babies' caps with which to cover her hair, boxes full of artificial flowers, tartan shawls, some imitation diamond stars, bolts of taffetas and lengths of classical drapery, a great collection of picture hats brought from Mexico, Morocco, California and Sussex, tricorne hats, casquettes, and, for more occasional use, a busby.

In assembling her rooms, Lady Diana attacks the procedure with a mannish nonchalance. Nothing is carefully calculated. Somehow the things that conform to her taste, the grey brocades, the oyster colours, the jardinieres, the baskets, seem to fall into her capable hands. Like the true artist, she is almost heavy-handed in her arrangement of flowers. As she thrusts a rose among the flowers of high summer, she asides with a wink, 'There's nothing like a rose for pulling up a mixed vase.'

Her frankness of manner is often baffling to those accustomed to the pretences of the *beau monde*. Nor has she any false modesty. As ambassadress to France, she was direct and outspoken. 'You're ten minutes too soon,' she said to a marquis who had suggested he would like to see her at the British Embassy in Paris and had arrived before the appointed hour. Intuiting that he wished some special help or service from her, she continued, 'And what can I do for you?' The Marquis, at first somewhat taken aback by the direct approach, at last began to explain his wishes, while Lady Diana, concentrating on all he had to say, proceeded to change her clothes in front of him. By the time the other guests had arrived at the appointed tea hour, she had completed her toilet and given her constructive suggestions for help.

Lady Diana knows the enjoyment of making an expensive gesture, but she also gains satisfaction from bringing economy to a fine art. Her dislike of waste is intense. During the last year of a war-scarred England she was on her way through the sitting room of her house at Bognor one early morning to milk her cow, when she noticed, among the litter of cards and ashes from the previous night's bridge game, that two of the players had left two half-drunk glasses of whisky and soda. Though she herself hates the taste of whisky, she exclaimed, 'Appalling waste,' and, making a wry face, drank both glasses to the dregs.

To enumerate Lady Diana's virtues is to risk being accused of exaggeration or prejudice. Yet who does not warrant high praise if not a beauty who is a wit, an enlightening *raconteuse*, and a brilliant correspondent (it may well be that she will live in posterity by her letters)? She is an artist in life with countless artistic gifts, a friend with unswerving loyalties, at once business-like, capable, imaginative and full of heartbreak, an eccentric who is frank and outspoken with the knowledge of when not to mention any given subject. Lady Diana, indeed, seems to be a woman with most of the rare qualities.

CONCLUSIONS

IT was Colly Cibber who said that one might as well be
out of the world as be out of fashion. But far more important than being stylish or *passé* is the question of our
attitude towards fashion. Those who disregard it completely
are the losers, for they miss the delightful multiplicity and
charm of the fads that reflect our deepest psychological needs.
He who ignores fashion ignores life itself.

In the course of this book I have hidden a number of general
ideas behind particular people and things; or perhaps the ideas
have emerged from a discussion of the individual. Having
arrived at the end of a voyage of discovery, I now begin to
realize the involved and complicated pattern that emerges from
individual threads. It would be difficult to extract any authoritative moral lessons or philosophic meaning, but a few con-
clusions are inescapable.

It seems obvious that changes in fashion correspond with
the subtle and often hidden network of forces that operate on

society—political, economic and psychological factors all play their part. In this sense fashion is a *symbol*.

Why should man, however, who is forever seeking eternal and changeless values, be so concerned with surface and fleeting ones? Is there a changeless spirit behind the endless mutations of life itself? Perhaps the truth is that no form of expression by man can satisfy him. In art as in fashion, new styles or forms seem only a ceaseless and urgent search for some ultimate form of expression. Born in a changing physical body, man seeks the absolute, yet ironically creates things which are as changing and ephemeral as himself.

Even these changes have a certain constancy, however. There are forms that reappear in various ages with only slight variations. It is surprising how certain peasant designs and materials resemble the costume of the early Egyptians. A modern woman, when she goes to the hairdresser, may be unaware that the Babylonians had created similar hair styles some thousands of years ago. Thus, though it is true that fashions, *per se*, are never revived, there are constants which manifest themselves anew throughout the years.

Eastern clothing shows the great aesthetic perfection that can emerge only from a long tradition of wearing the same kind of garment. In our Western world we can see the same example in church vestments, riding habits, uniforms and liveries, these forms of apparel being more rigidly subject to tradition because of religious, ritualistic or functional reasons.

Why does European fashion not tend towards some kind of simplicity and beauty, some tunic or toga that would serve for longer than a single decade? The answer undoubtedly lies in our deep-rooted perversity, our incessant inner need for change and more change. This desire for change is costly. Billions of pounds and dollars and francs and lire and kroner and piasters and pesos are spent yearly.

Those whose lives or work are involved in fashion breathe the air of instability: they are like the Mexican farmer who several years ago discovered a volcano growing in his cornfield. Those who work in fashion's sphere must expect the worst and should provide for an early demise. Unfortunately he who gets

The Empress of Japan, 1910

Hindu styles

caught in the wheels forgets the lessons of the past. We know that others die, but our own death is inconceivable.

Fashion, however, has its happier aspects as well as its vicious ones. Our latter-day promotion, also, though it has done much towards standardizing fashion and robbing it of its air of mystery, has raised the general level of taste. Much as one may disagree with many of the influences of the wholesale trade and its merchandise, it has helped to create a potential canon of taste. Utility and ready-made clothing are today fabricated along better lines than ever before. The average person all over the world has become more sophisticated in matters of taste.

Unfortunately tastes and values cannot escape a certain vulgarization when filtered down through a great number of people. One has only to examine the appalling styles and tastes displayed in the shops where cheap furniture and household objects are sold. The average person still accepts the most hideous designs in wallpaper, cretonnes, linoleum and crockery, and one wonders if public bad taste imposes itself on the manufacturers of furniture, clothing, china and moving pictures.

If you are a poor man in England, even presuming that you have good taste, it is hard to buy anything which is not inevitably of bad design. By contrast, in any European country, Italy or even France, you can go to any village, and though bad taste has already infiltrated even the smallest shops, there are still to be found good, simple designs in pure colours, the product of an artisanship, of a craftsmanship, which still flourishes even today. In England carpets, curtains, furnishing materials and other merchandise are nearly always in off colours: one can never buy a clear blue, but rather a grey-blue or green-blue; pinks are seldom clear but are called cedar or squashed strawberry, and seldom can one find a rich crimson red.

There is no reason why a miner's house should not be attractive: but the miner's wife seldom has access to anything but the hideous. It is the manufacturer who has the bad taste, it is he who believes that this bad taste is what other people want.

My aunt Jessie bought things that could last her for years, and certain suits that I myself bought twenty years ago I still wear today. But the lack of solidity and craftsmanship, the gimcrack way in which things are put together today, is only too soon apparent. Even serious artists today often paint with house paints or cheap colours instead of ground pigments. One such artist replied, when told that a canvas had cracked within a year: 'Do you want them to last forever?' This is indicative of the neurotic state of impermanence in which some of us find ourselves.

Impermanence and conformity seem to be the twin evils of our day, and fashion, as it was once, can ill exist between such poles. That it can exist with impermanence is a well-known fact: the Balinese have one of the most impermanent cultures the world has ever known, one that must constantly be remade and rebuilt, but they have lost neither their craftsmanship nor their inherited aesthetic traditions. We, on the other hand, live in a kind of impermanence which destroys tradition and replaces

it with nothing, Slowly but inevitably our values have deteriorated.

It seems odd that Americans, who adore individualism and are quick to realize it, should have a drive towards conformity comparable with their urge to be different. Certainly both in America and in Europe we have lost much of the ingrown sense of culture that we once possessed. In this respect we are far less fortunate than what remains of the so-called 'primitive' peoples, who in a few rare parts of the world are in harmony with their arts and their heritage. An Indian woman combing her hair reveals more 'culture' in the gesture than most Western women are capable of expressing today. When we watch a Venetian gondolier, his gestures of rowing are so beautiful that we know they have come down to us through hundreds of years. What is culture but a sense of the past continually revivified in the *present* act?

In this century of the 'average man,' even those who have

persevered in their individuality have become wary of display and are withdrawing from the public gaze. Nor can one blame them. The political and social ideas of our day have replaced self-expression by guilt, inhibiting the enjoyment of being unique. A society without this luxury loses many important cultural values. And since being unique has in the past often been the prerogative of princes rather than paupers, it seems to be dying out with the social inequalities that nurtured it.

But are extremes of individuality and democracy really incompatible? Will fashion, in the extravagantly romantic guise fostered by extremes of wealth, become non-existent? Few ladies are ladies of leisure today, and it is true that they have already abdicated the centre of the stage to a great extent. No longer do they become boldly authoritative leaders of style as they once did.

Whether the framework of high fashion be largely economic or not, it is certain that the wellsprings of a romantically ambiguous approach to fashion seem temporarily to have dried up. Try as one may, it is hard to avoid the conclusion that somewhere has passed a little glitter from the earth. The erstwhile mystery of clothing itself—a scarf worn by an enigmatic woman, an aigrette in a tart's hat, or a ribbon on a stocking—has faded into the hard realistic light of today, of serviceable needs, identical but practical uniforms, and a wholesale if anonymous excellence. Those ladies of Poiret who strode the lawns at Longchamps like fine Flemish horses have been replaced by a line of starlets, pin-up girls in bathing costume, and calendar art.

Yet it is always a danger to bemoan the lost glories of the past and the barbarism of the present. If every age is a birth and a dying, better to be on the side of the living than the dead. Glamour still flickers in unexpected guises, holding out a promise that our yearning renews itself like the phoenix. Every age has its need of romantic figures, though their expression may alter with altered times. If Forzane and Gaby Deslys have faded before the image of Marilyn Monroe and the Gabor sisters, only an inflexible nostalgia would deny the validity of the new expression of old ideals.

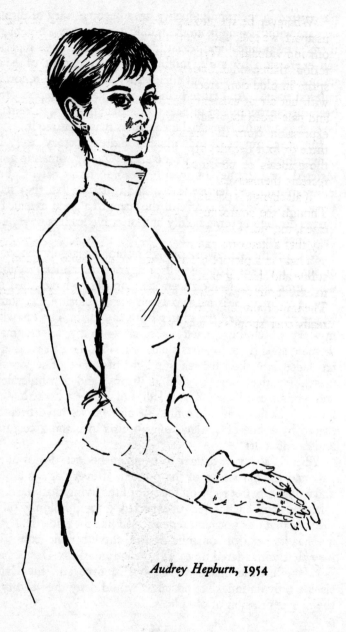

Audrey Hepburn, 1954

Whatever be the modern forces of anxiety that would pull us apart, we seek with greater boldness and intensity to express our individuality. Today's emphasis is accordingly less mysterious than candid. Stars such as Audrey Hepburn, a troubled sprite in blue dungarees, a citizen Puck; or Renée Jeanmarie, with her air of existential suffering, her peasant-cropped hair and pale-faced intensity—such figures may be a very different expression from the stagey, brilliantly artificial actresses of three or four decades ago, but they are living embodiments of those ideals of physique or personality that must eternally recreate themselves.

If all change is painful, it is as necessary as the air we breathe. Though the conformist pressures of modern life can be criticized, the individual expression still shines through. Who is to say that a neurotic gamine in Hamlet black is not as authentic as a lady in a picture hat and yards of crinoline? Fashion is the subtle and shifting expression of every age. It would be foolish to expect our social mirror to always send back the same image. The important thing, in the last analysis, is whether that image really corresponds to what we feel ourselves to be.

INDEX